THE ADVERSITY
OF DIVERSITY

Praise for *The Adversity of Diversity*

"Dr. Carol M. Swain and Mike Towle provide real insight into how the Left has hijacked diversity and injected woke indoctrination into all aspects of society. Anyone who believes in treating our fellow Americans in a fair and equitable manner should read this book."
— **Marsha Blackburn**, U.S. Senator

"Carol Swain is a courageous truth speaker who believes we can do better than the divisive DEI programs that have become common across America. Her co-authored book with Mike Towle, *The Adversity of Diversity*, seeks to bring healing and unity to an issue that has divided Americans for far too long."
— **Pete Hegseth,** *FOX & Friends Weekend* Co-Host & Bestselling Author

"Critical race theory was designed around two goals: expanding affirmative action and using it to use race to install political officers to undermine American institutions from within. The DEI industry became its action arm. This timely book by Carol Swain, written at a pivotal moment in this history, unmasks these programs (DEI and affirmative action) in beautiful prose and, most importantly, tells us what we should do next in this country that truly recognizes the sacred promise that all men are indeed created equal."
— **James Lindsay,** PhD., Author, Mathematician, Self-proclaimed professional troublemaker, Founder of New Discourses, and Co-Author (Helen Pluckrose) of *Cynical Theories: How Activist Scholarship Made Everything about Race, Gender, and Identity—and Why This Harms Everybody*

"Any member of a disadvantaged or underrepresented community seeking a role model for how to achieve the American dream should ditch their sense of entitlement, quit waiting on the government for a free ride, and follow the lead of Dr. Carol Swain, whose own path to success has been a true inspiration. Start your own uplifting journey by reading *The Adversity of Diversity* to get Carol's take on why affirmative action and diversity training have worked in tandem to sell Blacks and other minorities short in the realms of higher education and the workplace."
— **Robert L. Woodson**, Founder and President of the Woodson Center, 1776 Unites, and Voices of Black Mothers United

"Carol Swain's unusual background and accomplishments make her uniquely qualified to speak with authority on issues involving identity politics. Her co-authored book, *The Adversity of Diversity*, is a thought-provoking treatise that seeks unity around one of the most contentious issues of our day. She is my hero."
— **Arthur B. Laffer,** PhD, American Economist

"The Supreme Court's ruling against affirmative action has intensified challenges to diversity, equity, and inclusion (DEI) initiatives. Here, Dr. Carol Swain, a longtime critic of DEI programs, and co-author Mike Towle elaborate on the case against them and offer fresh ideas on achieving just racial progress. A vital perspective for all who wish to understand the full range of views in today's racial policy debates."
— **Rogers Smith,** Christopher H. Browne Distinguished Emeritus Professor of Political Science, University of Pennsylvania

"This book is a must-read for anyone who is a student of free speech, or who is seeking an in-depth understanding of the cultural battle lines being drawn today between freedom and forced adherence to the droning mantra of DEI. So many speakers on this topic take a curse the darkness approach. Swain and Towle present a refreshingly intellectual discussion of alternative solutions to the growing problem of woke indoctrination."
— **Larry Crain,** Author and Constitutional Lawyer

"*The Adversity of Diversity* is a road map to guide Americans out of the bondage of today's race-based hysteria and back into real unity; back to *E Pluribus Unum*, "Out of Many, One." As Swain lays out, the solutions are so simple we learned them in kindergarten: kindness, integrity, and mutual respect. Leveraging her life and experience, Swain exposes the fraudulent nature of divisive agendas like DEI and affirmative action and proves true the indelible, indisputable merit of merit."
— **Rebecca Friedrichs**, Author, Educator, Founder of For Kids & Country, and served as plaintiff in SCOTUS case *Friedrichs v. California Teachers Association.*

"Carol Swain has a unique ability to help us see what is true, right and good in diversity, equity, and inclusion conversations. I recommend this book to all who desire a path forward in the very confusing landscape around these issues. Her perspective is one that I trust."
— **Bobby Harrington,** D. Min., CEO RENEW.org and Discipleship.org, Lead Pastor, Harpeth Christian Church

"In their groundbreaking book T*he Adversity of Diversity*, Carol M. Swain and Mike Towle challenge the status quo of diversity, equity, and inclusion (DEI) practices. With keen insights and extensive research, they delve into the interplay between affirmative action, DEI, and critical race theory, providing a thought-provoking analysis that will reshape the conversation. This book offers a bold and compelling vision for achieving genuine unity in our workplaces and institutions. T*he Adversity of Diversity* is a timely and essential read for anyone seeking a transformative perspective on the legality of DEI and its impact on our society."
— **Dr. Robert J. Pacienza**, Senior Pastor of Coral Ridge Presbyterian Church, President of D. James Kennedy Ministries

THE ADVERSITY OF DIVERSITY

How the Supreme Court's Decision to Remove Race from
College Admissions Criteria Will Doom Diversity Programs

Carol M. Swain, PhD and Mike Towle

Foreword by Alan M. Dershowitz

BE THE PEOPLE
BOOKS

ISBNs:
Print: 978-1-7374198-2-2
eBook: 978-1-7374198-3-9

Cover design by Christian Hildago.
Cover photo of Carol Swain provided by Kevin Wimpy.
Page layout by Win-Win Words LLC.

Dr. Carol Swain's March 23, 2023, Statement to the Texas Legislature on Senate Bill 16 (diversity, equity, and inclusion [DEI] and critical race theory [CRT] in higher education) is available upon request. Contact her at info@carolmswain.com

Join the effort to help Reclaim America by making a tax-deductible contribution to Be the People Non-Profit, a 501c (3) that educates the public about the cultural, social, and economic issues of our day, https://bethepeoplenonprofit.com/

Personalized copies of *The Adversity of Diversity* can be ordered in bulk through Logos Books, logosnashville@gmail.com

Printed in the United States of America

To America's children. I want my great-grandchildren Hezekiah, Heavenly, and Haevyn to grow up in a world where they are neither advantaged nor disadvantaged because of their skin color or socioeconomic status. Likewise, Jackson, Olivia, and Karis, white children I love and respect, should bear no burden because of their race or socioeconomic status. What ultimately matters should be the content of their character.

— Carol M. Swain

To Andrew, for your support and inspiration.

— Mike Towle

Contents

Foreword

O N THE HEELS OF THE SUPREME COURT DECISION declaring race-based affirmative action in higher education unconstitutional, Swain and
Towle's *The Adversity of Diversity* puts forth a compelling case for questioning
the entire diversity, equity, and inclusion (DEI) industry that has departed
from any integrationist goals. It has become an aggressive force that takes
organizations away from their core missions and often transforms them into
divisive and disruptive institutions that openly violate the rights of members
of disfavored groups.

Swain and Towle argue that DEI programs often violate the equal protection clause of the Fourteenth Amendment and the 1964 Civil Rights Act
and its amendments, while doing nothing to genuinely promote racial healing and reconciliation. Swain's recommended solution of Real Unity Training
Solutions entails a return to core American principles that embrace nondiscrimination and equal opportunity in a meritocratic system that recognizes
individual rather than group rights.

Although I don't necessarily subscribe to all their arguments, and I applaud well-intentioned measures that have given members of underrepresented groups a boost toward pursuing their dreams of a quality college
education, the Supreme Court's ruling is one that I have sought for more
than fifty years. I wrote my first liberal essay against race-based affirmative
action in the 1970s, calling for affirmative action to be based on economic,
social, and personal characteristics rather than on race alone.

As a Jewish man of Eastern European heritage, I was subjected to discrimination while in law school and upon graduation. I graduated first in

my class at Yale Law School, only to get rejections from all thirty-two of the job applications I sent to Wall Street law firms. This wasn't because I didn't dress well, either.

Despite the SCOTUS ruling, I anticipate that some, if not many, schools will continue to bend the rules to fulfill their well-intentioned but ultimately dangerous racial "justice" agendas. It will take watchdog scrutiny and presumably more legal fights to hold these violators accountable.

As I reflect on the moment, I think about my journey as a civil rights champion to the position I continue to take that celebrates the Court's decision to reject race-based discrimination in college and university admissions. I have had the opportunity over the years to meet many brilliant racial and ethnic minorities, and I know that talent is not confined to one race. Fighting for racial justice has been a constant for me since college.

Not only did I participate in the civil rights activities of the early 1960s, but as a student I poured myself into organizations committed to fighting against racial discrimination. One of the highlights of my experiences was being in the crowd when Dr. Martin Luther King Jr. gave his famed "I Have a Dream" speech. Dr. King cast a vision that should continue to inspire all of us. His vision was to live in a nation where his children would be judged by the content of their character and not the color of their skin.

I believe that the demise of race-based affirmative action in college admissions should be accompanied by the elimination of most other nonmeritocratic criteria, such as legacy status, athletics, geography, and other nonacademic preferences. We should truly level the playing field by eliminating practices that create division while taking us further from King's vision and the constitutional protections we should welcome.

In this book, Swain shares her own affirmative action journey and the factors that enabled her to achieve the American dream. She and her coauthor have not given up on the nation's motto of *E Pluribus Unum*—out of many, one. Her vision for unity rather than what has become divisive training is one we can and should explore. One need not agree with all their observations and proposals to benefit from their wisdom.

— Alan M. Dershowitz

Felix Frankfurter Professor of Law (emeritus) at Harvard University Law School, and author of numerous bestselling books, including *The Case for Color-Blind Equality in an Age of Identity Politics.*

Preface

THE IDEA FOR UNITY TRAINING AND, SUBSEQUENTLY, THE SEED that would later become this book came to me in the fall of 2020. That is when the Council on National Policy invited me to participate in a panel on race relations. This was just a few months after George Floyd's death in Minneapolis.

The event was supposed to be a private, closed-door meeting barred to reporters, but it turns out there was a *Washington Post* reporter embedded in the audience who recorded part of my speech. I had spoken about the need for conservatives to compete in the diversity, equity, and inclusion (DEI) space. I knew then that many businesses across America were being forced to bring in DEI consultants to conduct race-sensitivity training, and I knew that such consultants disrupted workplaces while accomplishing next to nothing in terms of improving race and gender relations.

My motivation for launching my company, Real Unity Training Solutions, grew out of a heavy burden I felt for our nation. Like many Americans, I was deeply troubled by the weeks of nightly riots taking place in the wake of Floyd's death and the response coming from government leaders and corporations. Every time I picked up a newspaper, I read about yet another major corporation pouring money into Black Lives Matter or DEI/racial sensitivity training. This bothered me because I knew that racial reconciliation and healing could never come from a conflict model rooted in cultural Marxism. I saw crime escalate while law-enforcement personnel were demonized and placed in dangerous situations. I saw confusion from corporate leaders who were pouring millions of dollars into the coffers of activists' organizations and investing in individuals such as Ibram X. Kendi and Robin DiAngelo, seemingly in an attempt to "check the box" or virtue signal to the mob.

It is clear to me that organizations have mostly embraced the wrong approach to managing workplace diversity. They have gotten away from their original mission statements and founding principles, and they have waded into a minefield of distractions and corporate risk in their attempts to appease identity groups concerned only about their own radical social agendas. The result is chaos in our workplaces (much like in our streets). What is needed is a practical off-ramp from this failed approach that respects the dignity and talents of each person regardless of their race, ethnicity, or sexual preferences. In nearly all cases, such surface-level considerations matter little (or not at all) to the work that organizations are engaged in.

I also realized that companies paying for diversity trainers would never realize their goal of workplace racial harmony. That is because they were financing organizations that focus on conflict as opposed to working for healing and reconciliation. I knew there had to be a better way to properly counsel employees on racial issues in the workplace. Then one night I was awakened in the early-morning hours by the word *unity* bouncing around inside my head. I felt it in my spirit, as a Christian, that the solution to this worsening state of divisiveness was unity—unity training.

After I got out of bed, I ran to my computer and searched for the domain name *unity training*. It was taken, so I chose *Unity Training Solutions*. A few months later, I had an intellectual property attorney apply for a trademark, and we found more than five hundred applications pending for companies that would have *unity* in their name. As I perused some of the descriptions, I realized that most of them were rebranding their DEI programs as unity training in some form. What they were offering was clearly not my vision of how we can improve workplaces and learning institutions.

Since I am a public figure, I branded my company as Carol Swain's *Real Unity Training Solutions*. My vision is to provide leaders with tried and true principles that will get their organizations back on track with an approach that places teamsmanship and the needs of the organization above the identity-group politics that now dominate our environment. Knowledge of discrimination law, constitutional protections, compliance, and equal accommodations are essential for leaders, but the workplace should never become a setting for mandatory sensitivity training: this creates conflict and distracts workers from the jobs they were hired to perform.

One of the hallmarks of Real Unity Training as I envisioned it was respect for the individual. This means a return to the golden rule by which you treat other people the way you want them to treat you. This means not singling out a person because they happened to have been born into the wrong "group" or have the "wrong" attributes. One thing was clear: companies and organizations needed to get back to their mission statements based on the purpose for which they had been formed. The problem with this newfound focus on DEI and sensitivity training was that it steered business leaders away from their foundational goals and rerouted them toward social engineering and other practices and programs that divided the workplace.

Considering all that, my first goal, when consulting with companies, organizations, nonprofits, etc., is to offer leadership training to executives and managers in the areas of American civil rights and antidiscrimination laws. I was a political science and later law professor for more than twenty-eight years. On top of that, I have been a political advisor and member of a state advisory committee and the U.S. Civil Rights Commission—so these are areas about which I know something. It's important for leaders in any workplace to know and understand civil rights—something that most DEI experts apparently do not. Beyond that, the focus should be on building strong and effective teams, and this, in turn, requires effective communication.

Our unique approach at Real Unity Training Solutions is to embrace and value diversity. We believe a company's strength lies in its ability to mobilize the unique skills and talents of each employee. We believe that this can only be accomplished using a unity approach. The American dream and our nation's motto, *E Pluribus Unum*, are unifying principles that we use to guide our work with clients. We believe in optimism within a framework of the law—no guilt, shame, or oppression. Instead, we emphasize a renewed focus on the organization's mission.

I believe that I bring a unique perspective as a Black, conservative, Christian woman. I sometimes mention how my vantage point is informed by having been raised in abject poverty, having dropped out of middle school, and having worked alongside poor Whites. The Real Unity

Training Solutions approach is unique enough that it could be packaged like a Dale Carnegie course; yet it is rooted in common-sense values and principles.

In the wake of the U.S. Supreme Court's June 2023 decision eliminating the consideration of race from college and university admissions, everything is now in flux. DEI programs appear to be dying, and the SCOTUS decision is likely to have a trickle-down effect of further eroding DEI in colleges and in workplaces.[1] Unity Training is not just another diversionary program that reduces employee productivity and distracts employees from their jobs. Instead, Unity Training helps leaders rethink how to work with their employees.

The United States is presently in the grip of *extreme social division*—in large part about how to address race relations. Consider this segment of what the *Washington Post* reporter I referenced earlier wrote for publication following the Council on National Policy panel:

> In one of the sessions . . . former Professor Carol Swain, speaking on the panel about race relations, said that White people have lost their voice in America. She likened the Black Lives Matter movement to the KKK. "The Democratic Party is using Black Lives Matter and antifa the same way they used the KKK," said Swain, who is black. "They created the KKK; it was their terrorist wing to terrorize everyone." In response to questions, Swain stood by her remarks.[2]

I still do.

This book was written in anticipation of affirmative action being struck down, and my co-author Mike Towle and I put the finishing touches on an almost-completed manuscript two weeks after the Court decision was announced in late June 2023. I had long believed and espoused that affirmative action *had* to be struck down if the Supreme Court were to adhere to the U.S. Constitution. I believed that diversity, equity, and inclusion (DEI) would also have to fail and either die or be eliminated, because it, too, violates the Constitution in the same way as race-based affirmative action has. Not only did I believe that affirmative action had to be struck down for enabling discrimination against Whites and Asians, but also for its enabling law-breaking implications in other settings.

DEI and critical race theory (CRT), the latter of which we don't talk much about in this book (although you can read about it in my 2021 book

Black Eye for America), is another layer on top of the whole affirmative action scheme—yes, they go together. DEI pursues its goals in an aggressive manner that ignores civil rights laws and the Constitution. What else would you expect from a cottage industry that has grossed tens of billions of dollars? DEI sees itself as occupying the moral high ground (it does not) and as exempt from civil rights law (it is not). Affirmative action and DEI (and CRT) proponents believe their motivations are so noble as to be unbound by American law or by the U.S. Constitution. Where is the justice in that?

There are better ways to promote and to be a champion for diversity and to give a hand up to underrepresented groups applying to colleges or looking for workplace opportunities than making race the number-one factor in admissions, hires, promotions, and contracts. Affirmative action has been demeaning and disparaging to the accomplishments of people who belong to groups labeled as marginalized: it paints these people as victims and says that standards must be lowered to get enough of them. It pursues proportional representation rather than tweaking a system to one where you are now seeking the best talent you can get and assuming that that talent is available on a nonracial or nongender basis.

The whole argument, for instance, that math is racist[3,4] apparently gives racial ethnic minorities an excuse, I suppose, for not being successful in math as opposed to the reality that math is a challenge for many people of various ethnicities and that it requires a lot of practice and perhaps help from tutors. That doesn't mean you eliminate math-course requirements in schools or standardized college admission tests for applicants—such as the SAT and ACT—that include sections on math.

One last thing. I was pleased that Mike Towle accepted my offer to join me in researching and writing this book. We have worked together on assorted projects over the years. He is a former newspaper reporter, later an editor and general manager, and he has authored more than a dozen books of his own. As a white male and college graduate, Mike has had his own front seat to affirmative action and diversity training in play. I value his perspective on these interrelated subjects as well as his familiarity in taking a book manuscript through all the stages of self-publication. Because of that, I was able to get this book out quickly and as a first-rate product. Mike is also brilliant with titles, and I credit his advice and expertise in helping me find the right cover and title for my 2021 book *Black Eye for America: How Critical Race Theory is Burning Down the House*. I am blessed to have a partner who knows every aspect of the publishing business.

— **Carol M. Swain, PhD**
Nashville, Tennessee
July 16, 2023

Acknowledgments

I (CAROL) WOULD LIKE TO EXPRESS MY GRATITUDE to the Texas Public Policy Foundation (TPPF) for its support, as well as give a special shout-out to executive vice-president Jerome Greener. Greener impressed me with his compassion, intellect, and wisdom. In addition, Dr. Sherry Sylvester and Texas Senator Brandon Creighton invited me to speak to the Texas Senate about the problems with diversity, equity, and inclusion in higher education. Ken Oliver and Chuck Devore of TPPF were especially supportive of my work.

Other people who deserve recognition for helping me to bring this book to fruition include Christian Hildago, the cover designer; Mike Towle, my co-author; Sandy Norris, my assistant; Milena Ulrich, my research assistant; Michelle Hooper, who worked with me as I developed Unity Training and who conducted interviews of company owners and HR directors; and Jeff Ulmer, who supports my endeavors by doing whatever is needed.

Other people who deserve mention are Wallace Long, Gary Cooper, and Don Schmincke. Don is a leadership mentor who greatly encouraged me. Each of these men was helpful in giving advice and serving as sounding boards as I developed my ideas. Dr. Chris Schorr and Adam Bellow offered critically important insights that helped improve the messaging of the book. I would also like to thank my friends Donna Willis, Mary Poplin, Nan Bouchard, Lee Beaman, Mike Hardwick, Bob Woodson, Stephanie Huffman, and Dave Ramsey for their unwavering support. Lastly, I appreciate the prayers and support from Nancy Dunn's Sunday School Class and Forest Hills Baptist Church. In other words, it took a village to reach this point.

THE ADVERSITY
OF DIVERSITY

CHAPTER 1

RIP, Affirmative Action: Up Next, DEI?

"You do not take a person who, for years, has been hobbled by chains and liberate him, bring him up to the starting line of a race and then say, 'You are free to compete with all the others,' and still justly believe that you have been completely fair. . .

"This is the next and the more profound stage of the battle for civil rights. We seek not just freedom but opportunity. We seek not just legal equity but human ability, not just equality as a right and a theory but equality as a fact and equality as a result."[1]

— **President Lyndon Baines Johnson**, Howard University
Commencement Address, June 4, 1965.

Fifty-eight years later:
"[W]hat cannot be done directly cannot be done indirectly. The Constitution deals with substance, not shadows," and the prohibition against racial discrimination is "leveled at the thing, not the name." . . . A benefit to a student who overcame racial discrimination, for example, must be tied to that student's courage and determination. Or a benefit to a student whose heritage or culture motivated him or her to assume a leadership role or attain a particular goal must be tied to that student's unique ability to contribute to the university. In other words, the student must be treated based on his or her experiences as an individual—not on the basis of race. Many universities have for too long done

1

just the opposite. And in doing so, they have concluded, wrongly, that the touchstone of an individual's identity is not challenges bested, skills built, or lessons learned but the color of their skin. Our constitutional history does not tolerate that choice."[2]

— **U.S. Supreme Court Chief Justice John Roberts**, Majority Opinion, *Students for Fair Admissions v. President and Fellows of Harvard College*, June 29, 2023.

T RADITIONAL UNDERSTANDINGS OF EQUALITY AND JUSTICE are making a comeback in America. Credit that, in large part, to a recent pair of landmark U.S. Supreme Court decisions that came almost exactly one year apart. The first, which came on June 24, 2022, restored the right to life for the unborn in America by overturning *Roe v. Wade.* The second, announced on June 29, 2023, took a big bite out of affirmative action. It did this by ruling that race-conscious college admissions practices, long perceived by many Americans as a form of reverse discrimination, were unconstitutional and violated a federal law that applies to all colleges and universities "that receive federal funding, as almost all do."[3]

The deconstruction of affirmative action likely isn't finished, either. It is conceivable—in fact, expected—that the Court's 2023 position on affirmative action will expand to the workplace. Should this occur, it would mean the end of race-based favoritism in hiring and preferential sub-contracting awards for minority-led firms—components of the affirmative action mandate constructed from three similar executive orders issued by two U.S. presidents, both Democrats, during the 1960s. The first, Executive Order (EO) 10925, was signed and issued in March 1961 by President John F. Kennedy. Subsequent EOs signed by President Lyndon B. Johnson in 1965 and in 1967 expanded on JFK's original order.

The first of the three EOs had the most conspicuous impact and brought the term "affirmative action" into the American lexicon. JFK's EO10925 directed federal contractors to take "affirmative action to ensure that applicants are treated equally without regard to race, creed, color, religion, or national origin."[4] The first of LBJ's follow-ups, EO11246, linked civil rights enforcement to affirmative action by prohibiting employment discrimination by "those organizations receiving federal contracts and subcontracts," and established the President's Commission on Equal Employment Opportunities. Two years later, the tall Texan's companion EO11375 added sex (gender) to the list of protected criteria, presumably in light of the fact it had been omitted in his first executive order.[5]

Richard Nixon was the first Republican president to sign an affirmative action-related executive order, amending Johnson's EO11246. In 1969 Nixon pledged to " . . . promote the full realization of equal employment opportunity through a continuing affirmative program in each executive department and agency."[6] In short, government employment was now subject to affirmative action's provisions. Under Nixon's Philadelphia Plan, contractors were to establish "goals and timetables" for hiring members of "underutilized" groups and were expected to demonstrate "good faith efforts" to reach their goals. Goals soon evolved into quotas, and color-blindness under the law became color consciousness almost immediately after the passage of the 1964 Civil Rights Act.[7]

Sociologist John D. Skrentny has explained this shift as emanating from crisis management following the wake of urban riots that began in the summer of 1963 and culminated in 1967. Ironically, it was white male elites who felt the pace of progress was too slow and that something more radical than recruitment and outreach needed to be done.[8]

In response to the riots, President Johnson issued EO 11365 establishing the National Advisory Commission on Civil Rights that became known as the Kerner Commission. It concluded:

"Our nation is moving toward two societies, one black, one white—separate and unequal." The report was a strong indictment of white America: "What white Americans have never fully understood—but what the Negro can never forget—is that white society is deeply implicated in the ghetto. White institutions created it, white institutions maintain it, and white society condones it."[9]

AFFIRMATIVE ACTION:
NEVER ACTUAL LAW IN TRADITIONAL SENSE

For decades, affirmative action was widely treated (or feared) as if it were law. In reality, affirmative action had neither been created by legislation— i.e., voted on by Congress and signed into law by a sitting president—nor had it been added as an amendment to the U.S. Constitution. What affirmative action had going for it was the power and influence of the civil rights movement of the 1960s. That movement yielded the watershed Civil Rights Act of 1964 but also organized hordes of loyal, sharp-elbowed activists who aggressively pushed affirmative action and were never shy about getting into the faces (or inside the heads) of anyone reluctant to go along with their program.

I (Carol) was an eleven-year-old black girl living in the rural South when President Johnson signed the Civil Rights Act of 1964 into law. The Civil Rights Act prohibited government-sanctioned discrimination based on race, color, national origin, sex, or religion. It was seismic in its impact because it banned segregation in movie theaters, restaurants, and hotels. It meant that people like me were no longer barred from using public swimming pools or libraries, and it mandated that states not in compliance with the 1954 *Brown v. Board of Education* of Topeka, Kansas, ruling had to stop dragging their feet.

LBJ's Howard University speech referenced above was significant because it signaled that the federal government would use racial preferences to achieve equal results or in today's language, *equity—equal outcomes*. Affirmative action would use racial preferences to address the past and present effects of discrimination against the black descendants of slaves. In doing so, affirmative action contradicted the words spoken by the floor manager of the legislation, Minnesota Senator Hubert Humphrey. He vowed that the legislation would not lead to racial preference or quotas, and that if it someone could find where it did, he would "start eating the pages" of the bill. We assume he never did.

Today, in the wake of *Students for Fair Admission*, affirmative action remains operative in workplace settings. The United States thus remains mired in the uncomfortable and, ultimately, untenable position of ignoring key elements of civil rights law and the equal protection clause of the Fourteenth Amendment. Much the same can be said of the presence of diversity, equity, and inclusion (DEI) initiatives. Although distinct from affirmative action (AA), DEI has become the action arm for CRT to expand affirmative action into every sector of our society. According to CRT, every white person benefits from undeserved privileges connected to their whiteness, and every racial and ethnic minority, regardless of social status and wealth, is a victim. Lost in the new meaning of diversity is our national motto, *E Pluribus Unum—* out of many, one.

Let's break it down now. The "D" in DEI stands for Diversity, but diversity is no longer about integrating racial and ethnic minorities into institutions where they have been underrepresented. It is now about recruiting

4

members of historically marginalized groups and empowering them to maintain their separate identities. DEI's diversity is based on a conflict model of human relations that seems obsessed with differences and grudges about real and imagined historical wrongs.

The "E" in DEI stands for Equity, but equity is not about nondiscrimination and treating people fairly. Nor is it about ensuring equal opportunity. It is about equal outcomes based on group membership. Equity is also a key demand of CRT proponents. They seek equal outcomes for favored groups regardless of efforts, talents, or abilities.

The "I" in DEI is for Inclusion. Inclusion is not just about bringing people into institutions and areas of life where they were excluded. It is also about allowing them to maintain and celebrate their differences. That strikes us as the opposite of what the word *inclusion* actually implies. DEI opposes assimilation, merit, and integration. It embraces group differences and is at war with heterosexuality, the white race ("whiteness"), and core American values such as equal treatment under the law.

Affirmative action and DEI both share a common DNA with the equal opportunity movement that gained significant traction in the 1970s. Both are entrenched as practitioners and promoters of reverse discrimination. This is particularly true of DEI, which has shown significantly more bite than AA in brazenly putting Whites, especially white males, on notice by claiming that they bear the blame for nearly 250 years of alleged "sins" committed by America's founding fathers and by subsequent generations.

The Fourteenth Amendment was added to the Constitution following the Civil War to ensure equality under law and protection from racial discrimination for all Americans. The ongoing disregard of our Constitution and civil rights laws contributes to a crisis of credibility and to a climate of hostility that pits well-meaning Americans against one another. Our nation is deeply divided. The U.S. Supreme Court's decision in *Students for Fair Admission* is a step in the right direction, but there is more to be done. Interestingly, not a single U.S. president (not even the staunchly conservative Ronald Reagan)—there have been ten presidents since Nixon—has had the courage to issue an EO overturning any of the original three affirmative action EOs.

PROGRESSIVES AND REVERSE DISCRIMINATION

Unfortunately, America seems besieged by radical "progressives" intent on ignoring the equal protection clause of the Fourteenth Amendment and the Civil Rights Act of 1964 and its amendments. They do this by pushing divisive DEI training programs, which, to a great degree, have become closely aligned with the Marxist-driven philosophies and tactics of Black Lives Matter (BLM), antifa, and the National Education Association. It's like our Marxist-influenced "progressives" have put critical race theory, political correctness, wokeism, and cancel culture into a blender and mixed them all together, served cold in how they undermine traditional American freedoms, thought, and culture. They do this by promoting reverse discrimination, deterring free speech in part by silencing dissenting voices (with big help from Big Media, such as Facebook, and, at one time, Twitter). They take great delight in devaluing the citizenship status of Whites by tossing out false, incendiary labels such as "White privilege" and "White supremacy," as well as blanket accusations of Whites being "racist" at birth. This is not a joke, but it is a mess.

DEI would probably be more effective (at worst tolerable) if businesses and colleges treated their programs less like chasing a cure for cancer and more like an honest pursuit of healing the racial/ethnic divide eating away at America's soul. Unlike the traditional diversity measures once associated with affirmative action, DEI is more witch hunt than warm heart, more command and control than compromise and conciliation.

I (Mike) see DEI as a progressives-driven "front." It is the clichéd dry-cleaning shop hiding the operation that manufactures reverse discrimination to support the far-Left liberal cause. Diversity training is predicated on a Marxist-driven lie known as White oppression and Black victimization, which is foundational to critical race theory and the DEI action-driven enforcement arm. DEI is a rallying cry for BLM proponents who take pleasure in painting white people as inherently privileged and innately racist, although white progressives attempt to dodge such labels for themselves by adopting and parroting the lines of the activists. As a white man, I wonder how white progressives reconcile themselves with these prejudicial beliefs. Let's do a little experiment. If you are white and lean politically left, try this exercise: Look into a mirror and ask yourself, "How am *I* also not a beneficiary of White privilege, and why am *I* exempt from being declared racist at birth? After all, I *am* white." In this scenario, white progressives should, in fact, be their own worst enemies—purveyors of White privilege and White supremacy just because of their skin color. Picture the white, male C-level executive who institutes mandatory diversity training for his employees, aiming for a more diverse workplace. Now try to imagine such a white power broker, in support of diversity and true servant leadership, voluntarily firing himself (and refusing his golden parachute) to create an opening tailormade for a minority manager seeking such a promotion.

Here's the stark truth about DEI: Diversity programs and those who enacted them have generally failed to make their workplaces more diverse, even while pandering to minorities (and alienating Whites). In fact, *most* diversity programs have failed to increase diversity, period. That's in large part because, since the 1970s, companies have switched to oppressive strategies such as diversity training to reduce bias, hiring tests and performance ratings connected to hires and promotions, and grievance systems to help employees call out managers for unacceptable behaviors (i.e., bias in the workplace). These dated practices, Dobbin and Kaley say, cobble an environment of "force-feeding" that promotes bias more than squelches it.[10]

It's not just the failures in achieving desired diversity numbers, either; there are also DEI systemic abuses (i.e., attempted cheating) that along the way have proven costly for companies and organizations. Such instances include firing white employees for apparently bogus reasons, and then hiring minority replacements as a quick and easy boost to their diversity numbers. This gives a whole new perspective to "cooking the books."

David Duvall is a former senior vice president of marketing and communications for North Carolina-based Novant Health, a nonprofit health care organization of thirty-five thousand employees scattered across many states. Without warning, and despite lacking a paper trail proving that Duvall had been warned about what was later revealed as alleged subpar work performance, Novant fired Duvall, a white male, in July 2018. They then ordered him off the premises immediately and reportedly hired two minorities—a white woman and a black woman—to split duties in sharing Duvall's former workload.[11]

Duvall filed a federal lawsuit claiming that Novant had violated the Civil Rights Act of 1964 by firing him to achieve racial and gender diversity. Despite the insistence by Novant's legal representation that Duvall had actually been terminated due to job performance, which Novant claimed was not indicative of the caliber of leadership someone in his position needed, the jury sided with Duvall. He was awarded $10 million in punitive damages in October 2021. Duvall's court documents also revealed that other white men at Novant had been fired without warning and replaced by minorities, including women.[12]

S. Luke Largesse, Duvall's attorney, said that his client's lawsuit was not an indictment of the existence of diversity and inclusion programs, adding that, "The lawsuit was only about the need to run such programs lawfully. We believe the punitive damages award was a strong message that an employer cannot just fire employees based on their race or gender to create opportunities to achieve diversity targets. That is plainly unlawful and very harmful, and that is what the jury denounced here."[13]

DIVERSITY: A LIFE OF ITS OWN

Diversity is no longer just a nice word depicting a workplace organically composed of a variety of races, ethnicities, faiths, and gender identifications. The word has taken on a life of its own; it represents an obsession gripping our nation, a concession to the PC police. The idea of *diversity* represents the key ingredient in identity politics—if you identify as someone who fits into a highly sought-after diversity demographic (for example, a trans woman such as Dylan Mulvaney), then you suddenly have a huge advantage in today's DEI environment. In sports, for example, there's the biological male at birth who switches genders—or even just gender identification—and suddenly gains an enormous competitive advantage participating in events against nontrans girls or women. Case in point is transgender athlete Lia Thomas, who in 2022 won an NCAA Division I swimming championship competing in the women's division[14]—and who sometime soon after was photographed wearing an antifa T-shirt. This is progress?

One of the poster women for the progressives' diversity juggernaut is Karine Jean-Pierre, President Joe Biden's press secretary. It is not enough that Jean-Pierre speaks for the president at White House news conferences, taking and sometimes even answering questions from the media. She also has used the White House press secretary's podium as her own bully pulpit, such as to promote her membership in the LGBTQ+ community. During an April 2023 press briefing, she added a personal note emphasizing her key role in the diversity movement, saying, "So this week is Lesbian Visibility Week, and as the first openly queer person to hold the position as press secretary for the president of the United States, I see every day how important visibility and representation are. Today I am honored to welcome the casts of the *L Word* and *Generation Q*, two Showtime series that chronicle the friendship, the love, the challenges, and the triumphs of strong, funny, and resilient queer women."[15]

I (Carol) once posted this comment on social media: "I feel sorry for this incompetent young lady who makes a mockery of true diversity. Her sexuality is the *only* thing about herself that she seems to value. It's too bad she was placed in such a visible position. Contrived diversity hurts qualified Americans of all groups."

All that might soon be changing, however, and for the better.

THE SUPREME COURT AND ORAL ARGUMENTS

Legal experts and higher-education officials on both sides of affirmative action saw the Supreme Court's 2023 ruling against affirmative action coming from miles away, dating back to October 31, 2022. That is when SCOTUS members gathered to hear oral arguments surrounding two similar cases involving similar 2014 lawsuits, one filed against Harvard (a private institution) and the other naming the University of North Carolina (public). The common link between the two cases is an organization known as Students for Fair Admissions (SFFA), which had filed the suits, both claiming that the respective schools' admission policies "discriminated against White and Asian applicants by giving preferences to Black, Hispanic, and Native-American students." In their defense, the two universities claimed their race-conscious admissions policies were necessary to establish and maintain diversity in classrooms, an affirmative action goal considered key to student learning in general.[16]

Edward Blum, creator and president of the plaintiffs' SFFA organization, didn't see the rationale for all the fuss from affirmative action supporters in the months leading up to the Court's ruling. "Ending the consideration of race and ethnicity in college admissions is not a controversial goal," Blum wrote in an email to the *Chronicle*, an independent news organization of Duke University, which itself was following the case closely for its own sake (it was one of seventeen universities that filed an amicus brief on Harvard's behalf, stating it was an invested party). "Those who advocate for the continuation of race in admissions are working against the convictions and preferences of the majority of America's racial minorities," Blum added. In saying this, he also referred to a 2022 Pew Research survey that showed 74 percent of all Americans, including 59 percent of Blacks, 64 percent of Asian Americans, and 68 percent of Hispanics, do not believe race should be a factor in college admissions.[17]

This has not been Blum's first rodeo when it comes to fighting legal battles aimed at overturning race-based college admissions preferences and other similar types of race-preferential maneuvers. He represented (after having searched for a plaintiff, and found) Abigail Fisher. She was a white student whose application for admission to the University of Texas at Austin (Blum's alma mater) was turned down in the wake of UT's decision in 2003 to abandon its race-neutral admissions policies in favor of adding race and ethnicity to its fifteen admissions criteria. Although the Supreme Court in 2013 upheld the right of UT—and therefore other college institutions—to pursue diversity as a compelling educational interest, in its decision it also put out the stern word that universities "should first try race-neutral means of achieving diversity before implementing affirmative action," as reported by the *Boston Globe*.[18]

Blum's support of race-neutral policies and practices extends into other fields as well. Soon after he and his wife moved into Houston from the suburbs in 1989, Blum noticed there wasn't a Republican running in his local congressional district's race. When he queried the local Republican Party office to ask why, he was told the district was a majority-minority district and a Republican candidate wouldn't stand a chance. Two years later, Blum ran for the seat and won the Republican primary but later lost to his Democratic opponent in the general election. During his campaign, however, he discovered something that didn't look right. Neighborhoods in his district had been redrawn to bolster minority voting power. This lit a fire in Blum, and he put together a legal team that sued the state of Texas over its allegedly unconstitutional gerrymandering practices—spending eight thousand dollars a month of his own money along the way. Vengeance, to a certain degree, was his. The U.S. Supreme Court found that three of the state's districts were indeed snubbing the Constitution by factoring in race in configuring districts.[19]

So, what does all this about Blum have to do with diversity and diversity training on college campuses and in the corporate world and other workplaces? For one thing, it apparently helped fuel his commitment to end the injustices inherent in reverse discrimination. A word to the wise: Blum apparently isn't finished, and the possibilities are intriguing. Consider what the

Boston Globe reporter Hilary Burns reported in her profile piece on Blum: "Blum has ambitions beyond academia, with litigation in the works to end race-based initiatives in other aspects of American life, including employment diversity programs, corporate board diversity quotas, and government contracting requirements."[20]

Finally, a few words from Blum himself: "The nation cannot remedy past discrimination with new discrimination. There are ways in which individuals and groups who have been on the fringes of opportunity can be brought in, but raising the bar for certain races and lowering the bar for others cannot be the solution to equal opportunity."[21]

Originally scheduled for two hours, the Supreme Court's October 2022 hearings involving the two lawsuits naming Harvard and the University of North Carolina as defendants, reportedly lasted upward of five hours, with the Court's conservative majority spending much of that time grilling affirmative action proponents. Justices Clarence Thomas and Samuel Alito—both among SCOTUS's 6-3 conservative majority—each questioned some of the semantics. "I've heard the word *diversity* quite a few times, and I don't have a clue what it means," said Thomas, an African American. "It seems to mean everything for everyone." Alito said he was baffled by what "underrepresented minority" meant. Fellow Court conservatives Justice Amy Coney Barrett and Chief Justice John Roberts insisted that affirmative action defenders specify an expected end date for when their goals would be met, with attorneys for the universities unable to do so.[22]

The case against Harvard showed that the institution's admissions criteria included a subjective measure of an applicant's traits such as "likability, courage, and kindness, and effectively creating a ceiling for those students [namely, Whites and Asians] in admissions."[23] The subjective "personality test" gave school officials a means to admit lower-qualified students and weed out superior White and Asian applicants without having to defend their admissions policies that were biased against Whites and Asians.

DIVERSITY RULES

Diversity is at the heart and soul of affirmative action, which explains why diversity, equity, and inclusion (DEI) is closely associated with affirmative action, a connection that does not bode well for DEI programs following the Court's decision to strike down race-based admissions in higher education. Whether they know it or not, "companies may be directly impacted by the decision," because of "potential legal challenges to their programs," as stated in a client report released in March 2023 by the Morrison Foerster Law Firm. It noted that "[e]mployers are also increasingly having to navigate the growing trend of state legislation and measures seeking to limit workplace DEI efforts."[24]

It stands to reason that the greater a link that can be established between affirmative action and DEI, the more likely lawsuits challenging the constitutionality of workplace-based diversity programs could mushroom in number. The argument for a historical link between affirmative action and diversity training, or as it is sometimes called "diversity management," appears buttressed by a 1998 paper co-written by Erin Kelly and Frank Dobbin, now college professors. Their premise in "How Affirmative Action Became Diversity Management" is that corporate affirmative action programs actually *became* diversity programs.[25] The question becomes: How did this happen?

To answer this, Kelly and Dobbin argue that Ronald Reagan and his decision after taking office in 1981 to pull back the reins on regulatory oversight and enforcement impacted programs covered by antidiscrimination laws. By 1981, both affirmative action and the Civil Rights Act of 1964 had been in effect more than fifteen years. Many employers had already established diversity programs to manage compliance with the two federal edicts, and they were not about to abandon their efforts because of changes in regulatory oversight. Those efforts had included the establishment of Equal Employment Opportunity (as created by the Civil Rights Act of 1964) and affirmative action offices and activities, which corporations deemed fit and necessary to continue in operation if they were to achieve their affirmative action diversity goals.

Much of the responsibility for diversity training/management's survival, as suggested by the authors of the paper (published in the April 1998 edition of *American Behavioral Scientist*), went to the EEO/AA specialists running the programs. In defense of their work, "they touted the efficiency of formalizing human resources management through such antidiscrimination measures as grievance procedures, formal hiring and promotion systems, and systematic recruitment schemes. Later they invented the discipline of diversity management, arguing that the capacity to manage a diverse workforce well would be the key to business success in the future."[26]

That success in large part remains missing in action. It's time to do something about it, and, in Real Unity Training, a proposed alternative solution is presented. Diversity done the correct way enhances institutions and can lead to creative problem-solving breakthroughs. It also can lead to more harmonious workplace relationships that can flourish in an atmosphere of mutual respect.

It is time for a different approach. It has been almost sixty years since the Civil Rights Act of 1964 sought to eliminate discrimination based on immutable characteristics. Colleges, universities, corporations, and governmental agencies opened their doors and pursued aggressive outreach and advertising to bring underrepresented racial and ethnic minorities into the system. I (Carol) benefited from these efforts. In fact, statistics show that the jump in the enrollment numbers of previously underserved minorities started to rise dramatically in the late 1960s. Many prestigious universities in 1969 enrolled more than double the number of black students from a year earlier, a big bump in numbers attributed to the muscle of the whole civil rights movement in league with affirmative action. Columbia University president Leo Bollinger, who had been a first-year law student at Columbia in 1968, remembers the racially based dynamics of that era well. "In that time," Bollinger told the *New York Times*, "there was a sense, pure and simple, that universities had to do their part to help integrate higher education."[27]

HOW AFFIRMATIVE ACTION HELPED RADICALIZE AMERICA

Affirmative action has from its start been bombarded with complaints, and, surprisingly, the gripes have mostly come from racial and ethnic minorities who feel that they should be further along. They want more positions of power and more opportunities than they currently have. They are annoyed that, after all these years of purported progress, there still are not enough racial and ethnic minorities in certain fields or in certain positions of power; therefore, they believe they are not being well represented in society. Along those lines, we have seen progressive activists such as Derrick Bell, the father of critical race theory, argue that anything Whites do, they do to benefit themselves.[28]

Such dissidents would argue that racism was structural, that it was a systematic entity, not just a collective of random acts of bias or discrimination. That helps explain how and why DEI apparently emerged in tandem with the CRT movement birthed on university campuses, which now reaches into every sphere of American society, including the U.S. military.

Progressives dissatisfied with the pace of progress imposed DEI and CRT on top of affirmative action without much complaint from civil rights advocates who now push for outright discrimination against Whites and Asians. DEI's critical race theory component allows supporters to discount history, facts, and statistical data and anchor their claims on their lived experiences. The lived experiences shared through storytelling, recounting the injustices, outweigh anything a white person has to say about a race-related issue. In other words, an outsider's opinion doesn't count, as in, "How can they possibly know what it's like to be victimized?"

Supporters of affirmative action, and therefore DEI advocates, reject color-blindness; they say it is an impossibility. They do not believe in a meritocracy in which a black man or woman will be fairly and properly rewarded and/or compensated for their work or school performance and achievements. Instead, they believe there should be racial preferences. Not only that, but those preferences should also be only for people who have been discriminated against.

Progressives deny the accomplishments of millions of successful Blacks from all walks of life who have overcome tremendous odds to make their mark on America. A few that come to mind: Bob Woodson, Henry Lewis Gates, Ben Carson, Thomas Sowell, William Julius Wilson, and Toni Morrison, as well as historical figures like Booker T. Washington, W. E. B. Du Bois, and Madam C. J. Walker.

When I think about my own success as a middle-school dropout who became a university professor, I think about the opportunities created by the passage of civil rights legislation. By the time I reached college in the late 1970s, affirmative action had a decade of existence under its belt. It was the law of the land, and I benefited from encountering people who encouraged me to further my education in an environment where the Whites I met wanted me to succeed. What benefited me the most was their goodwill in an environment that prohibited racial discrimination and encouraged institutions to look for talent among underrepresented populations. I was the right person at the right time to take advantage of a new America.

CHAPTER 2

Carol's Educational Journey in an Affirmative Action World

"The Congress of the United States has never founded schools for any class of its own people. . . . It has never deemed itself authorized to expend the public money for rent or purchase of homes for the thousands, not to say millions of the white race who are honestly toiling from day to day for their subsistence. A system for the support of indigent persons was never contemplated by the authors of the Constitution; nor can any good reason be advanced why as a permanent estab-lishment it should be funded for one class or color of our people." [1]

ONCE AGAIN WE HEAR FROM A PRESIDENT JOHNSON speaking during the tu-multuous sixties, like how we led off the first chapter of this book. Except this time, it is not LBJ being quoted, but rather Andrew Johnson, the "other" presidential Johnson, who ascended to the U.S. presidency on April 15, 1865, after the assassination of Abraham Lincoln. Andrew Johnson's quote was in reference to the establishment by Congress of the Freedmen's Bureau in the immediate aftermath of the Civil War. It was designed to offer aid to the newly emancipated black slaves. Their newfound freedom was hailed as life-chang-ing, yet it was accompanied by the realization that freed slaves had suddenly been bequeathed the stark reality of starting a new life from scratch, many without a home of their own, a job, or two pennies to rub together.

Andrew Johnson vetoed the Freedmen's Bureau, only for the hostile Republican Congress to override the veto before it nearly succeeded in getting Johnson removed from office.* Johnson's dislike of the proposed Freedmen's Bureau was not born out of racist spite toward black slaves and not wanting to help them in a time of need; it was because the bill ignored poor Whites, many of whom were as destitute as the poorest slaves following the abject death and destruction from the Civil War. In short, Johnson saw the Freedmen's Bureau as a potential source of what almost exactly a hundred years later would become known as "reverse discrimination" as it relates to affirmative action.

Years ago, I (Carol) observed that the first expression of affirmative action, or in this case reparations, came with accusations of reverse discrimination. Newly freed slaves never got their forty acres and a mule, but private philanthropy and government programs have spent trillions of dollars trying to address past and present discrimination against the descendants of slaves. Unfortunately, present-day affirmative action programs disproportionately benefit the foreign born and those who are affluent. Note that Vice President Kamala Harris, former President Barack Obama, and numerous "black" members of Congress are not descendants of slaves.

In fact, inner-city and poor blacks have *not* been the biggest beneficiaries of affirmative action. Occasionally, some of us slip through the gatekeepers, but for the most part the mobility has not been what one would expect. In 2004, the *Journal of Blacks in Higher Education* reported that in the "late 1960s major universities were recruiting low-income or so-called ghetto blacks. Not so today." Most Blacks at Harvard University and other elite institutions hail from *middle- or high-income families.* The article referenced a 2004 interview in which Professor Henry Louis Gates Jr., then director of the W. E. B. DuBois Institute for African and African-American Research at Harvard, told the *London Observer,* "The black kids who come to Harvard or Yale are middle class. Nobody else gets through." Gates and his colleague, law professor Lani Guinier, noted that two-thirds of the blacks at Harvard were like Barack Obama and Kamala Harris, in that they were the offspring of immigrants most often from West Africa or the Caribbean.[2]

---

* Andrew Johnson, William J. Clinton, and Donald J. Trump are the only US presidents to be impeached by the US House of Representatives (twice for Trump). None of the men were convicted by the US Senate or removed from office, although Democrats, with the help of an unabashedly compliant left-leaning mainstream media, has gone after Trump nonstop with one flimsy charge after another since he won the election in 2016 and even after he left office in early 2021, their obsession to either get him removed from office (that didn't work) or to derail his 2024 re-election bid.

Affirmative action in some form has been around since I (Carol) was in grade school. When I was in second grade, President Kennedy signed Executive Order 10925 requiring government contractors to "take affirmative action to ensure that applicants are employed, and that employees are treated during employment, without regard to their race, creed, color, or national origin." The goal of nondiscrimination was later codified in federal law when Congress passed the Civil Rights Act of 1964 following the longest debate in congressional history. South Carolina Democrat Senator Strom Thurmond's filibuster of the civil rights action lasted twenty-four hours and eighteen minutes, a record that still stands.

CIVIL RIGHTS MOVEMENT SET THE STAGE

By the time I was born, the civil rights movement was scoring victories that helped set the stage for future success. I was born in 1954, the year that the U.S. Supreme Court issued its ruling in the *Brown v. Board of Education* school desegregation case, but I attended segregated schools until 1968. After completing the eighth grade, I dropped out of school, as all my siblings would eventually do. I married at sixteen and had my first child at seventeen.

I obtained my high school equivalency in 1975, and in 1976 I began my academic journey in college, which culminated in an associate degree in business, followed by a bachelor's degree in criminal justice with the distinction of *magna cum laude*, a master's and a PhD (in political science), and a Master of Legal Studies. I wasn't finished. After earning my PhD from the University of North Carolina, I paused my academic studies to take a tenure-tracked position at Princeton University. Then in 1999, circumstances caused me to resume my schooling while taking a sabbatical to earn a Master of Studies from Yale University. After having earned early tenure at Princeton University in 1994, I moved to Nashville in 2000 to teach at Vanderbilt University where I was promoted to full professorship and a joint position in the law school.

Liberals would argue that I used affirmative action to attain success and now I want to pull up the ladder after me. Such an assessment would miss the fact that I worked a full-time job nights and weekends while I was in college and managed to graduate with high honors. Although I was aware of affirmative action, I knew I was smart and I wanted to show that I could compete with the best regardless of race. It was difficult, and sometimes I struggled, particularly with math and science, but I had a strategy, a plan, and a can-do attitude that enabled me to silence the naysayers. Academia was never my idea. White progressives and conservatives recognized my talent and pushed me along a path I never consciously chose.

What benefited me the most was the kindness and benevolence of good people who wanted to see me succeed. They saw potential in me I was unaware of. These people became mentors and encouragers who pushed me far beyond the narrow limits of my imagination. Through it all, I was driven by a desire to prove myself capable. I never wanted to be the weakest link of the affirmative action hire. Consequently, I refused to apply for the minority positions being offered in political science where job candidates competed within their own groups. I insisted on competing in the general population of applicants and was willing to start at a mid-ranked school and work my way up to Harvard or Princeton. I was persuaded to start my career at Princeton University by an older conservative white man who said, "If you can start at the top, do so. Those other places will always be waiting." Princeton University chose me, and I chose them. I announced when I was hired that I planned to earn early tenure and I did. When I was hired, I had a Harvard University Press contract on my dissertation and I had a National Science Foundation Grant that enabled me to collect data that would turn the dissertation into the prize-winning book *Black Faces, Black Interests: The Representation of African Americans in Congress.*[3]

Black Faces, Black Interests was selected out of 611 titles by *Library Choice Journal* as one of the seven outstanding academic books of 1994, and it won three national prizes. It was the winner of the 1994 Woodrow Wilson prize given to the "best book published in the United States during the prior year on government, politics, or international affairs." It also won the 1995 D. B. Hardeman Prize for the best scholarly work on the U.S. Congress during a biennial period and was a co-winner of the V. O. Key Award for the best book published on Southern politics. *Black Faces* was also cited by Justice Anthony Kennedy in *Johnson v. Degrandy,* 512 U.S. 997, 1027 (1994) and twice by Justice Sandra Day O'Connor in *Georgia v. Ashcroft,* 539 U.S. (2003). Several outside offers of tenure, including one for an endowed chair, soon followed the publication of my book.

I negotiated for early tenure at Princeton, a move I later regretted for how it created animosity among other faculty because the tenure period is normally a seven-year process. By negotiating for early tenure, I was following the examples of white men and women who were highly sought after.

I wanted tenure to prove that a person from my background could earn early tenure. My strongest supporters have always been older conservative white men; my greatest opposition has come from progressive Whites who have often joined forces with black liberals to create roadblocks for me.

Academia was never an easy fit for me. Since affirmative action was the dominant focus of institutions, my awards and accomplishments were discounted. In other words, winning the career prize for political scientists did not mean the same thing to the world that it would have meant had I been white. In 2017, I relinquished my tenure, left academia, and have never looked back. Academia equipped me to do what I do today. I can speak to these issues from a vantage point where I believe I have seen it all. Hopefully, my journey can help others trying to understand and navigate the uncertainty of a world without affirmative action and hopefully without the divisive presence of the DEI purveyors of racism.

DEI: A COTTAGE INDUSTRY

Before diversity, equity, and inclusion became a cottage industry that often gives advantages to members of historically marginalized groups, it focused on less-controversial goals of nondiscrimination, outreach, and advertising. Nondiscrimination and the search for talented, hardworking minorities were powerful motivators for institutions. That involved searching for talented members of underrepresented populations and offering them employment and educational opportunities while publicizing opportunities nationwide to the general population. White men benefited from the advertising of open positions that helped weaken the word-of-mouth "old boys' network."

If institutions were good at recruitment, and honest about their motivations, they were often successful in bringing in people from underrepresented groups and helping them get up to speed. That was the kind of affirmative action from which I benefited as did millions of other people who have been successful in a similar manner since the passage of civil rights legislation in the 1960s. I was a child of that era and a beneficiary of a regime of nondiscriminatory, active recruitment of people from underrepresented populations. Although I graduated *magna cum laude* while working full time and raising two boys, I confess that my Graduate Record Examination (GRE) scores were not outstanding. Also, while in the community college, my lack of a high school background meant that I took remedial courses in math that would later prove crucial to my success in academia. Remedial math helped prepare me for the statistics courses required of social scientists. In fact, my first book and dissertation contained the obligatory regression analyses expected of PhD graduates.

During those years in school, I had an equal opportunity to succeed or fail. Academic leaders and mentors at my schools were looking for bright minorities, so I made sure I was there right in front of them so they could see me. I neither expected nor wanted special treatment. I was able to get admitted to colleges and earn scholarships based on my being an industrious worker who defied stereotypes such as Blacks being inherently unqualified, or lazy, or worse.

I benefited from people looking for talented minorities. For me, it was mostly white men who pushed me further than I intended to go; starting out I was just going to get a two-year degree so I could get a job. I never intended to pursue a PhD, or even become a professor at elite institutions (let alone two such institutions); it was just people I met along the way pushing me because they saw that I was bright. I was able to get attention that a white or Asian student would not have gotten as an honor student. I defied the odds—people knew my name. I profited a lot just from good, old-fashioned common sense and mentorship.

After unsuccessfully applying for jobs as a store manager, I was told I needed a four-year degree. At the same time I also decided I needed to distinguish myself on applications by becoming an honors graduate. Just "make it happen" was my philosophy. That is how I *really* caught people's attention. I checked out library books and purchased others on how to make As in college, how to take essay exams, and how to take objective tests. Then I applied the principles. So, I had a strategy. I knew that if I excelled, it was going to propel me far. Once, when I was struggling in a finite math class at Roanoke College, I dropped the course and, with the professor's permission, I attended the class until the course ended. I took the course for credit the following semester and earned an A.

Many white progressives have been found to hold racist views about the genetic abilities of Blacks. I will never forget when Francis Lawrence, president of Rutgers University in New Brunswick and a staunch supporter of affirmative action, spoke to faculty members about the need to lower expectations for Blacks. In what he thought was an off-the-record conversation, Lawrence stated that Blacks "don't have that genetic, hereditary background to have a higher average" on standardized admissions tests. After his remarks met with calls for his resignation, Lawrence said that he misspoke and didn't really believe what he stated.[4] Surprisingly, he survived the scandal and many high-profile Blacks came to his rescue.[5] Many white progressives, by their actions, indicate they hold the same set of beliefs. That is why they are quick to set up separate graduations, dorms, and class sections for minority students and faculty.

DIFFERENT EXPECTATIONS

White progressives genuinely believe that racial and ethnic minorities are incapable of meeting the same standards as white students. They will not come right out and say that, but their actions speak what their mouths rarely allow to slip out. They also dismiss the minorities who are well qualified and excel in academia and elsewhere. These minorities are the exceptions that prove the rule. The problem now for progressives is that there are not enough of these exceptional underrepresented minorities to satisfy the liberal appetites for proportional representation. So, instead of trying to increase the pool of qualified students, they have been artificially lowering the standards—both to get a desired number of minority students into the school and then to keep them there in good academic standing. Simultaneously, they are getting rid of advanced placement courses, honors courses, and standardized admissions tests. These are among many examples of "affirmative action" in action that make it clear it has been a breeding ground for what we now know as DEI and CRT—outgrowths of affirmative action that play up the victimization angle for Blacks. At the same time they seek to put Whites in their place once and for all, which is in the back of the room, if in the room at all.

It is a similar situation in many high schools. In my home state of Virginia, for example, there were reports in early 2023 of seventeen schools in Fairfax County whose school officials had reportedly failed to notify those students who had achieved National Merit Scholar status. That denied those students the opportunity to tout that recognition on their college applications. It was alleged that school district officials had withheld notice from the award-winning students because they did not want to hurt the feelings of students who fell short of achieving such status. Fairfax County public schools superintendent Dr. Michelle Reid denied the "hurt feelings" allegation, saying the delayed notice for the students was the result of "human error." Reid also disputed a claim made by Virginia

Governor Glenn Youngkin, who, upon hearing the news about the schools, said this was a "maniacal" attempt by the school district to ensure all students receive "equal outcomes."[6] Or what is otherwise known as *equity*.

BLOWING OFF SOME DUST

While writing this chapter, I was performing some light spring cleaning when I opened a drawer and found my senior thesis on affirmative action—the one I referenced earlier—that I had written forty years earlier. That was in 1983 while I was an undergraduate at Roanoke College. I picked it up and read back through its bound pages, all of which had been typed on an old typewriter. I was struck by how well the premise of the paper holds up even today. Remember, too, I was a Democrat at the time, and yet I saw a big problem with affirmative action. Two things really got my attention re-reading my paper: first, how several extended parts of it still resonate and are applicable for present-day discussion, even offering uncanny glimpses of affirmative action's future, and, second, that I got an A+ on it.

Here's an excerpt from that paper that seems as timely today as it was when I was in my twenties:

> Before entering college and the job market, my knowledge of affirmative action stemmed from media accounts. I expected much from the program, considered all Whites opposed to the program racist, and expected my share of the reparations. It took several years of increasingly political awareness and program examination for me to become thoroughly disillusioned with affirmative action. I resent the program that sometimes places incompetent individuals in positions of token authority. Their inevitable foibles are often purposely used to attest to the inadequacies of the program. Furthermore, I resent situations in which competent and sometimes superior minorities are forced to prove that their achievements are earned and not conferred benefits.
>
> Because of these things, I often find myself arguing with white males who say, "You've got it made, you're a black female" or "Why should you study so hard—you've got affirmative action to help you?" The most irritating statement that I've received from these white males was one in which the man lamented, 'I've been looking for a job for two years; if I were a black female, I'd have one.' The average white male seems to believe that minorities are reaping great benefits at his expense. Indeed, he sees us as having food stamps, welfare, practically free education, job preferences, and Medicaid all paid for out of his tax dollars. Moreover, he is quick to point out that he is not responsible for our inferior social status. He be-

lieves that affirmative action is the unjust visiting of the "sins of the father, upon the child."

If nothing else, the fact that there is a 1983 paper of mine that has a timeless feel to it says that I have aged well, too, if I may say so myself.

A SENSE OF BLACK ENTITLEMENT

The main thing I wanted to show in bringing that paper out of mothballs is how I took such a conservative stance so long ago, when I was still a Democrat. I have always believed that common sense and, as Spike Lee might concur, doing the right thing at any given time and with any given issue, are more important than pledging blind loyalty to a political agenda. In writing about affirmative action, I observed that a lot of Blacks I encountered forty-plus years ago had one of two mindsets: either they believed they were *entitled* to have admissions standards lowered far enough to meet them where they were, or that without affirmative action around to give them a lift they were incapable of success.

Both beliefs were lies. One lie likely prevented students from becoming doctors and lawyers because the academic standards they encountered once they got into a school (thanks to affirmative action) were not as low as they thought they would be—you still must do the work once you get there. If you have a GPA of less than 2.0 and think you are going to be a doctor or lawyer, think again. Not even affirmative action is going to climb that mountain for you. For the Blacks who believed they were incapable of achieving success *without* affirmative action, they were crippled, too.

I have always believed that people are motivated by incentive and will strive to meet any standard standing between them and their life's goal. There was a time when students coming out of high school and wanting to go to elite schools such as Harvard, Yale, Duke, Stanford, etc. thought they knew exactly when they needed to be competitive for admission at elite colleges and universities. Everyone who wanted to go to the Ivy League thought they had to be exceptional. Harvard University, which has never discriminated against Blacks, has always had some among its alumni. Students who wanted to go to a particular school figured out what they had to do to get there. The rules have changed dramatically as DEI has been layered over old-fashioned affirmative action. The quest for equity (*equal results*, not to be confused with *equal opportunity*) stacks the deck against those who played by the old rules. I, for one, do not believe that the elimination of racial preference will yield lily white or Asian institutions; there will always be high-achieving, privileged racial and ethnic minorities who will figure out what they have to do to attain their dream. Bright students will conform their behavior to the environment and the incentive structure placed before them.

Affirmative action, now in its sixties, has had staying power but has taken some legal hits over the years—such as in Michigan. That is where, in 2006, 58 percent of voters approved a ballot initiative banning affirmative action in the state. Not only did the ban affect college admissions, it also put a stop to taking race into account in hiring and contracting. The initiative was challenged the very next day, leading to an eight-year legal fight that moved its way up through courts. Finally, in April 2014, the U.S. Supreme Court ruled that the ban was legal, prohibiting preferential treatment based on race, gender, ethnicity, or national origin.

The Michigan case dates back to 1995. That is when Jennifer Gratz, a young white woman, sued the University of Michigan in Ann Arbor after her application for admission to the prestigious school was rejected. This was despite her 3.8 grade-point average and participation in a variety of extracurricular activities. Gratz, thirty-seven when SCOTUS ruled in favor of the affirmative action ban, predicted at the time that more of the country would follow suit. "I think that this ruling took us one step closer to equality," she said.[7]

I never wanted my two sons to know about affirmative action while they were in high school. I never talked about it around them because I never wanted them to think they could coast because of their race. Affirmative action sends the signal to young minorities that they can be less competent and still get to the same place as their hardworking classmates who happen to be white and end up at lesser institutions. My older son, a factory worker, did not go to college and my younger son became a businessman. For the longest time, my younger son would not apply for work while listing his business as a minority-owned business because he felt it limited his opportunities. Eventually, when he was seeking to subcontract with major firms, he then designated his business as minority owned, as he was advised to do by the corporations wanting to hire his agency. Many corporate and governmental agencies have to solicit bids from a certain number of minority-owned businesses to meet mandated quotas and expectations. The system incentivizes white women and racial and ethnic minorities applying for and taking advantage of whatever programs and funds are available. I have my own businesses as well and have avoided applying for the designation of minority-owned business even though I would certainly qualify as a Black and as a woman.

THE MISMATCH THEORY

Progressives and well-meaning conservatives who push for lowered admission standards for racial and ethnic minorities are often doing more harm than good. Back in 2012, Richard Sander and Stuart Taylor Jr., both UCLA law professors, wrote an important book titled *Mismatch: How Affirmative Action Hurts Students It's Intended to Help, and Why Universities Won't Admit It*. Sander and Taylor found that racial preferences often put students at a competitive disadvantage when they found themselves among classmates who were more academically prepared. The affirmative action admittees often found themselves doomed for failure. Eventually, many of the minority students, who could have been successful at a lower-tiered university, never finished. As a consequence, colleges and universities are producing far fewer lawyers, doctors, and engineers than would be expected. Minority law students who manage to graduate fail the bar exam at four times the rate of white students.[8] Of course, Sander and Taylor's study was conducted before DEI's big push for equal outcomes. There has been a move to eliminate tests that disproportionately fail minorities.

We do know that aggressive affirmative action and DEI programs are putting minority students into institutions where many are not prepared to excel. Whenever failure occurs, institutional racism can always be blamed, but not one's level of preparation or intellectual prowess.

When I started college, I began by enrolling at a community college— no affirmative action necessary to attend Virginia Western.

Once I had gotten to Virginia Western and made the dean's list a couple of times, I became receptive to pushing myself to excel. Feedback from prospective employers indicated I needed a four-year degree to become a store manager. I knew from the applications that I needed to distinguish myself if I wanted to get a high-paying job. I either purchased or checked out library books on how to make A's in college, how to write essays, and how to take multiple choice exams. I applied the principles and they worked. My journey took me to Roanoke College, a four-year liberal arts college in Salem, Virginia, then to Virginia Tech, and then to the University of North Carolina at Chapel Hill for my PhD. I would later earn another master's degree in law from Yale University. This was after I had earned tenure at Princeton and before I moved to Nashville to start my full professorship at Vanderbilt. There are minorities (and Whites, sometimes) who are bright and have done well in high school who could do well at the "typical" four-year undergraduate school, but because of affirmative action or sports recruitment, end up instead going to more selective schools where they struggle, and some drop out. If they had gone to a college or university more closely aligned with their academic record, perhaps even a two-year college first, more could have been successful, and some would have graduated at the top of their class rather than in the lower tier. As a GED holder, I needed the community college stint to prepare me for my educational journey. It filled in the gaps and made up for the high school instruction I lacked. My remedial math course prepared me for college math and statistics I would later take at the four-year-college and in graduate school.

I believe my nontraditional path would work for other would-be college or trade school graduates. More strategic choices and planning should be encouraged for young people, and not just for Blacks. It can work for anyone who needs more preparation: the diamond in the rough, for example.

Creative new thinking has come from Harvard University economist Roland Fryer, who happens to be black, like me. In a *New York Times* article titled "Build Freer Schools and Make Yale and Harvard Fund Them," Fryer noted that the current approach to student recruitment to Ivy League schools is deficient:

"Right now, colleges take the supply of qualified minority students as fixed. They might run a summer enrichment program for local kids, but they don't intervene in students' education in systemic ways. They don't teach the higher-order skills that students need to get into college. They don't cultivate the grit and resilience that kids need to navigate a challenging curriculum after they are admitted. They rely on existing schools to do that—and if those schools routinely fail minority students, well, that's a problem with the precollege pipeline."[9]

Fryer's solution, which is one I wholeheartedly endorse, is for elite institutions to operate and fund feeder middle and high schools for promising students who lack access to a quality education. As far as I am concerned, this approach would be a better use of their vast endowments than the DEI programs and lowered admission standards they fought tooth and nail to retain. To adopt this approach, colleges and universities would have to believe that racial and ethnic minorities are capable of learning and competing with members of the majority group on an equal basis when given the right opportunities.

CHAPTER 3

Diversity Training:
A Corporate Conundrum

"Our greatest asset in protecting the homeland and advancing our interests abroad is the talent and diversity of our national security workforce. Under my Administration, we have made important progress toward harnessing the extraordinary range of backgrounds, cultures, perspectives, skills, and experiences of the U.S. population toward keeping our country safe and strong. As the United States becomes more diverse and the challenges we face more complex, we must continue to invest in policies to recruit, retain, and develop the best and brightest from all segments of our population. Research has shown that diverse groups are more effective at problem solving than homogeneous groups, and policies that promote diversity and inclusion will enhance our ability to draw from the broadest possible pool of talent, solve our toughest challenges, maximize employee engagement and innovation, and lead by example by setting a high standard for providing access to opportunity to all segments of our society." [1]
— **President Barack Obama**

THAT IS THE CRUX OF AN OCTOBER 2016 MEMORANDUM titled "Presidential Memorandum—Promoting Diversity and Inclusion in the National Security Workforce." President Barack Obama issued the memorandum less than four months before completing his second term in office. His stern message was directed at the more than three million people who at the time comprised the U.S. national security workforce. That labor pool, according to the memo, entailed the departments, agencies, offices, and other entities found within the "diplomacy, development, defense, intelligence, law enforcement, and homeland security" assets of our federal government.[2]

Obama's eight-page decree encompassed more than twenty-six hundred words and included five major directives outlined in five sections composed of a total of thirteen subsections. A lot to digest there, pushing hard for a PC version of DEI. It offered extensive detail about the procedures and measures these federal departments were to follow and prioritize in focusing their efforts—as prefaced in the memo's titles—specifically in the areas of *diversity* and *inclusion*. The expressed tenor of Obama's directive presumably put diversity and inclusion—you could also include *equity*, albeit unmentioned here, to complete the familiar DEI triumvirate—ahead of other factors such as mission readiness, exclusively merit-based promotions, and quality of training on the pecking order of success criteria for our national security workforce.

Several questions are begged. Was Obama suggesting that solely by increasing the percentage of Blacks and other minorities working in these departments (e.g., defense and homeland security) that their mission readiness would be improved—that more problems would be solved, and with better solutions? And exactly what research was he referring to when he mentioned that "diverse groups are more effective at problem solving than homogeneous groups"? Also, which "homogenous" groups was he referring to (with "homogenous" likely being code for "too white")? He then wrote, "We must continue to invest in policies to recruit, retain, and develop the best and brightest from all segments of our population." Wasn't that already being done?

Obama in his memo called for such geeky-sounding directives as "collection, analysis, and dissemination of workforce data," "aggregate demographic data," "New Inclusion Quotient (New IQ) index score," "barrier analyses related to diversity and inclusion," "voluntary applicant flow data," a requirement that "agencies shall ensure their SES CDP comports with the provisions of 5 C.F.R. part 412, subpart C, including merit staffing and assessment requirements,"[3] and, well, you get the gist. There is nothing like a slew of newly required mind-numbing, time-eating number crunching to further bog down federal government workers while giving America a skewed view of presidential support of the so-called merits of DEI. Notice, too, the timing of Obama's memo—barely a month before the 2016 election, no doubt so he could show his liberal Democratic base just how genuine his pandering embrace of them was (it didn't work, obviously—Hillary lost). It also sent a late presidential-term shot across the bow of America's corporations, companies, and other organizations, producing a trickle-down effect that served as a warning that they had better get in line with DEI practices as well, or else.

Clearly, DEI, and its forerunner—known simply as diversity and inclusion—had been around decades before Obama fired off his warning-shot memo in October 2016 as part of his farewell tour from the White House. He wasn't breaking new ground on the DEI philosophy and its practice; he was putting his fingerprints on something that stipulated how it would (as opposed to "should") be done. Its roots, as pointed out earlier, date back to the 1960s and the creation of "affirmative action" as introduced in executive orders by JFK and augmented by his successor, LBJ, both of which addressed the workplace as well as college and university admissions offices. What had changed, though, by the time Obama got his boost into the White House, thanks to the political world's version of "affirmative action," is that diversity and inclusion has expanded unchecked into an industry all its own. No longer are DEI programs just an appendage to human resource departments in businesses and on college campuses.

In the last eight to ten years, what we now know as DEI has become a potent and influential cottage industry with a cumulative budget nationwide in the tens of billions of dollars. We now have DEI departments, many led by what's called a chief diversity officer, or something similar, cluttered with untold thousands of DEI professionals whose generous livelihoods are carved out of resources that include taxpayer money as well as dollars that might have otherwise been budgeted for HR departments. As the dominoes start to fall backward with the Supreme Court's blow to affirmative action, DEI professionals and their supportive allies in the far-Left ranks are desperately scrambling to validate their continued employment in these roles so they can save as much of that pie as possible for themselves.

DEI PROGRAMS EXPOSED

DEI programs and consultants often use methods that violate the Civil Rights Act of 1964 and the equal protection clause of the Fourteenth Amendment. The Supreme Court decision in the Harvard and University of North Carolina cases shines a spotlight on race-based discrimination and exposes programs for what they really are and what they actually have created in our society. The workplace is rife with political correctness and demands for group privileges that often violate civil rights protections for groups that are not considered historically marginalized. That includes, for example, white males, Christians, and heterosexuals who just want to do their jobs in an environment free of the pressures of social engineering.

Start with their destructive effects on corporate strategy, developing a culture that distracts from profits and market performance, stifling conversation at board meetings that leads to costly nonsensical decisions, stimulating unproductive behavior, and creating a contrarian subculture. Yet DEI advocates and far-Left liberals cling to a false narrative, faithfully parroted by a compliant mainstream media, that diversity, equity, and inclusion remain the key ingredients to success in the corporate world and across all workplace environments. You have those three things in place (or at least believe you do) and the rest is gravy. Probably not. How about market share for your business? Net profits? Year-over-year growth? For many business leaders, those do not seem to matter as much as DEI metrics.

One thing DEI has down cold with all its programs, training, and behavioral edicts is putting white people, especially males, in cages and making them grovel to toe the company line. If you don't embrace the philosophies of aggressive race or gender-based affirmative action, the LGBTQ+ movement, critical race theory, and Black Lives Matter, then it's time to hit the bricks. The same goes with colleges and their DEI mafia with strong-arm tactics of their own, such as if you want an A or B in that history or English class, you had better get in sync with your professor's worldview on gender, race, and American history.

We get it that, legally speaking, the First Amendment and its declaration of free speech applies only to the government's attempted intrusion into our free speech, but you get our drift—the "spirit" of free expression should be voluntarily exercised by all citizens (and their workplace bosses) in all walks of life. It is sad to see how much the far Left insists on trampling on those rights through tactics such as compelled speech in corporations and other organizations insistent on their employees kowtowing/pandering to the politically correct agendas of DEI advocates and activists.

Take it from James Damore, who had been a senior software engineer at Google for four years when in 2017 he got fired for what he described as "perpetuating gender stereotypes."[4] It is not enough that workers—which includes managers and executives—tolerate and are courteous to minority and minority groups (such as LGBTQ) whose lifestyles conflict with a worker's religious beliefs; they also must embrace and endorse such lifestyles, or else. Damore's religious beliefs were not on trial in his case; his rejection of political correctness and right to express his opinions were. His DEI faux pas was a ten-page memo in which he called for the company to back off its obsessive (my word) push for gender diversity in the workplace. Damore's memo zeroed in on Google's diversity and inclusion strategies, among them an unconscious bias class the company was encouraging employees to take, as if they had a choice. He reportedly also argued that gender gaps in the workforce do not necessarily "imply sexism" and that "discriminating just to increase the representation of women in tech" (is) "misguided and biased" (and) "unfair, divisive, and bad for business."[5]

Although Damore was accused of using stereotypical misconceptions about men and women in stating his case, the memo also came out at a time when Google had just updated its internal diversity metrics, apparently admitting that its workforce demographics were skewed heavily male and white. Simultaneous to this, the U.S. Department of Labor had put Google under the microscope amid reports of wage discrimination whereby female employees were allegedly being systematically underpaid. Reaction inside and outside the company over Damore's memo was divided.[6] Some supporters of Damore's right and, in some cases, rationale in writing the memo turned up the heat on Google over the issue of the software engineer obviously not being allowed to speak freely due to his being fired over the controversial memo.

Google isn't the only high-tech company that has stubbed its toe in the diversity, equity, and inclusion world; Mozilla is another. Mozilla forced the resignation of CEO Brendan Eich in 2014 when it learned that he had made a modest personal contribution of a thousand dollars—*six years earlier*—in support of a gay-marriage ban in California that has since been overturned.[7] When it comes to public and workplace firestorms (especially in California and particularly when it involves a corporate executive supporting a conservative cause), there's nothing so inspiring as going after a company bigwig with a huge public profile when there is no statute of limitations or minimum dollar amount constituting an unacceptable or even unethical political contribution. It is bad for business, apparently, and Eich was toast.

No way Mozilla was going let this one go (other than Eich being shown the door). As Associated Press reported, "Eich's abrupt departure has stirred the debate over the fairness of forcing out a highly qualified technology executive over his personal views and a single campaign contribution *six years ago*. And it raises questions about how far corporate leaders are allowed to go in expressing their political views."[8] In a DEI world, not very far at all, especially when said corporate leader is white and male, as Eich is. Not just any white male, mind you: Eich not only created JavaScript, but he also had a hand in writing the code for Netscape's Navigator web browser, and he later cofounded Mozilla.[9]

AMERICANS DID NOT SIGN UP FOR THIS

Before you ask, I'll tell you what's wrong with this picture. It is the distasteful type of diversity that is being pursued by activists today, the one that has been politicized and distorted beyond recognition. This diversity is not the one we signed up for. Diversity's destiny is aimed in the wrong direction. This current version of diversity is not connected to the kind of diversity that we can all pretty much accept and celebrate, the one that we know it when we see it, the one in which everyone can be comfortable that a variety of people are all being given the same opportunity and can blend together without being told how to act. The one in which no single demographic benefits at the expense of another (reverse discrimination). We seek a pure, undefiled brand of diversity absent of legalistic gibberish, rules, and regulations tailored to fit a certain political agenda.

The problem with this altered state of diversity is that those who are running today's diversity, equity, and inclusion industry want people to come into businesses or colleges and universities with group identities. These purveyors of DEI nonsense want to establish affinity groups, then maintain those identities without ever really assimilating (which is foundational to proper diversity), and then to make sure these groups get special protection. They are pushing for proportional representation—actually, *more* than proportional representation. That is, they are not saying that when you get to 14 percent Blacks or 18 percent Hispanics (consistent with the proportional makeup of the general U.S. population), you're done; they want bigger and bigger numbers because they believe they are entitled to special treatment. They are pushing and promoting a tact openly hostile to Whites, knowing in this current environment of PC on steroids they will get little pushback, because few opponents dare to try—even when right, they lose.

In my 2002 book *The New White Nationalism in America: Its Challenge to Integration*, I warned that multiculturalism and identity politics, and their attendant language, fostered an environment that would lead to increased racial and ethnic conflict. And it has. The diversity "solution" needs fixing. What is being done now with the likes of DEI and CRT is geared directly and purposely toward creating group conflict that has reached the level of intense tribalism. There is nothing about the current DEI approach that seems geared toward bringing people together—no natural blending, integration, or assimilation. It is mostly about conveying the message that it is time for heterosexual white men and women to step aside, that they have had their privileges long enough, and now it is time for members of historically marginalized groups to rule and reign. At the same time, the DEI/CRT movement is sending a message that violence and crime emanating from Black and Hispanic communities is justified because of historical injustices and that antifa members are just freedom fighters who deserve the kid-gloves approach they receive in most cities where they cover their faces like Klansmen and engage in violent behavior against anyone who gets in their path.

Corporate/workplace diversity training (again, what we now call DEI) dates back to the late 1960s and into 1970s. It was a response to the birth of affirmative action and federal legislation that gave us the 1964 Civil Rights Act. Title VII of that landmark Act made it illegal for employers with more than fifteen employees to "discriminate in hiring, termination, promotion, compensation, job training, or any other term, condition, or privilege of employment based on race, color, religion, sex, or national origin."[10] Maybe that explains why those early years of diversity training focused primarily on legislation and compliance (i.e., lawsuit avoidance) in response to a spate of discrimination lawsuits filed with the Equal Employment Opportunity Commission (EEOC).[11]

"Most training during this era was primarily the imparting of knowledge with recitations on the law and company policies, a litany of do's and don'ts and maybe a couple of case studies for the participants to ponder," researchers Rohini Anand and Mary-Frances Winters wrote in "A Retrospective View of Corporate Diversity Training from 1964 to the Present," which was published in 2008. "The length of training varied widely from one hour to a full day, with a typical length of four hours."[12]

DIVERSITY TRAINING: THE EARLY YEARS

In those early years of diversity training, companies and their executive leaders were diligent about compliance, but they were also content to check whatever boxes needed to be checked to mitigate any complaints or lawsuits that otherwise might come their way. Put it another way, they were going through the motions, albeit while playing by the rules of conducting such diversity training, although rank-and-file employees going through such training—it was usually conducted by HR managers already in place—might remember what they were taught and told, only to forget it days later. But other problems surfaced as well. For instance, because such training at the time focused on underrepresented minorities (think Blacks) and women, those groups' nonmembers—to include white males, of course—felt purposely excluded and came to see such training as preferential treatment of others. As Anand and Winters also point out, the training content itself did not sit well with members of the dominant group (again, white males) because the instruction failed to make much of a connection between recommended changes in behavior among employees and improved business results.

One aspect of the 1960s-1970s diversity training environment that today's social justice warriors can applaud is that industry giants IBM and Xerox jumped into diversity training with both feet. IBM showed its enthusiasm by boldly stating that diversity is a moral imperative, while Xerox put into place an overtly social responsibility tact in creating a diversity training program that went above and beyond what the law called for. No surprise there, though. Rochester, New York—Xerox's home base to this day—had been rocked by riots in the mid-sixties and in 1971 was hit with a class action discrimination suit.[13]

Some fifty years later, diversity/DEI training has morphed into something almost unrecognizable to what C-level and HR executives were dealing with in the Aquarius days of yesteryear. In case you have not noticed it, this whole DEI/CRT/BLM and even LGBTQ+ alphabet-soup programming—with their seething watchdog influence over corporate America and workplace diversity training in general—is all part of the American version of Marxism. I have seen presentations of these agendas; critical race theory comes straight out of Marxism. That's not us stretching things to the nth degree to make a connection; by their very nature and definition, CRT, critical queer theory, and so forth are subcategories of Marxism. If you are a far-Left progressive and either do not know that or deny that connection, then you have not done your required reading of the Marxist playbook—it is the overarching umbrella. You need to do your own homework; it's your philosophy we are talking about here, after all. At the end of the day (and morning, afternoon, and night for that matter), Marxism in its radical nature is all about upending society. It is not about bringing people together, or racial healing, or reconciliation, or bringing about any type of unity into America. It is all about division.

THE BLACK LIVES MATTER FACTOR

As much as BLM has been a ringleader—you, too, LGBTQ+—in this "progressive" crusade to hold corporations hostage to their whims, and as much as BLM has gotten into the heads of the likes of National Football League Commissioner Roger Goodell, it's interesting to note that as of this writing in June 2023, BLM is apparently on life support, teetering on the edge of bankruptcy.[14] Chalk that up to the reported failures of individual leadership that has allegedly pocketed millions of dollars in wealth/real estate holdings for themselves, much of it eagerly donated by corporations such as Warner Bros., looking to promote their "antiracist" agenda, all the time making no secret of their ties to Marxism.

Yes, BLM's questionable business dealings and accounting practices have earned the race-driven organization a spot in this discussion about diversity training. How so? It's how the likes of Warner Bros. have signaled their antiracist virtues[15] by sending big bucks to BLM, which apparently makes up for any deficiencies they might have in their own in-house DEI training programs. Law professor and legal scholar/commentator Jonathan Turley put it thusly: "(BLM co-founder Patrisse Marie Khan-Cullors) was previously open about her lack of interest in working with 'capitalist' elements. Nevertheless, BLM was run like a Trotskyite study group as the media and corporations poured in support and revenue. It was glaringly ironic to see companies like Warner Bros. falling over each other to grab their own front person as the group continued boycotts of white-owned businesses. Indeed, if you did not want to be on the wrong end of one of those boycotts, you needed to get Cullors on your payroll."[16] And what a payoff it was for Cullors and others in charge at BLM. Tens of millions of contributed dollars (or what Don Corleone might call "protection money") flowed into their coffers at Black Lives Matter Global Network Foundation, more than $6 million of which went to Cullors and other Canadian activists for the 2021 purchase of a Toronto mansion.[17]

When I (Carol) see a white male child, I see someone who is going to have a lot of problems down the road because of the color of his skin. At this point in history, the tables have seemingly been turned against Whites. Unless DEI is reined in like affirmative action was in higher education, white poor and working class youth will remain members of a disfavored group likely to experience race-based discrimination in some sectors of society. Only a strong commitment to nondiscrimination can create a more just system where no one is advantaged or disadvantaged because of their skin color.

When I (Carol) give presentations to homeschooling families, I emphasize the need for them to know the truth about DEI and CRT; otherwise, when their kids finish their education and enter colleges and universities or the work world, they are going to be blindsided by what they encounter. White males will encounter prejudicial information telling them that their race is responsible for the injustices around the world and that they bear guilt for the unfortunate situation many racial and ethnic minorities experience. The goal is to indoctrinate them with white guilt and shame so that they will embrace the call to antiracism and devote their lives to the noble cause of social justice. The CRT/DEI-related bullying and shaming on college campuses have traditionally begun when the student begins to receive literature from the institution, and orientation week is like drinking water from a firehose for many students raised in traditional Christian families. Unfortunately, some young people will be in for a massive cultural shock when they encounter the world of work and life on the modern campus. It will not matter whether the institution is Christian or secular. The playbook seems to be the same everywhere.

We need to prepare for life after race-based affirmative action because of its clear implications down the road for the DEI officers and trainings that have engulfed every sector of our society, including the U.S. military, medical schools, and the aviation industry. We need to be prepared to have substantive conversation about what we believe is important about people, the teams they form, and the missions of our institutions. We do know from the higher education examples that led to the end of affirmative action that all the courses, protests, DEI deans, and cultural engagement employees failed to advance racial healing or reconciliation. Instead, they have supported seg-regation and resegregation with their separate dorms, separate class sections, separate this, and separate that. *That* has been hugely divisive. People in the corporate world then need to know that those students educated under that system described above have taken their values into their corporate world. Now it's your problem, C-level executives on down. Instead of being able to focus on true success-or-failure criteria, such as profit margins, year-over-year growth, market share, and adherence to the mission of the founders and owners, you are having to babysit, nurse, and otherwise deal with all those issues related to the diversity dynamic.

That could soon be changing. For the better, of course. We hope.

CHAPTER 4

A Not-So-Inconvenient Death: The Martyrdom of George Floyd

"Never allow a good crisis to go to waste. It's an opportunity to do the things you once thought were impossible."[1]
— **Rahm Emanuel**, White House Chief of Staff under President Barack Obama, 2009-2010, writing for the *Washington Post*, March 25, 2020

"The murder of George Floyd on May 25, 2020, unleashed a tidal wave of pledges of support for greater diversity, equity, and inclusion (DEI) across corporate America and beyond. Companies scrambled to voice their support for Black Lives Matter; they created and filled new positions for chief diversity officers, and announced their commitment to increasing their efforts to hire and retain more people from underrepresented, underprivileged, underappreciated segments of the population."[2]
— **Paolo Gaudiano**, writing for *Forbes*, June 27, 2022

THE FIRST PART: HORRIBLE NEWS, *PARTICULARLY* FOR THOSE PEOPLE who knew and loved George Floyd, but good news for the DEI industry. It finally had found its best rallying opportunity in years.

Rahm Emanuel was right.

Emanuel, a former Illinois congressman and eventually a mayor of Chicago after leaving his White House post less than two years after being appointed to it by President Obama, has never run from his controversial quote (on loan from the archives of noted political theorist and radical activist Saul Alinsky). In fact, Emanuel wrote about seeing the brighter side of a national crisis or tragedy in his March 25, 2020, editorial in the *Washington Post*. This was days after the U.S. started shutting down in the wake of the arrival of the COVID-19 crisis, and exactly two months ahead of Floyd's death attributed to the hands (or bent knee) of a white cop in Minneapolis.[3]

Worth noting, giving the historical significance of Floyd's death, is the initial autopsy report by the Hennepin County Medical Examiner's Office. It described Floyd as having COVID with the cause of death listed as a "cardiopulmonary arrest complicating law enforcement subdual, restraint, and neck compression." Fentanyl and methamphetamine were in his bloodstream and he suffered from heart disease and hypertension. Independent medical examiners hired by the family concluded that the death was homicide with one of the expert witnesses describing him as being in good health.[4]

To bring perspective to Emanuel's quote above, it helps to know that he at one time was tagged as a "bulldog" or "attack dog," dating back to his days as an aide in the Bill Clinton administration. Referring to the spreading pandemic in that *Post* article, Emanuel said that then-President Donald Trump was "outmatched by the moment," and, furthermore, immediate mobilization was needed "to think strategically not only about how to address the virus but also about how the United States can come out stronger on the other side."[5] On this side, however, thousands of Americans a week were already dying from a rampant global virus. Opportunities during tragic times like this can only arise in the eyes of sociopathic beholders—such as BLM, antifa members, and other racially divisive activists.

Emanuel's seemingly ruthless words could be interpreted as even more fitting in the aftermath of the death of Floyd, a black man who, while on the ground and in police custody, succumbed as Minneapolis cop Derek Chauvin kept him pinned to the ground with a knee.[6] As news of the manner of Floyd's death flashed across America, anti-White activists went to work as if on cue. The death of Floyd, a black man, at the hands of a white cop was their green light, a chance to seek "social justice" by wreaking havoc nationwide through violence, protests, and destructive acts such as burning businesses. People died. It wasn't long before local government officials and angry citizens started calling for the defunding—some even mentioned "disbanding"—of police departments, as rioting and related violent crime spiked in many areas.

This all had the appearance of mass insanity, except it wasn't. If you look closely in the right places, you will see that these waves of protests, violence, and destruction, to include the burning of businesses, were part of the radical progressive playbook, to include the parts about being orchestrated and well-funded. There was nothing random or authentic about any of it. All it takes to put the master plan in motion is a spark that lights the fuse, and Floyd's death was that spark. The fact that the perpetrator was a white cop was a bonus. It was too good a crisis to pass up. It screamed *opportunity*. Alinsky and Rahm were right. And Floyd? He was as much a useful patsy as he was a mourned martyr.

CORPORATE AMERICA TOLD TO JUMP, BUT HOW HIGH?

Much of corporate America immediately went into overdrive launching their own crisis responses, and they knew what needed to be done to save or preserve face: just as Gaudiano described above, underneath the Emanuel quote. Many companies, perhaps sensing they were about to be pressured or even bullied at the end of a proverbial bayonet, pledged to beef up and push harder than ever before with their DEI programs and practices, all in the spirit of workplace affirmative action guidelines. It was also to make a public showing of their enhanced efforts to fight racism in their communities. If BLM leaders had asked (told) corporate executives and board members to jump, they likely would have responded, "How high?" What choice did they have?

Here's a choice, as reported in the *New York Post* on July 10, 2020. Within weeks of Floyd's death, the city of Seattle's Office of Civil Rights sent out an email invitation asking, "white city employees" to be present for a training session titled "Interrupting Internalized Racial Superiority and Whiteness," a presentation intended to help white employees examine their "complicity in . . . white supremacy" and "interrupt racism, in ways that are accountable to black, indigenous, and people of color." It was also reported that Seattle's trainers explained to seminar attendees that "white people have internalized a sense of racial superiority, which has made them unable to access their 'humanity' and caused 'harm and violence' to minorities."[7]

Christopher F. Rufo, author of that *New York Post* piece, noted in his story that James Lindsay, also a noted critic of DEI training, had opined that content of that training session, as described here, wasn't "the language of human resources; it is the language of cult programming—persuading members that they are defective in some predefined manner, exploiting their vulnerabilities and isolating them from previous relationships."[8]

DEI training? How about we instead call it what it really is: BCW Training—Boot Camp for Whites? Seattle in recent decades has painted itself as a champion of the political correctness movement to include standing guard as a true DEI trooper, a lightning rod for diversity and diversity training notoriety. Which brings us to Seattle-based Starbucks. You might remember hearing about the April 2018 incident at a Starbucks facility in the Philadelphia area. That was the one in which two lack men who had entered the Starbucks were asked to leave after they had been spotted by Starbucks employees sitting at a table for quite a while without ordering anything. The two men, who declined to leave when asked by management, claiming they were waiting for a business associate. That meeting never took place, however, because the two men eventually were led out of the facility in handcuffs by police who had been called by a store manager.[9]

Enter Shannon Phillips, a regional Starbucks manager in the Philly area. She was fired after having defended a white restaurant employee who, in turn, had been put on administrative leave for alleged discriminatory conduct. For sticking up for the employee put on leave, Phillips herself was fired. About a year later, Phillips filed a lawsuit saying, by her being fired, she had been discriminated against because of her race. A classic case of reverse discrimination. No White privilege there. Four years later, though, in June 2023, a New Jersey jury returned a verdict of $25.6 million in favor of Phillips. That included $25 million for punitive damages and $600,000 in compensatory damages, according to the law firm that represented Phillips.[10] Soon after the original incident, Starbucks closed about 8,000 of its stores for an afternoon of mandatory anti-bias training for 175,000 of its employees. Looney Tunes stuff like this is going on all around America, masquerading as diversity/DEI training and being forced down the throats of workers who have no option but to listen to this nonsense and try to swallow it (or not).

Wokeness has its cost. By July 2022, Starbucks was in the news again because of its decision to close sixteen stores in urban areas (five of those in Seattle) because of crime and rampant drug use. Backtracking on its free public use of bathrooms, Starbucks store managers now have the discretion about when to hand out the key. Keyed bathrooms have now become the norm even in cities as far flung as Nashville.[11]

A STICKY SITUATION

Granted, the Floyd aftermath simultaneous to the COVID outbreak was a sticky time to be a company executive or business owner. Corporate America was already reeling from having to wrestle with panicky local, state, and federal authorities issuing mandates and protocols regarding which businesses were deemed essential and which were not. Not to mention how to handle such issues as masks, social distancing, and, eventually, vaccine distribution and administration amid misinformation and false narratives relative to proper health care of apparent COVID patients.

The elephant in the room: what to do about diversity, equity, and inclusion (DEI) programs in workplaces now that it was time once and for all to put white people—especially *white males*—and most especially *conservative white males*—in their rightful place and to stamp out so-called White privilege and White supremacy. DEI advocates, managers, and trainers now had a renewed and enhanced level of clout they had never had before; meanwhile, Marxist-influenced progressives were rubbing their hands in gleeful anticipation of what they could get away with next. Floyd's death had essentially weaponized DEI practices and training against Whites—not a chance of a two-way street here.

History was repeating itself from more than fifty years earlier. Just two or three years after the Civil Rights Act of 1964 was signed into law, America witnessed its worst race riots ever. At the time, in the late sixties, affirmative action, racial preferences, and what was then simply called diversity training (all things most Americans say they no longer want or need) were designed to appease would-be rioters. So much for that. For decades, the Left has used a strategy of violence and protests to get what they want. It's their nature. They create a narrative out of thin air that may or may not be true, but repeat it enough times prominently—with the help of much of the media—that anyone content like sheep to buy into the liberal malarkey, accepts the liberal narrative as gospel *truth*. It was *not* the down-and-out people who were rioting now, it was the elites. Alinsky would have been proud if he had still been alive to see this, and no doubt Rahm is nodding his head as if to say, "See, I told you this stuff works. If you build it (a crisis), they (opportunists) will come."

Since the Floyd debacle, the dial on the divisiveness quotient of DEI training has been cranked up to high; it's in the red of the danger zone. This first started becoming evident while Barack Obama was in the White House.

No coincidence there. Under him, DEI became more aggressive. At the time, I was still a university law professor and aware of what was happening at colleges and universities. Because of trickle-down orders and mandates from the Obama administration, prospective employees and students were forced to take certain oaths or write and sign statements declaring their support for various forms of diversity. This now included far-Left agendas espousing LGBTQ+ principles, even when those ran counter to a prospective employee's or student's faith/religious beliefs. That is known as compelled speech, or compelled acts, and goes against the grain of the U.S. Constitution as well as Christian morals and ethics. Tolerating homosexuality, queerness, or transsexualism is one thing; being forced to embrace, promote, or endorse those lifestyles is another—it's likely in violation of free speech as stated in the First Amendment. Marxist progressives have been empowered and emboldened to shove those types of shenanigans upon applicants, apparently nonchalant to the possibility that courts could rule them as sexual harassment.

While we were working on this book, the Texas senate passed a bill that would prohibit universities from forcing applicants to swear such oaths or sign such statements. It was signed into law, making Texas the second state (Florida was the first) to ban DEI programs at public universities. (See Appendix B.) Such programs should be prohibited at every college and university in the nation because they are based on practices and approaches that violate the rights of nonfavored groups. A number of Women's Studies programs have for decades been requiring job applicants to express support for LGBTQ+ lifestyles. At some of the more elite institutions, it is a given that new directors of such programs must be either a member of the LGBTQ+ community or someone with a track record that can easily demonstrate their commitment by writing or signing a statement swearing to such.

One distinction needs to be pointed out here. Leftist advocates for diversity training and similar programs keep insisting that DEI, affirmative action, and the teaching of CRT are three separate entities that must be treated distinctively from one another—that, for example, DEI and affirmative action are not the same (they are, in fact, the same). Leftists have long said they are different so that if the Supreme Court were to strike down or at least considerably weaken affirmative action (which it did, ultimately), DEI would be less likely to be affected. Therefore it could continue unscathed as the $50 billion industry it is, still employing tens of thousands, all with expectations of continued job security. Well, not so fast, obviously.

In its original form, in the late sixties, diversity training was. in fact . . . drum roll . . . diversity training. As it should be. That is no longer the case. *Diversity training has morphed into something more resembling divisiveness training.* I'd even go so far as to say it is divisiveness indoctrination, a form of social re-engineering. The Left's aim is for it to be a mechanism that promotes social justice.

If your workplace has scheduled one of those special days where everyone must, say, wear a purple ribbon to virtually signal their approval, support, or endorsement of a certain cause or movement, and you either refuse to wear the purple ribbon or choose to stay in your office all day while not taking it off, you risk punishment if what you are doing is considered rejection of that day's mandated cause, or borderline insubordination.

As of 2023, instances of reverse discrimination continue to dot the American landscape. Another notable example involved the University of Minnesota, which faced backlash in 2023 after its Office of Undergraduate Studies launched a taxpayer-funded summer research program that was made available only to nonwhite students. In fact, it was a paid undergraduate internship program (each student selected for the program received a $6,000 stipend) in which applicants were required to submit demographic information about themselves.[12]

Where's the fairness in that? Not much diversity being practiced there.

"There is no good form of racial discrimination," Bill Jacobson, president of the Equal Protection Project said, referring to the University of Minnesota case. "It's shocking that a major university would so openly make educational opportunities open only to students of a certain skin color. . . . U. Minnesota's conduct is inexcusable."[13]

College campuses are ripe for (and rife with) a variety of diversity-related issues. One credo in all this: Be careful what you say or write, as I found out the hard way concerning a newspaper column I wrote some years back, critical of and questioning certain tenets of Islam related to violence. I first experienced it at that time when I was still a college professor and wrote the opinion piece criticizing Islam. Apparently offended by what I wrote (that is what is now known as a *microaggression*), a hipster-identifying student from California wrote to all my website advertisers telling them that if they didn't stop advertising with me, he was going to organize a boycott of their businesses. A couple of them quietly ended their advertising for me with only the staunchest conservatives being undeterred by the threats.

For many people, this has become the American way of doing business. That could be construed as blackmail or extortion, unless you are an under-represented class of people, i.e., "minorities." Some groups have stepped up their aggressive, intrusive attacks against conservatives or corporations that don't give them special treatment.

Case in point is LGBTQ+, a far-Left cause which has become powerful and even ruthless in how they target businesses. The message: you'd better play ball with them, and they get to make all the rules. That is going on all over the country, and it's no longer just about getting a fair shake, equal rights in the workplace, and respect in the court of public opinion; it's about forcing onto us their views, beliefs, and lifestyle and gender-related choices—some of them of highly questionable moral character, such as drag queens instruct-ing and even touching children at public events. Recall how, during Pride Month in June 2023, LGBTQ+ (lesbian, gay, bisexual, transgender, queer, etc.) groups and activists were celebrated nationwide the entire month, such as in pregame events at Major League Baseball ballparks. Some of the dis-plays were overtly distasteful and of a crude sexually suggestive nature, all the while getting gobs of favorable national attention from hordes of media apparently eager to help promote the cause.

Because LGBTQ+ influence and activities have likely been riding the coattails of George Floyd's martyrdom and the aftermath of his death, cor-porations and other businesses across America have been put on notice that gender- and sexuality-identification issues in the workplace require imme-diate attention and remedial action. In an upside-down world where trans-actress and influencer Dylan Mulvaney (who transitioned from male to female in 2021) has become a national icon representing and promoting brands such as Nike, Anheuser-Busch, and Kate Spade, much of corporate America has hustled to climb aboard that bandwagon to protect the viability of their own names and brands. The incentive that has whipped them into shape? A scoring system known as CEI, which stands for corporate equality index, managed by the Human Rights Campaign (HRC), reportedly the largest LGBTQ+ political lobbying group in the world.[14]

Funded in part by millions of dollars donated by George Soros's Open Society Foundation, as well as other entities' contributions, according to the *New York Post*[15], HRC issues report cards that keep the U.S.'s biggest corpo-rations "in line" by grading them on a 100-point scale, measuring how well they implement certain criteria: workforce protections (no employment discrimination based on sexual orientation of gender identity); inclusive benefits (such as providing health care for same-sex couples); supporting an inclusive culture (i.e., trans-inclusive restroom/facilities policy); corporate social responsibility (marketing to LGBTQ+ consumers, for example); and responsible citizenship (you lose points for donating to organizations that advocate against LGBTQ+ equality). James Lindsay, a prominent political commentator and anti-DEI proponent, describes the HRC's administration of the CEI to be "like an extortion racket, like the Mafia."[16]

SOMETHING CALLED
THE 'CORPORATE EQUALITY INDEX (CEI)'

CEI is part of a larger, growing entity known as ESG (Environmental, Social, and Corporate Governance), which has been described as an "ethical investing" operation "increasingly promoted" by the nation's three biggest investment firms—Blackrock, Vanguard, and State Street Bank. ESG funds are invested in companies that obediently oppose fossil fuels, favor unionization, and place a higher priority on racial and gender equity than they do merit-based hiring and board selection.[17]

According to the *New York Post*, this triumvirate of firms is among the top shareholders of most U.S. publicly traded companies. That puts them and their ESG orthodoxy in position to wield considerable control over many of the top corporate management teams and boards, "and they determine in many cases executive compensation and bonuses and who gets re-elected or reappointed to boards," says entrepreneur and *Woke Inc.* author Vivek Ramaswamy, an announced Republican candidate for president in 2024. "They can make it very difficult for you if you don't abide by their agendas."[18]

Going against LGBTQ+ training in your workplace can be hazardous to your career's health. Raymond Zdunski, a western New York account clerk for a public organization that provides education materials to school districts in the state, was fired in 2018 for refusing to attend mandatory LGBTQ+ training. He sued, stating that the scheduled training sought to change "his religious beliefs about gender and sexuality . . . and would have caused him to violate the religious teachings to which he adheres." About four years later, a district court judge dismissed the lawsuit, claiming that Zdunski's claims were unsupported. The 2nd U.S. District Court of Appeals upheld the lower court judge's ruling, saying Zdunski had failed to provide "sufficient evidence" backing up his claims.[19]

The Left and its constituent companies, organizations, and associations are effective at intimidating conservative businesses, using pressure tactics that interfere with not just freedom of speech but also the freedom of commerce. Right now, this is "their time" and it is open season on Whites and conservatives, in particular—Asians, too, to some degree, at least in educational circles. The pendulum has swung in favor of the Left and DEI programs, especially in the three years since Floyd's death. It's payback time, and Whites and conservatives are victims of old-time holdups, just like in the old Westerns with the shoot-'em-up bad guys robbing a train.

The ramped-up DEI intrusion we have seen in the three years since Floyd's death has been described as an "ideological creep." That was the phrase the *Epoch Times* used in a headline over an article in which it was reported that the "DEI industry is on a mission creep, and while anti-DEI measures seem to be curtailing woke brainwashing in some workplaces, DEI promoters have been busy insinuating it into others." Such as making DEI training a required element of continuing education for practicing lawyers, with eleven states now making it mandatory for attorneys to accrue "diversity and inclusion" course credit hours to keep their law-practice licenses.[20]

It is a similar story in the healthcare field. In 2022 the Association of American Medical Colleges published its official DEI competencies to be adapted into curriculum development for medical schools, post-graduate residency programs, and faculty training. Those competencies reportedly include one that describes "the impact of various system of oppression on health and healthcare (e.g., colonization, White supremacy, acculturation, assimilation)."[21]

Much of the mainstream media has remained faithful to the enhanced "wokeness" of the DEI industry, especially over the last three years, consistently giving glowing reports of "how well" DEI training has done in addressing such problems as White privilege and White supremacy, and supposedly making our country—at least our workplaces—much safer and more cognizant of the value of social justice and DEI's positive effect on the world.

GOODBYE TO 'EQUALITY'; HELLO TO 'EQUITY'

On the one-year anniversary of George Floyd's death, CNBC reported on corporate America's progress in terms of reforming their workplace practices to fight against and reduce racism. CNBC asked a half-dozen business executives, activists, and thought leaders involved in this reform what progress they had seen in the previous twelve months. Walmart President/CEO Doug McMillon mentioned, ". . . we've seen the private sector step up in response to racial injustice and inequity . . .". Maxine Williams, Facebook Chief Diversity Officer: " . . . companies are becoming more bold in acknowledging inequities . . .". Carlos Cubia, Global Chief Diversity Officer at Walgreens Boots Alliance: "The racial equity movement opened not only eyes, but minds." Then there is this, from Connie E. Evans, President and CEO of Association for Enterprise Opportunity: "There must be a long-term approach to promoting equity for black and brown business owners . . . " and, "Companies will also fall short if they have not made internal changes to address equity . . .". [22]

Consider what each of those comments had in common. The use of the word *equity* in one form or another, a word which many people believe to be synonymous with *equality*, when in fact it is not. Progressives have slyly sneaked *equity* into many conversations about race, diversity, inclusion, and affirmative action. Equity, in this context, means that, as a member of an underrepresented group, you will not only be given a boost in the hiring process (diversity) and an inside track for positions of added influence (inclusion), your performance metrics on the job will receive a favorable grade, score, or rating higher than your actual performance should have earned. It's much like being graded "on the curve" during exam time in school.

I (Carol) know of numerous business owners who have developed and cultivated highly successful workplaces with motivated employees representing healthy mixes of races, beliefs, and backgrounds by implementing and promoting unifying business practices that build morale and lift bottom lines. Some of the things these innovative entrepreneurs and companies have in common are commitments to caring for employees and encouraging them to care for themselves; inspiring ideas, creativity, and clear, open communication; active listening with consistency and empathy; ensuring leadership fully understands the organization's mission and vision, and can clearly articulate and model it to others; and embracing and celebrating diversity according to biblical principles, which by their very nature are inclusive, as well as other virtuous practices.

Those precepts and guidelines might sound radical to many people, and that is a shame because they are all rooted in what we know to be traditional, foundational values easily understood and appreciated by people from a variety of backgrounds. Put it this way: Which of those practices and precepts would you consider to be poisonous to the workplace in terms of divisiveness? None, right? It shouldn't take a presidential executive order or an act of Congress to make mandatory what needs to be done. We have lost our way.

"If profit is a part of any business, then social responsibility should be its soul," we were told by Rebecca Weber, Chief Executive Officer of Association of Mature American Citizens (AMAC), a U.S.-based conservative advocacy organization and interest group with more than two million members. (Note: Weber is among about a dozen corporate human resources executives/managers interviewed for general background information used in this book.) "We feel a responsibility to take care of our associates. Their health needs and their families will always come first, before the demands of business. We demonstrate that through our flexibility. We have the right people and they don't take advantage or abuse it.

"Our work comes and goes, but at the end of our lives we don't really remember the business deals but we do remember our loved ones. We encourage building those memories. Our mission is focused on faith, family, and freedom, and we apply that to the way in which we manage people. We allow people to take off for different faith holidays they celebrate. We don't want to lose sight of what is most important—health and families."

Most American companies stuck and reliant on DEI programs are going about it wrong: pursuing, chasing, and conducting what has become a common type of in-house business strategy rooted in affinity groups, suspicion, intolerance, workplace bias, reverse discrimination, divisiveness, and, ultimately, self-destruction. In fact, those factors have started to take their toll on the DEI industry, pushing it toward irrelevance and eventual obsolescence in a world where affirmative action has long outlived its constructive purpose. DEI continues to miss the mark on how to heal this country, both in the workplace and extending into the home.

There is a better way, and we will soon get to more details of what *real* unity training should look and feel like as a worthy replacement for DEI training.

CHAPTER 5

DEI Training and
Its Descent into Divisiveness

"The idea of diversity is that you're bringing people with different perspectives together in order to create something that is a more profitable or productive whole. When you have functional diversity, it actually does seem to produce results. It does seem to actually help you overcome bigotry if that's a thing that is still a problem for you. But there are ways that work, and there are ways that don't. . . . For example, putting people in mixed groups and having them work toward a common goal, they tend to forget about the differences and work toward the common goal, and to bond in the process. This is actually something that is well-known and has evidence. . . .

"I don't want to give this idea that diversity means communism. I want to make the argument that diversity is a very colonized tool that has been purposed, and the reason that diversity has been so interesting . . . is because there were some big open doors created for it by the Supreme Court primarily that opened the door to gigantic industries for diversity trainers, whose manuals started coming out in the seventies. Now, people like Robin DiAngelo [American author of such titles as White Fragility, Nice Racism, *and* Seeing Whiteness] *write these manuals and make obscene money.*

"There is a difference between how normal people would view diversity—some functional goal is being achieved by bringing people with different perspectives together—vs. how the woke are going to see diversity, which is

going to be in terms of that the only relative thing is power dynamics in terms of creating difference. [For them it comes down] to identity politics."[1]

— **James A. Lindsay,** American author and cultural critic, excerpted from a segment of his April 2023 New Discourses video presentation, entitled "The Marxist Roots of DEI Workshop: Session 2—Diversity." This excerpt was edited for clarity and length.

D IVERSITY, EQUITY, AND INCLUSION (DEI) IS SHORTHAND for the present-day mantra of the type of workplace training—to include higher-education institutions—that not so long ago was known simply as "diversity training." It has been called other things over the years, some even suitable for printing in this book. The earlier version of what we now know as DEI was designed to fit the law of the land (Civil Rights Act of 1964, Title VII, etc.), and compliance was the order of the day. But that train has left the tracks and we are left with a fountain-gushing divisiveness across our great land.

DEI has become one of the worst purveyors of reverse discrimination ever conceived in America. And that's what we're going to talk about in this chapter: what DEI has done to contribute heavily to rampant divisiveness in this country and what kind of fate the future holds for DEI. Not a good one, we can assure you, although the Supreme Court's recent weakening of affirmative action on the educational side is likely to have a significant trickle-down effect on DEI's future. There isn't much of a chance that loyal advocates of DEI are going to be able to tap dance their way around this.

Your days are numbered, DEI, and that includes the wasting of tens of billions of dollars that have funded this not-so-little cottage industry for years, to include gifting healthy salaries to tens of thousands of diversity, equity, and inclusion executives, directors, managers, and rank-and-file employees who, in already starting, are wise to be hitting the bricks looking for a way to salvage their careers. Those early birds will eventually be joined by battalions of their compadres as DEI programs continue to be phased out. Throw away the book and start over, if at all.

As we finish this chapter, literally only two weeks after the Supreme Court's affirmative action ruling was announced, the trickle-down effect as it relates to DEI has already started. On July 13, as reported by the *Wall Street Journal,* Republican attorney generals from thirteen states sent a letter to *Fortune* 100 companies (e.g., Coca-Cola, Microsoft, and Johnson & Johnson) warning them against using race-based preferences in hiring, promotions, and contracting. "We urge you to immediately cease any unlawful race-based quotas or preferences your company has adopted for its employment and contracting practices," the letter reportedly said. "If you choose not to do so, know that you will be held accountable."[2]

Although the Supreme Court ruling applied only to the educational component of affirmative action, it could be eventually used as precedent should any legal action be filed contesting the constitutionality or legality (i.e., per the Civil Rights Act of 1964) of workplace affirmative action, which as of this book's publication remained in place.

One of the Cadillacs of DEI-type programs has been the Division of Diversity and Community Engagement (DCE) at the University of Texas in Austin. The publicly funded school reportedly has spent more than $13 million per year floating its DEI program, with almost all of that—$12.2 million—covering the salaries for 171 jobs, according to documents acquired by the *Epoch Times*. Another $1.4 million in pay was spread among fourteen associate deans who comprised what has been known as the Coalition of Diversity, Equity, and Inclusion officers. All this for what has been described as "a contentious sociopolitical movement that has taken hold in America's institutions."[3] Texas taxpayers' money goes beyond the university setting as well. UT Austin's diversity division also funds salaries at what is called the UT Elementary School, which serves pre-K through fifth-grade students as an open-enrollment school.[4]

The University of Texas at Austin has company when it comes to schools forking over big bucks for their DEI-related programs. During the 2021-2022 school year, The Ohio State University paid out $13.4 million for its 132 DEI administrators. At the University of Florida, the figure was believed to be a little over $5 million, which represented just a small piece of the $34 million the entire Florida system reportedly paid out for DEI, although those days might be over. In April 2023, Florida Governor Ron DeSantis, who has announced his 2024 run for the presidency, signed legislation defunding DEI in state-run institutions.[5] Texas Governor Greg Abbott soon thereafter signed similar legislation for the state of Texas's higher education programs.

RESISTANCE TO SUPREME COURT RULING ALREADY UNDERWAY

Sherry Sylvester, Distinguished Senior Fellow at the Texas Public Policy Foundation, recognizes the beginning salvos of a war. She has written about the efforts to "defy the law." Valerie Sansone, an assistant professor of higher education at the University of Texas at San Antonio, revealed the secret plan: "Conversations of how to push back are being conducted in hushed tones—not in whispers, but not entirely out in the open either. . . .We're not necessarily using our state university emails to communicate about this. You've got to be a little smarter than that."[6] Sylvester points out that, "Sansone and her DEI colleagues in 'the resistance' are fighting the basic premise of all civil rights legislation and the equal protection clause of the Fourteenth Amendment to the Constitution—that there should be no differential treatment in America on the basis of race."

Cracks in the walls of the DEI industry have been popping up in greater frequency over the last few years. You might say the DEI rubber band that has been stretched to its limit in recent years to accommodate Marxist-influenced spin-offs such as BLM, wokeness, CRT, affirmative action, and other openly anti-white organizations and movements, is starting to snap back. We've watched and put up with this stuff long enough, even though there still are millions of misguided people left in this country willing to bend and maybe break laws to support this racially divisive abomination (sounds like "Obama nation," right?).

DEI training breeds racism, pure and simple. Its workers and advocates know that, and they don't care that the rest of us know that. They believe they are in total control of this stuff, and that there is nothing the rest of us can do about it. Well, not so fast. Diversity training not only creates negative consequences, but it also creates discomfort for all who must sit through it. DEI further hardens racial attitudes toward it, feeds into the growth of white grievance as a factor in the rise of the alternative right, bolsters rather than lessens the victimization/white privilege narrative, and exposes differences between people (identity politics) versus promoting a healthy, common identity.

Once that rubber band snaps back and whips a few progressives in the face, they will know it is time for their DEI programs (or what they will eventually be called) to focus on true, color-blind diversity and inclusion. Let's get back to basics. They will likely have to abandon their role in the "antiracist" narrative that until now has blamed, accused, chastised, disparaged, threatened, and even physically harmed Whites for every negative thing imaginable. The most prominent wave of knee jerk reverse discrimination came in the wake of the death of George Floyd, which we covered in Chapter 4.

Some of these antiWhite shenanigans are so blatantly prejudicial and unprofessional that when you hear about them, you might assume they are fabrications of one of those phony websites that create and publish outrageously false news story as a form of satirical humor. No one is laughing now. Just like the news story that came out in late June 2023 about a former Penn State University English professor suing the school for reverse discrimination, claiming that the school had forced him to instruct students that the English language embodied White supremacy. Almost unbelievable, but true. Zack DePiero, who, fed up with this extreme antiWhite freak show, finally walked away from teaching English at Penn State Abington. In his lawsuit, he alleged that his direct supervisor, Liliana Nayden, had supported the belief that "White supremacy exists in the language itself, and, therefore, that the English language itself is 'racist.'"[7]

Furthermore, as presented in DePiero's lawsuit, the school stirred him and other Penn State faculty members to attend and take part in antiracist workshops and training, including one that was titled "White Teachers Are the Problem." There were other similarly absurd charges made in DePiero's lawsuit, all of which combined—and if true—paint Penn State as an institution that is off its rocker. "DePiero told Fox News Digital that he felt the university's approach to diversity and inclusion produced a "cultlike environment where you had this Original Sin. . . . In this case, I'm white. I need to repent for that sin."[8]

Here's what some numbers are telling us about what's really going on present-day with DEI training programs. According to Washington, DC-based HR Dive, which, as stated in its LinkedIn profile, "provides in-depth journalism and insight into the most impactful news and trends shaping workforce management,"[9] cited a November 2022 survey conducted by ResumeBuilder.com and Pollfish. The survey found that 52 percent of hiring managers employed by a company with a DEI program reported that their company practiced reverse discrimination. This wasn't just any run-of-the-mill survey knocked out with a few dozen phone calls in a single afternoon. "Of the 1,000 hiring managers surveyed, 873 work for companies with a DEI initiative," HR Dive reported. "Nearly half say they've been told to prioritize diversity over qualifications (although slightly more than half say they weren't told this). About one in six say they've been told to deprioritize White men when evaluating job candidates. A quarter (25 percent) strongly believe, and 28 percent somewhat believe, they could lose their job if they don't hire enough diverse candidates. More than 600 of the managers surveyed identify as White, according to the survey data."[10]

Hiring employees to fulfill the mission of improving diversity numbers doesn't address one problem DEI managers and specialists are facing—job security. In the early weeks and months following the death of George Floyd, business leaders were bullied by the likes of BLM into ramping up their DEI programs and diversity hiring at breakneck speed, although what any of that had to do with bringing back Floyd to life or making up in any way for the isolated act of a white Minneapolis cop's poor, fatal decision is anyone's guess. No matter, three years after Floyd's death touched off a nationwide glut of rash, frantic C-level moves that were more about social appeasement than common sense and bottom-line responsibility, DEI programs are on thin ice. Diversity hiring has slowed in recent months, and minority hires (just like many of their White fellow employees) are losing their jobs as large corporations down to smaller businesses make layoffs. Why should DEI program managers, officers, and their own rank and file be exempt from mass layoffs? Welcome to the real world, folks. You wanted equality (or what you call "equity") and now you get it going out just as you got it while getting in or going up.

REVs. JESSE JACKSON AND
AL SHARPTON KEEP A CLOSE WATCH

No discussion of Black activists'-driven shakedowns would be complete without an honorable mention for Revs. Jesse Jackson and Al Sharpton on the subject of applying persuasive pressure to White-led corporations, organizations, sports entities, etc.—especially when high-profile racial issues are involved. It's not like BLM has a patent or monopoly on this stuff. If some sort of concession (such as business owners getting with the program and hiring and promoting more Blacks whenever a black man in the act of being arrested dies at the hands [or under the knee] of a white cop) isn't coming, then perhaps a persuasive comment about boycotts or other stringent measures might do the trick, assuming the right kind of person is doing the asking.

Jackson and Sharpton both are seasoned veterans of how this works, occasionally turning up like bad pennies when there is a high-profile, racially connected event or incident begging their intercession and "mediation" skills. When duty calls, with any luck, there is a healthy honorarium, contribution, or perhaps even a "tithe" or "offering" awaiting the inevitable "sales pitch" accompanied by woke's version of passing the plate. Terms (not ours) such as "race baiter"[11] and "shakedown"[12] have been used to describe Jackson's and Sharpton's respective *modi operandi*.

There's a story here. Jeanne Hedgepeth, at the time a Chicago-area high school teacher, in 2021 posted a social media comment in which she called Jackson and Sharpton "race baiters" while also criticizing the rioting that ensued after George Floyd's death, describing the violence as a "civil war." Elsewhere in her post, she also had the audacity to compare the progressives' use of the term "white privilege" to everyone else's use of the N-word. And for that, Hedgepeth was fired from her job, after which she filed a federal lawsuit against officials and board members affiliated with the school district in which she had taught.[13] It would seem freedom of speech—even freedom of *reasonable* speech, in Hedgepeth's case—has no place in parts of Chicago, which just happens to be one of Barack Obama's former hometowns. Does that surprise you?

Both NASCAR and the National Football League, vanguard organizations of the sports world, can vouch for the Jackson/Sharpton factor. According to Kenneth R. Timmerman, author of *Shakedown: Exposing the Real Jesse Jackson*, it was Peter Flaherty, president of the conservative National Legal and Policy Center (based on Washington, DC), who in the early 2000s first brought to light that Jackson had allegedly pressured NASCAR his concern about the lack of success of its black drivers on the stock-car circuit. Nervous about a possible Jackson-inspired boycott, NASCAR reportedly ponied up $250,000 in sponsorship fees for Jackson's groups to get the good reverend to walk away.[14]

Some twenty years later, Sharpton got his turn to play sports-league overlord when the NFL got hit with a lawsuit from former Miami Dolphins coach Brian Flores. A black coach, Flores alleged there is an underlying culture of racism within the league that blocks black coaches from getting head-coaching jobs. In response, the NFL began studying alternatives to its long-standing Rooney Rule, which requires teams to interview at least one minority applicant whenever looking to fill a head-coaching vacancy. Sharpton was one of several civil rights leaders who met with NFL Commissioner Roger Goodell to discuss more effective options to the Rooney Rule, with

Sharpton suggesting racial quotas with deadlines, saying the league "must have firm targets and timetables." This coming from a "civil rights leader" who has "incited antisemitic riots and pushed fake hate crimes before they became a popular hoax topic," according to a report in the *Washington Examiner*.[15]

You get the picture. Such is the state of racial equality in America. It's not in good hands.

Meanwhile, back in workplaces across America, some see these "sweeping layoffs" of DEI staffers and diversity hires made to improve the numbers as a phenomenon whereby companies are reneging on promises made in the chaotic aftermath of the Floyd killing, and there is a Republican backlash involved as well. That's what reliably liberal mouthpiece news.bloomberglaw.com has been reporting: Workplace diversity and inclusion efforts adopted in the wake of George Floyd's death and ensuing protests are fading as "sweeping layoffs blunt companies' bold commitments to boost underrepresented groups in their C-suites and ranks," reporter Khorri Atkinson wrote in a March 2023 piece under the headline "Corporate Diversity Pledges Fizzle Amid Layoffs, GOP Backlash." He added, "More than 300 DEI professionals departed companies in the last six months including Amazon.com Inc., Twitter Inc., and Nike Inc.," according to a February 2023 report done by Revelio Labs, a workforce analytics firm. "These diminishing roles have left observers questioning whether the sense of urgency to create workforce diversity that corporate leaders made almost three years ago was genuine or simply a reactionary business decision to mitigate reputational risk."[16]

It was in all probability more of the latter.

Corporate leaders—no question—proverbially knocked over office furniture while jumping through hoops to make a good showing during the ruckus that followed Floyd's death. In the court of public opinion, they had no choice at the time. But now that these same corporate leaders are faced, as usual, with pinched dollars in a tightened economy amid the realization that their DEI programs really are fostering a growth of reverse discrimination versus a decline in available capital, it was time to cut bait. This sort of thing happens across all industries in the corporate world—it's called "rightsizing," and across the board it can be detrimental to everyone's job security. Get used to it, even though you don't have to like it.

Think about it: Why should DEI staffers—or Blacks and other workers from underrepresented groups in general—be exempt from downsizings/lay-offs when market conditions or other factors are forcing the hands of company leaders to let workers go? As is often expressed at such unfortunate times in coarser language that most Americans can understand, "stuff" happens. Job (in)security-related anxiety weighs heavily on the minds of workers across the board, regardless of race, creed, faith, gender, etc. It's a fact of life, and blaming and bullying businesses into enacting reverse discrimination policies isn't going to change that.

NO ONE IS IMMUNE

Here's one truth about the DEI industry, which is vulnerable to the same sort of vagaries, ups, and downs that all other industries face from time to time during the constant ebb and flow of commerce—no one is immune. Sometimes you win and get a boost; sometimes you lose and pink slips go out. DEI got its boost after Floyd's death, and BLM, etc. were suddenly empowered to make big demands helped by the compliant mainstream media; now that worm has turned, so to speak.

Let's face it: DEI, at least how it is perceived by its many detractors, is merely a front for the woke industry. George Floyd dies in the presence and hands of police and now, suddenly, corporations have to make it a top priority to step it up in beefing up their DEI programs (Note: DEI job listings grew by more than 123 percent in 2020 in the immediate aftermath of the Floyd-related political and racial unrest[17]) and hiring more under-represented workers. What's the connection there? What does Floyd's death—or his life, for that matter—have to do with workplace staffing dynamics?

Again, those companies and corporations cutting their DEI programs are doing it because they know those programs and training are useless. All they really accomplish is to keep conflict going because that's exactly what their job is, even though, of course, you will never see that written in a mission statement or annual report. If heterosexuals and homosexuals, and Whites and Blacks and Hispanics, get along, there's no need for a diversity officer because all they know how to bring to the table is how to foster conflict by accusing Whites of being White supremacists, or heterosexuals of being homophobes, just by their very existence. If you are born White in this woke world, you are born a racist; no ifs, ands, or buts. How crazy does this world have to get?

The DEI juggernaut is starting to fray around the edges; that's even before we get into the increased threat of lawsuits likely to come against workplace-diversity manipulations as affirmative action continues to lose more of its bite. Contributing to DEI's pending demise are the cracks we are now seeing with BLM. Its Marxist roots are being revealed more and more, bit by bit, and its questionable accounting practices and spending (tens of millions of dollars reportedly unaccounted for) are apparently putting it on the fast track toward bankruptcy, as covered earlier in this book.[18] Why does the financial health and bold presence of BLM even get mentioned here in the same breath as DEI? It is because BLM is, in a sense, an outside agency that acts as the enforcement arm of DEI, giving business leaders pause and perhaps a proverbial kick from behind whenever they might think that a watered-down diversity program will suffice for their corporations, companies, and organizations. And if BLM is an enforcer keeping business leaders accountable and in check, much of the mainstream media is the public-relations agency that keeps liberal entities in the headlines, providing a positive spin on such entities as DEI, as needed.

The Court's decision to eliminate the educational component of affirmative action, while not (yet) directly affecting workplace DEI/affirmative action programs and practices, could "encourage (legal) challenges" to those things, Morrison Foerster Law Firm wrote in a March 2023 advisory it sent out to its clients, three months ahead of the Court's announcement of its 6-3 decision. "Depending on the Court's reasoning," the firm's advisory continued, "the importance of diversity as a compelling interest more broadly could be impacted and might indirectly undercut some of the rationales used to support DEI initiatives and affirmative action measures in the workplace. As a result, employers should understand the differences between permissible and potentially unlawful DEI and affirmative action programs."[19] Okay, that last part is true, on paper at least, but it still doesn't insulate business leaders from the court of public opinion, which can be easily swayed by intense public pressures. That, of course, includes major squeezes put on business leaders by threats (e.g. threats of boycotts, or worse) from race-based or other minority activist groups such as LGBTQ+ demanding favoritism with their hiring, promotion, retail-oriented, etc. decisions when they hit the streets demanding it, such as what transpired post-Floyd.

WHY DO DIVERSITY PROGRAMS FAIL?

Theories abound as to why diversity programs—such as DEI or as it was referred to until recent years as simply Diversity and Inclusion (DI)—have stumbled or just outright failed. A 2021 *Forbes EQ* commentary highlighted four reasons for DEI's relative failure: 1. No long-range plan ("ineffective alignment of the long-term D&I program goals with the organizational strategic plan creates gaps in program delivery and affects sustainability"); 2. Lack of commitment to the program ("If the program is not enforced and modeled by leadership, employees will lack the motivation to buy-in."); 3. Poor instructional delivery model (leaving "the employees lacking in understanding the significance of the new information presented to them."); and 4. Lack of representation ("Everyone must have a seat at the table.").[20] Of course, we presume that the author of that piece would agree that Whites, Jews, and other non-minority groups have places reserved for them at that table. Also, we are certain that DEI advocates, to be just and fair, would insist that any incendiary race-targeted terms such as "White privilege" and "White supremacy" should be scrubbed from any language used in DI/DEI training and seminars. (Note the sarcasm.)

Until George Floyd's death sent corporate executives, business owners, DEI managers, etc. into knee-jerk, scurrying-around mode attempting to appease the likes of BLM with bolstered DEI efforts, diversity training had for years been focused on compliance to avoid lawsuits. That's what it was all about—do just enough to stay out of court and avoid humongous settlements. That brings us back to what we mentioned earlier: diversity training aimed to curtail bias in the workplace; hiring tests and performance review ratings aimed at mitigating signs of bias in recruiting and job promotions; and grievance processes to give employees an open door to challenge managers on diversity issues: "Those tools are designed to preempt lawsuits by policing managers' thoughts and actions," Frank Dobbin and Alexandra Kalev wrote in their comprehensive study on diversity training that was published in a 2016 edition of *Harvard Business Review*. "Yet laboratory studies show that this kind of force-feeding can activate bias rather than stamp it out. As social scientists have found, people often rebel against rules to assert their autonomy. Try to coerce me to do X, Y, or Z, and I'll do the opposite just to prove that I'm my own person."[21]

After explaining in detail why typical mandatory diversity programs often offer poor returns, Dobbin and Kalev examined a number of alternative approaches to diversity that more effective programs were utilizing—a common element to their success being a more positive framework. "The most effective programs spark engagement, increase contact among different groups, or draw on people's strong desire to look good to others," they commented while zeroing in on several types of programs that seem to work well, such as those that emphasize voluntary training, self-managed teams, cross training (exposing managers to a variety of groups of people instead of favoring one or another), college recruitment targeting women, college recruiting targeting minorities (focusing on historically Black schools), mentoring, and diversity task forces (promoting social accountability and encouraging members to bring solutions back to their respective departments).[22]

The kind of diversity training that Dobbin and Kalev describe—placing positivity over finger pointing—does exist in some workplaces and other organizations that endorse teamwork and managers and employees working toward a common goal, while striving for solutions instead of blame. One company that has steered itself away from being dependent on a formal in-house DEI program is FrankCrum, a professional employer organization (PEO) company that has been around more than forty years. It provides businesses with such services as payroll and human resources (HR) administration, employee benefits/retirement, workers' comp and safety, and HR risk mitigation and employment practices liability insurance (EPLI). I (Carol) spoke with FrankCrum's vice president of human resources, David Peasall, in 2021 about his company's DEI awareness and management:

> I've listened to several DEI trainings . . . It seems the action message was that I need to survey my own employees to find out and document who has what sexual identities and preferences, understand everyone's race and ethnicity, and then make changes. It was very difficult to understand next steps. I'm asking myself, "I'm to ask employees what, exactly? And why would they tell me?" There are laws and common-sense business practices against making employment decisions based on personal characteristics versus objective good business reasons, and for the past fifty-plus years we've been trained that these topics are none of the employer's business. So, now I'm to make it my business and find out this personal information? And this will increase sales and our company's performance?

Peasall also volunteered how FrankCrum isn't about trying to force healthy work environments; it is more about nurturing them. There is a lesson here that DEI proponents could learn:

> Today we talk about 'safe' environments for employees to be in. I see it safer for them to know they can come to work and not be subjected to divisive and polarizing political and social topics. You can come to work and not worry about whether or not to participate, and your manager's perception of you for not participating, in groups formed to talk about feelings and personal information about social, religious, or political topics. That sounds like a good recipe for making people feel divided from each other and distracted from the job they're paid to perform. If they do want to be involved in these topics, they can go on social media and be part of a group outside of work, meeting with their friends and neighbors. But if we're going to respect each other's opinions here at work, we aren't going to spend time on this. Instead, we'll join together to be focused on the mission of the work and how that purpose unites all of us in a common way.

One thing is clear: What the world needs now is to be prepared to talk about what happens *after* affirmative action, and how DEI programs in higher education have not advanced racial healing or reconciliation. What they *have* done is support segregation and resegregation because they've endorsed having separate dorms, separate class sections, separate this, separate that. They've been divisive. People in the corporate world need to know that students who were educated under that system of DEI took their values into the corporate world. Consequently, instead of corporations being able to focus on the profits and the mission of the founders and owners, they are having to babysit, and nurse, and deal with all these issues related to the diversity regime.

IDENTITY POLITICS HARD AT WORK

The problem with diversity programs we see today is they are looking for people to go into their companies or organizations with group identities and affinity groups, and pretty much maintain those identities and get special protections without any expectation to assimilate with others. It seems DEI and CRT in their present state are geared toward creating hostilities and conflict. There's nothing about their agenda that seems to be about bringing people together. It's about mostly saying that white people need to step aside, they've had their time, they've had their day, and, you know, it's now time for minorities to rule. At the same time, it's turning a blind eye to all the violence that's taking place.

I believe I have a solution to all this that can help heal America, and it's called unity training—not the divisive diversity training we have grown accustomed to encountering. Carol Swain's Real Unity Training Solutions offers an off-ramp for institutions that want to do the right thing within the legal framework provided by the U.S. Civil Rights Act and the Constitution's equal protection clause.

CHAPTER 6

Real Unity Training:
An Antidote to DEI's Divisiveness

"Eliminating racial discrimination means eliminating all of it. And the equal protection clause, we have accordingly held, applies 'without regard to any differences of race, of color, or of nationality'—it is 'universal in [its] application.' . . . For '[t]he guarantee of equal protection cannot mean one thing when applied to one individual and something else when applied to a person of another color.' . . If both are not accorded the same protection, then it is not equal."[1]

— **U.S. Supreme Court Chief Justice John Roberts**, Majority Opinion, June 2023, *Students for Fair Admissions v. President and Fellows of Harvard College*

"While I am painfully aware of the social and economic ravages which have befallen my race and all who suffer discrimination, I hold out enduring hope that this country will live up to its principles so clearly enunciated in the Declaration of Independence and the Constitution of the United States: that all men are created equal, are equal citizens, and must be treated equally before the law."[2]

— **U.S. Supreme Court Justice Clarence Thomas**, Concurring Opinion, June 2023, *Students for Fair Admissions v. President and Fellows of Harvard College.*

ALTHOUGH BOTH U.S. SUPREME COURT CHIEF JUSTICE JOHN ROBERTS AND JUSTICE CLARENCE THOMAS (above) were addressing the Court's 6-3 verdict to strike down race as a factor to be used in college admissions, their words could just as well apply to the current state of workplace DEI programs and training. That is another place where equal protection has been shelved such that one segment of the population (Blacks and Hispanics) get preferential treatment and another segment (Whites, mainly) are often disparaged and left feeling alienated. That is likely about to change, however, as the dominoes from the 2023 Court decision start falling in a direction opposite the upside-down world that now surrounds us.

Let us also go back nearly twenty years to 2004. That's when Barack Obama, then a member of the Illinois State Senate, gave a keynote speech at the Democratic National Convention that stirred the hearts and minds of his fellow Democrats and parts of the rest of the nation. It was a well-written speech, a classic; Obama read it aloud well. His speech not only essentially launched his quest to the White House, it also unwittingly (to him, apparently) included a segment that could be interpreted as contrarian to the divisiveness that has been wrought in today's model of diversity training. It is a model in which black and white nations separately exist, the former being the beneficiary of a form of preferential treatment that seemingly violates the U.S. Constitution; the latter has been victimized by reverse discrimination while being disparaged as purveyors of "white privilege" and "white supremacy."

Let us show you what we mean. Here's an outtake from Obama, speaking at the 2004 Democratic National Convention:

E Pluribus Unum. Out of Many, One.

Now even as we speak, there are those who are preparing to divide us, the spin masters, the negative ad peddlers who embrace the politics of anything goes. Well, I say to them tonight, there is not a liberal America and a conservative America—there is the United States of America. There is not a Black America and a White America and Latino America and Asian America—there's the United States of America. . . .

I stand here today, grateful for the diversity of my heritage, aware that my parents' dreams live on in my two precious daughters. I stand here knowing that my story is part of the larger American story, that I owe a debt to all of those who came before me, and that, in no other country on earth is my story even possible.[3]

Illinois State Senator Barack Obama spoke words that Americans wanted and needed to hear. The man who mesmerized the world in 2004 certainly would not be at all in favor of how diversity, equity, and inclusion training has evolved in the 2020s. We know what he appeared to be was not actually who he was.

I (Carol) remember the speech vividly. In fact, I wrote an essay for *Ebony* magazine that was published in December 2006. Not only did I say America was ready for a black president, I wrote: "The first successful black candidate will be a person like Barack Obama or Gen. Colin Powell, both of whom embody the American dream."[4]

Obama and I seemingly shared a deep appreciation for *E Pluribus Unum*—it is the foundation for my Real Unity Training Solutions, LLC, which grew from an idea I birthed during the summer of 2020. Over the past two years, I have been observing American politics and developing what I believe is a better approach to healing group conflicts, especially between Whites and Blacks. So in one sense, Obama (or at least the version of him who spoke so eloquently and inspirationally nineteen years ago) and I had one thing in common—we did not want to see a separate Black America and White America (which is what DEI is striving to give us). We preferred one unified nation where diversity can be pursued and celebrated instead of weaponized in pitting one segment of America against the other. Unfortunately, the Obama who assumed the presidency in 2008 bore little resemblance to the man we adored in 2004.

Race-based solutions that discriminate against Whites and Asians cannot continue to exist. The trickle-down effects of the Court's landmark 2023 ruling into the workplace are already being felt and stimulating changes in workplace diversity programs. Hopefully, plenty more of that is on the way.

EQUIPPING CEOs AND LEADERS

Real Unity Training Solutions has evolved into an approach that focuses on equipping CEOs and other leaders rather than attempting the impossible task of trying to change the culture of an organization. It is the role of the leader or CEO to set the tone for the organization. Our vision is designed to help leaders return to the basics of running an organization without having to deal with the distractions and conflict that the DEI approach inevitably creates when it divides the workplace into warring affinity groups. Our goal is to equip these leaders with information on how they can achieve diversity without reaping divisiveness; how they can attain equal opportunity without the false promise of equity's equal outcomes; and how they can accomplish integration of individuals without the group demands of an inclusion model that encourages affinity groups (where identity groups self-segregate to gripe about their workplaces or learning environments). We respect the autonomy of the individual and believe that talent is distributed without regard to race, sex, religion, or sexual orientation. What matters is the skill, attitudes, and dedication of individuals to the mission and purpose of the organization. This is part of getting back to the basics. It is common sense and must be done within the confines of civil rights laws and constitutional protections.

Along those lines, there is plenty of room for improvement in how training is conducted in America, and, as touched on in chapter 5, there is a variety of great ideas begging to be implemented by fair-minded managers. Even staunchly Left-leaning advocates have come to the realization that bullying Whites and directing phony blame at them—especially white males—are counterproductive tactics that are failing to achieve the kind of diversity, equality, and inclusion that all of us can agree are beneficial to all groups.

Organizations can never bring about reconciliation using a conflict model. With the type of workplace diversity training we have seen in recent years, its proponents cannot point to any successes; at least not authentic ones, just false narratives to support the continuation of conflict-based DEI. Diversity was a more laudable goal when its proponents adhered to the original civil rights goals of nondiscrimination and equal opportunity; that was before identity politics took on its sharp edge. It was not long after the passage of the civil rights action that blatantly reverse discrimination and group entitlement to the extreme reared their heads in far flung organizations.

I (Carol) can attest to the fact that the Civil Rights Movement helped people like me, for whom doors were opened. We were given an opportunity to prove ourselves in an environment where we had an equal opportunity to succeed or fail. That all seems like ancient history now. I believe if we go back to the original intent, the original premise, the original vision of affirmative action as created by President John F. Kennedy and augmented by President Lyndon Johnson in the sixties, we land at the Civil Rights Act of 1964 which prohibited group discrimination and sought to use outreach, nondiscrimination, and advertising to reach underrepresented persons who previously experienced discrimination because of their immutable characteristics. Most Americans were certainly on board with the strides we made toward achieving a color-blind society. We were equal under the law, but individual prejudices and biases continued to exist in the hearts of men and women. That is human nature. We had to learn to get along and respect each other as individuals, not as members of discrete groups.

CUSTOMIZED TRAINING BASED ON NEEDS

One of the things I believe is needed is customized training based on the needs of a particular company as defined by its CEOs and owners who operate from a particular vision of where the companies need to go and what is bogging them down. Carol Swain's Real Unity Training Solutions is intended to replace and certainly improve on the one size-fits-all model that most DEI-equipped companies advocate—the one that has morphed into something unrecognizable when placed alongside what the presidential executive orders for affirmative action, the Civil Rights Act of 1964, equal opportunity, and even the U.S. Constitution together laid out as a path to constructive diversity.

Much of the diversity training I am aware of uses a one-size-fits-all model for tackling issues involving groups deemed historically marginalized: women, racial and ethnic minorities, and members of the LGBTQ+ communities. Too many DEI trainers come across as angry individuals who show open hostility toward groups considered privileged. A better approach is one that is customized for the organization; it should begin with the vision of the owner and founder which ties into the company's reason for existence. Workplace assessments are important. That is because, in some cases, there are no problems until the DEI officers or trainers arrive with their push for mandatory indoctrination. In some cases, there might not be any DEI-related issues at the company or organization, and if it is not broken, there is nothing to be fixed. Like the old saying goes, "If it ain't broke, don't fix it." (You'll only make things worse.)

It is critical for leaders and supervisors to know the civil rights laws of the land so that workers can be informed and lawsuits avoided. We believe the current approach is a failure and that there is no need or benefit to temporarily take employees off the job, even for less than a day, to be coached by DEI instructors. We have heard of situations where someone internally pushed for a sensitivity or DEI coach to be brought into the organization where employees were forced to attend. What sometimes happens is the workplace is left worse off. Workers who were previously satisfied with their jobs and with their work environment end up leaving. That kind of voluntary attrition does not make your company more genuinely diverse or more successful, assuming you measure success by the bottom line. If your diversity percentages are up, but your bottom line is bottoming out and workforce departures outpace the new hires, you have a problem. In such a divisive environment, Whites might feel like they have been singled out and beaten up; minorities might feel like they've gotten the worst end of a bad deal, and that they should be further along in their careers than they are. DEI is a lose-lose proposition.

Even if you really stretch things and cast DEI—at least as it is being practiced in 2023—in a positive light, assessing and attempting to discuss its value nonetheless stymies business leaders and human resource executives and managers across the board. Even rank-and-file employees see a fuzzy picture regardless of their viewpoint. For instance, the *Wall Street Journal* in a July 2023 piece mentions Clayton Homes, a Tennessee-based builder of mobile and modular homes that employs about 26,000 workers. About half of those employees claim the company's diversity measures don't, well, measure up; the other half say those diversity protocols go too far, implying those measures are unfair to them.

"There are people who say, 'I really wish we were more diverse,' and I've also seen people say, 'Stop being so woke,' " says Sarah Sharp, a human resources vice president at Clayton. She also pointed out how she is attempting to enhance objectivity when it comes to hiring, her aim being to attract and promote more underrepresented people while at the same time expressing these initiatives in a manner of language that shows overall fairness.[5]

Also cited by the *Wall Street Journal* is a growing trend in which white men say they are taking it on the chin in the workplace, no thanks to diversity programs and measures. "Jonathan McBride, a global managing partner who leads the DEI practice for recruiting firm Heidrick & Struggles, says the companies he works with worry about alienating some workers and say feelings of belonging are dropping among white men, as shown in internal surveys," *WSJ* reporters Te-Ping Chen and Ray A. Smith wrote. Likewise, research conducted by a unit of executive search firm Spencer Stuart found that more than half of white men surveyed reported not being valued at work or were "not given full credit for their contributions."[6]

In the wake of the Supreme Court's June 2023 decision to remove race as a factor in college admissions, workplaces are already feeling the effects even though they were not addressed in the Court case. Companies must work more diligently in preparing their employees by informing them about civil rights laws. Such knowledge is not only power, but can also be a source of unity, bringing people together.

A core value of unity training is treating other people with respect regardless of which group they belong to. Like we stated earlier, though, it also means that you are not celebrating one group of people's special day at the exclusion of other groups' special days. Other than major holidays, it is probably best to celebrate no one group's special day and to end the preachy nonstop emails that come from DEI's influence on human resources offices. Unity training is about making sure the workplace is a place where, when you are on the clock, you are focused on the mission of the organization, not on catering to or pandering to the social or cultural distinctions of a particular group. Along with that, diversity training and management should not be part of some sort of social engineering platform. It should be a place where people come to do a job and work as a team around the goals of the organization. That is not difficult to grasp.

A HISTORY LESSON IS IN ORDER

It bears repeating that people need to know the history of our nation and our civil rights laws against discrimination. Workers should be educated about the laws of the land that affect how they should interact with one another; that goes beyond just lawsuit avoidance. There is nothing wrong with that kind of training, except we don't see much of that. In fact, that is what *honest* unity training should do—educate leaders and managers about the laws of the land and the history of civil rights; then make it clear to them that civil rights protect everyone, including men and Whites. Beyond the basics, we then need to be reminded of the wisdom of leaders such as Stephen Covey, who authored the classic book *The Seven Habits of Highly Effective People*[7] and the impressive work of Patrick Lencioni, author of T*he Five Dysfunctions of a Team.*[8] At the end of the day, leaders and CEOs need guidance and a work environment that, to the extent possible, avoids direct engagement in the shifting politics of the day.

The reverse discrimination promoted by race-based diversity training and affirmative action stigmatizes the accomplishments of racial and ethnic minorities who are high achieving. Everyone's hard work and earned accomplishments can be discounted as a by-product of race-based policies. Once again, to reinforce where I am coming from, I believe we would have a better work environment if more people knew and practiced the Golden Rule. If it is wrong to discriminate against Blacks and Hispanics, it is also wrong to discriminate against Whites. If bullying and shaming is harmful to black and brown children, it is also harmful to white children.

I consider myself an astute observer of the passing parade. I seek to apply common sense to the world around me, and I sometimes see trends before others do. With race-based affirmative action, I saw the handwriting on the wall years ago when I authored my book *The New White Nationalism in America: Its Challenge to Integration.*[9] Back in 2002, I saw how identity politics and multiculturalism were dividing Americans in undesirable ways. The result was a rising White consciousness and identification as a discriminated-against group. Our society has moved in a direction where unity is more difficult because fewer people know the Constitution or the lofty vision cast by the Declaration of Independence—even fewer know the Judeo-Christian values that undergirded our nation. What I recognized then—and even more so today—is the dangerous collision course we are on when it comes to race relations and the tribalism of multiculturalism. Our current approach has created a devil's brew for racial conflict and hatred.

Although the days of diversity training that play on identity politics, reverse discrimination, and bashing and disenfranchising white people are not yet over, they should be, sooner rather than later. What would work in place of contemporary diversity training is a race-neutral outreach to people who are disadvantaged with more of a focus on social class and less—much less—on race. Do that, and businesses doing all the hiring will sweep in a lot of people and many of them will *still* be underrepresented minorities, and that's what everyone wants. You will also get rid of some of that resentment that poor or working-class Whites now hold, and that will be because that gets you back to something closer to the original version of meritocracy. A lot of what progressives have been doing in recent decades has actually *reversed* the gains that people—namely minorities to include Blacks—had already been making.

It is important to remember that the tenets and original intent of affirmative action and what we now know as diversity, equity, and inclusion are very closely related, in a sense synonymous with one another. It's important to embrace this when examining the overarching influence and outcomes yet to be that will follow the Supreme Court's decision to significantly diminish the use of racial preferences in American universities. A similar fate awaits the use of racial preferences in workplace hiring and promotions, with or without a Supreme Court ruling of its own (yet). In their book, *Mismatch*, [10] Richard Sander and Stuart Taylor Jr. say that such preferences hinder underrepresented minorities far more than they help them. In an online summary of their book, which we first mentioned in chapter 2, the authors go on to explain how "dramatic new data and numerous interviews with affected former students and university officials of color . . . show how racial preferences often put students in competition with far better prepared classmates, dooming many to fall so far behind that they can never catch up. . . . Even though black applicants are more likely to enter college than whites with similar backgrounds, they are far less likely to finish; why there are so few black and Hispanic professionals with science and engineering degrees and doctorates; why black law graduates fail bar exams at four times the rate of Whites; and why universities accept relatively affluent minorities over working class and poor people of all races." [11]

What this tells me, and what I have seen with my own eyes in many college classrooms as student and, later, professor, is that because of affirmative action, many students from underrepresented groups get recruited into Ivy League or other academically elite schools and end up unable to succeed. What I believe ensues is anger and often an embrace of Marxist theories of oppression. This results in protest and activism rather than study and high achievement in some cases. In hindsight, many of the students who graduate at the bottom of their class at an elite institution would have been better off starting out at a state institution where the admissions and academic standards might better match their profile. My own academic journey followed that latter pathway and took me to a PhD and, eventually, tenured academic positions at Princeton and Vanderbilt universities. I had help and encouragement along the way from mentors who did not look like me; many of them were successful older white men who wanted to see me succeed. With their encouragement and mentorship, which were not forced, I aimed high. The stepladder approach enabled me to go far beyond what would normally be expected from a person with my background.

GOAL SHOULD BE RACE-NEUTRAL RECRUITMENT

No doubt there have been many minorities over the years who have been destined for success, only to end up recruited into situations that put them in over their heads from their start, and from that it is difficult to recover. With race-neutral recruitment, support from professors and grad students, remedial help where needed (math for me when I was in school), and just understanding the circumstances that people come from, schools and students can succeed and advance. They can get good jobs for which they will be properly suited without the crutch of a system that focused on group membership and less so on individual accomplishments. People will thrive when they are in the right environment. Unfortunately, affirmative action programs have placed a stigma on every racial and ethnic minority, so much so that we currently have a presidential administration where high-profile leaders tout their group identities rather than their qualifications for the job. Whether they know it or not, their presence in a position attained through identity group politics hurts every qualified member of their group who worked their butts off to attain their positions. The only important factor should be one's qualifications for a position and how well they perform. Membership in a historically disadvantaged group should be irrelevant in most situations.

Targeting any special group or labeling them as evil or deficient because they are male, or because they are white or Asian, should not be the main idea of an effective training program. Civil rights laws protect individuals. We should all be searching for diamonds in the rough and talented people who want to better themselves and will take advantage of opportunities offered on a nonracial or nongender basis. A successful training program zeroes in on the mission as originally expressed—and presumably still applicable present-day—by the founders of the organization. In its optimal application, it brings together employees around that mission without singling out or denigrating any group. It does not allow fear to prevent leaders from standing strong and doing the right thing rather than the trendy thing for their organization. WorldBlu, founded by Traci Fenton, is a prime example of a leadership organization that helps business owners and CEOs move beyond fear toward freedom to innovate and build a healthy organizational democracy within the workplace that advances the mission of the institution.[12]

Real Unity Training Solutions believes that the secret to building strong teams is respecting and harnessing individual talent. Our goal is to help leaders of corporations, businesses, nonprofits, religious institutions, and other organizations achieve their goals by providing viable alternatives to the divisive and counterproductive critical race and gender theories that have divided Americans and disrupted institutions. We respect everyone's civil rights and equality under the law. We encourage Americans to rediscover and re-embrace our national motto: *E Pluribus Unum* (out of many, one). We also encourage other companies with a similar vision to compete in this space because knowledge is power, and the system is so broken that no single company could meet the needs of all. We encourage leaders and CEOs to have the courage and freedom to explore new and better ways of helping their organization become the best they can be while harnessing and developing the human capital entrusted to them as leaders who lead by example and not by fear and intimidation.

Following are Real Unity Training Solutions' twelve core values, in no particular order:

Core Values and Principles
- We want institutions to succeed.
- We believe unity is positive and productive.
- We believe the citizens of our nation share more similarities than differences.
- We respect the differences of others.
- We care about justice and fairness.
- We believe that customer service should be a top priority.
- We believe in traditional "success principles" of hard work, integrity, and accountability.
- We have no hidden agendas.
- We are truthful with our clients and our team.
- We believe in transparency and honest dialogue.
- We are financially responsible.
- We accept personal responsibility for our results.*

Unity training involves common sense, understanding the Constitution and the law; respecting and being tactful with one another; working as teams and celebrating the victories, big and small; encouraging one another; and being an active listener and observer, all at the same time all the time. There are numerous challenges and obstacles lurking to prevent you from being able to pull this off—to achieve constructive diversity training without of-

---

* This information and more about Real Unity Training Solutions is also available at our website, www.unitytrainingsolutions.com.

fending anyone. One of the elephants in the room is the rampant divisiveness in our nation, spilling over into the workplace, where there is evidence of "wokeness" around almost every corner. When we interviewed Mike Hardwick, the founder, president, and CEO of Tennessee-based Churchill Mortgage, which employs eleven hundred workers servicing forty-six states, he brought up the issue of divisiveness. Mike described it in terms that sound an awful lot like a description of wokeness:

"Our [surrounding] culture these days is radically different than it's been for most of my business career," Hardwick said. "There is so much divisiveness in our society today. That's a sad reality. You find yourself checking a lot of your thoughts because you have to be more cautious in how you express yourself. And that's not all bad. Because it goes back to this—when we express our thoughts, shouldn't we do so with respect to everybody? Different opinions, feelings and thoughts are okay, but can't we do that respectfully?

"When people respect each other, they can communicate better with each other, find areas of agreement. There's more peace and harmony through that effort than the railing, hollering, marching, raising banners, cussing that a lot of people tend to do. I don't know that anger has ever produced a lot of good. Respect, patience, seeking to understand others, I have found, works better more often than not."[13]

Let me close by repeating something I said in an October 28, 2022, article that appeared in *The Federalist*. Suitable for this book, the title of that article was "A Plan to Make 'Diversity, Equity, and Inclusion' Die." Exactly.

> I have always believed in America. I'm a product of the American dream. I have had faith in the Constitution, and the Bill of Rights, because that distinguished us from other nations. So there's a part of me that's very troubled at where our nation is at this point in time, but I try to stay optimistic because I believe that whatever we may think separates us, we are Americans at the core and . . . what unites us is far greater than what divides us.[14]

Notes

Preface

1   Ian Bremmer, "The U.S. Capitol Riot was Years in the Making. Here's Why America Is So Divided," *Time*, January 16, 2021, https://time.com/5929978/the-u-s-capitol-riot-was-years-in-the-making-heres-why-america-is-so-divided/, viewed July 24, 2023.

2   Robert O. Harrow Jr., "Videos Show Closed-Door Sessions of Leading Conservative Activists: 'Be Not Afraid of the Accusations that You're a Voter Suppressor,' " *Washington Post*, October 14, 2020, https://www.washingtonpost.com/investigations/council-national-policy-video/2020/10/14/367f24c2-f793-11ea-a510-f57d8ce76e11_story.html, viewed July 15, 2023.

3   Melinda D. Anderson, "How Does Race Affect a Student's Math Education," *Atlantic*, July 2017, https://www.theatlantic.com/education/archive/2017/04/racist-math-education/524199/, viewed July 24, 2023.

4   Rachel Crowell, "Modern Mathematics Confronts Its White Patriarchal Past," *Scientific American*, August 12, 2021, https://www.scientificamerican.com/article/modern-mathematics-confronts-its-white-patriarchal-past/, viewed July 24, 2023.

Chapter 1

1   Lyndon B. Johnson, "Commencement Address at Howard University: 'To Fulfill These Rights,'" www.presidency.ucsb.edu, June 4, 1965, https://www.presidency.ucsb.edu/documents/commencement-address-howard-university-fulfill-these-rights, viewed April 10, 2023.

2   U.S. Supreme Court Chief Justice John Roberts, "Majority Opinion: 'Students for Fair Admissions v. President and Fellows of Harvard College,' " June 29, 2023, https://supreme.justia.com/cases/federal/us/600/20-1199/#tab-opinion-4758916, viewed July 10, 2023.

3   Mark Sherman, "Divided Supreme Court Outlaws Affirmative Action in College Admissions, Says Race Can't Be Used," Associated Press, June 29,

2023, https://apnews.com/article/supreme-court-affirmative-action-college-race-f83d6318017ec9b9029b12ee2256e744, viewed July 12, 2023.

4   Carol M. Swain, *The New White Nationalism in America: Its Challenge to Integration* (New York City: Cambridge University Press), p. 139.

5   "A Brief History of Affirmative Action," Office of Equal Opportunity and Diversity," https://www.oeod.uci.edu/policies/aa_history.php#:~:text=11246%20in%201965.-,Executive%20Order%2011246,receiving%20federal%20contracts%20and%20subcontracts, viewed April 11, 2023.

6   Genevieve Carlton, PhD, "A History of Affirmative Action in College Admissions," best colleges.com, updated December 7, 2022, https://www.bestcolleges.com/news/analysis/2020/08/10/history-affirmative-action-college/, viewed April 12, 2023.

7   Jane Holzka, "Philadelphia Plan," encyclopedia.com, https://www.encyclopedia.com/history/encyclopedias-almanacs-transcripts-and-maps/philadelphia-plan, viewed July 17, 2023.

8   John David Skrentny, *The Ironies of Affirmative Action: Politics, Culture, and Justice in America* (Chicago: University of Chicago Press, 1996).

9   National Advisory Commission on Civil Disorders, *The Kerner Report* (Princeton, NJ: Princeton University Press, 2016) p. 2.

10   Frank Dobbin and Alexandra Kaley, "Why Diversity Programs Fail," *Harvard Business Review,* July-August 2016, https://hbr.org/2016/07/why-diversity-programs-fail, viewed April 26, 2023.

11   Michael Levensen, "Jury Awards $10 Million to White Male Executive in Discrimination Case," *New York Times,* October 28, 2021, https://www.nytimes.com/2021/10/28/us/david-duvall-firing-lawsuit-diversity.html, viewed April 25, 2023.

12   Levensen, "Jury Awards $10 Million to White Male Executive in Discrimination Case."

13   Levensen.

14   Hannah Grossman, "Trans Swimmer Lia Thomas Photographed Wearing 'Disturbing' Antifa Shirt: 'Doesn't This Make So Much Sense?'," FoxNews, July 19, 2023, https://www.foxnews.com/media/trans-swimmer-lia-thomas-photographed-wearing-disturbing-antifa-shirt-doesnt-this-make-sense, viewed July 25, 2023.

15   White House, "Press Briefing by Press Secretary Karine Jean-Pierre and the Cast of 'The L Word' and 'The L Word: Generation Q,' " April 25, 2023, https://www.whitehouse.gov/briefing-room/press-briefings/2023/04/25/press-briefing-by-press-secretary-karine-jean-

pierre-and-the-cast-of-the-l-word-and-the-l-word-generation-q/#:~:text=Today%20I'm%20honored%20to,funny%2C%20and%20resil-ient%20queer%20women, viewed May 25, 2023.

16   Stephanie Saul, "If Affirmative Action Ends. College Admissions May Be Changed Forever," *New York Times*, updated January 26, 2023.

17   Sana Pashankar, "If Affirmative Action is Overturned, How Could It Change Duke Admissions?" the *Chronicle*, Duke University, February 13, 2023.

18   Hilary Burns, "Meet Edward Blum, the Man Behind the Harvard Affirmative Action Case," *Boston Globe,* May 29, 2023, www.bostonglobe.com/2023/05/29/metro/harvard-affirmative-action-case-meet-ed-blum/?p1=Article_Recirc_Most_Popular&p1=Article_Recirc_Most_Popular, viewed May 29, 2023.

19   Hilary Burns, "Meet Edward Blum, the Man Behind the Harvard Affirmative Action Case," *Boston Globe*, May 29, 2023.

20   Burns, "Meet Edward Blum, the Man Behind the Harvard Affirmative Action Case."

21   Burns.

22   Stephanie Saul, "If Affirmative Action Ends, College Admissions May Be Changed Forever," *New York Times*, updated January 26, 2023.

23   Saul, "If Affirmative Action Ends, College Admissions May Be Changed Forever."

24   Morrison Foerster Law Firm, "Are Workplace Diversity Programs in Jeopardy if the Supreme Court Ends Affirmative Action in College Admissions?" March 29, 2023, https://www.mofo.com/resources/insights/230329-are-workplace-diversity-programs-in-jeopardy, viewed May 24, 2023.

25   Erin Kelly and Frank Dobbin, "How Affirmative Action Became Diversity Management: Employer Response to Antidiscrimination Law, 1961 to 1996," *American Behavioral Scientist*, April 1998, https://scholar.harvard.edu/dobbin/publications/how-affirmative-action-became-diversity-managementemployer-response-antidiscrimi, viewed May 22, 2023.

26   Kelly and Dobbin.

27   Genevieve Carlton, PhD, "A History of Affirmative Action in College Admissions," best colleges.com, updated December 7, 2022, https://www.bestcolleges.com/news/analysis/2020/08/10/history-affirmative-action-college/, viewed April 12, 2023.

28   Derrick A. Bell, *Race, Racism and American Law* (Boston: Little Brown, 6th ed., 2008), viewed July 25, 2023.

Chapter 2

1   Carol M. Swain, *The New White Nationalism in America: Its Challenge to Integration* (Cambridge, UK: Cambridge University Press, 2002), p. 156, from Richardson, Messages and Papers of the Presidents, Vol. 2, pp. 398-405, cited in Albert P. Blaustein, *Civil Rights and the American Negro* (New York: Washington Square Press, 1969).

2   "Most Black Students at Harvard Are From High-Income Families," *Journal of Blacks in America*, 2004, https://www.jbhe.com/news_views/52_harvard-blackstudents.html, viewed May 25, 2023.

3   Carol M. Swain, *Black Faces, Black Interests: The Representation of African Americans in Congress* (Boston: Harvard University Press, 1993, 1996).

4   Roger E. Hernandez, "Skirting the Real Issue—Racism," Washington Post, February 10, 1995, https://www.washingtonpost.com/archive/opinions/1995/02/10/skirting-the-real-issue-racism/1f3aba94-6da6-4845-99f6-ed6b1a914cdb/, viewed June 10, 2023.

5   Adam Tanner, "Why a Racial Remark at Rutgers University Stirs Such Emotion," *Christian Science Monitor*, February 13, 1995, https://www.csmonitor.com/1995/0213/13031.html, viewed June 10, 2023.

6   Alex Oliveira, "Virginia School Chief Denies National Merit Awards Were Withheld Due to 'Equity' Amid Claims 17 High Schools Delayed Handing Out Accolades to Avoid Hurting Other Students' Feelings," DailyMail.com, January 25, 2023, https://www.dailymail.co.uk/news/article-11676761/Virginia-school-chief-denies-National-Merit-Awards-withheld-equity.html, viewed April 12, 2023.

7   Maggie Severns, "Woman Who Killed Affirmative Action," *Politico*, April 24, 2014, https://www.politico.com/story/2014/04/jennifer-gratz-affirmative-action-michigan-105913, viewed May 2, 2023.

8   Richard H. Sander and Stuart Taylor Jr., *Mismatch: How Affirmative Action Hurts Students It's Intended to Help, and Why Universities Won't Admit It* (New York: Basic Books, 2012) p. 368.

9   Roland Fryer, "Build Freer Schools and Make Yale and Harvard Fund Them," *New York Times*, July 5, 2023, https://www.nytimes.com/interactive/2023/07/05/opinion/affirmative-action-college-admissions.html, viewed July 25, 2023.

Chapter 3

1   President Barack Obama, "Executive Order on Diversity, Equity, Inclusion, and Accessibility in the Federal Workforce," The White House, June 25, 2021, https://www.whitehouse.gov/briefing-room/presidential-actions/2021/06/25/executive-order-on-diversity-equity-inclusion-and-accessibility-in-the-federal-workforce/, viewed June 3, 2023.

2   Obama, "Executive Order on Diversity, Equity, Inclusion, and Accessibility in the Federal Workforce."

3   Obama.

4   Aja Romano, "Google Has Fired the Engineer Whose Anti-Diversity Memo Reflects a Divided Tech Culture," vox.com, August 8, 2017, https://www.vox.com/identities/2017/8/8/16106728/google-fired-engineer-anti-diversity-memo, viewed May 12, 2023.

5   Romano, "Google Has Fired the Engineer Whose Anti-Diversity Memo Reflects a Divided Tech Culture."

6   Romano.

7   Associated Press, "Mozilla CEO Resignation Raises Free-Speech Issues," as it appeared in *USA Today*, April 4, 2014, https://www.usatoday.com/story/news/nation/2014/04/04/mozilla-ceo-resignation-free-speech/7328759/, viewed May 13, 2023.

8   Associated Press, "Mozilla CEO Resignation Raises Free-Speech Issues."

9   "Mozilla CEO Resignation Raises Free-Speech Issues."

10 Rohini Anand and Mary-Frances Winters, "A Retrospective View of Corporate Diversity Training from 1964 to the Present," *Academy of Management Learning & Education*, September 2008, pp. 356-372, https://journals.aom.org/doi/abs/10.5465/amle.2008.34251673, viewed May 25, 2023.

11 Anand and Winters, "A Retrospective View of Corporate Diversity Training from 1964 to the Present."

12 Anand and Winters.

13 Anand and Winters.

14 Jonathan Turley, " 'What's More Tragic Is Capitalism': BLM Faces Bankruptcy as Founder Cullors Is Cut by Warner Bros.," jonathanturley.org, May 28, 2023, https://jonathanturley.org/2023/05/28/the-stuff-that-dreams-are-made-of-blm-faces-bankruptcy-as-founder-cullors-is-cut-by-warner-bros/, viewed June 7, 2023.

15 Turley, " 'What's More Tragic Is Capitalism': BLM Faces Bankruptcy as Founder Cullors Is Cut by Warner Bros."

16   Turley.

17   Turley.

Chapter 4

1   Rahm Emanuel, "Let's Make Sure This Crisis Doesn't Go to Waste," *Washington Post*, March 25, 2020, https://www.washingtonpost.com/opinions/2020/03/25/lets-make-sure-this-crisis-doesnt-go-waste/, viewed June 11, 2023.

2   Paolo Gaudiano, "Two Years After George Floyd's Murder, Is Your DEI Strategy Performative or Sustainable," *Forbes*, June 27, 2022, https://www.forbes.com/sites/paologaudiano/2022/06/27/two-years-after-george-floyd-is-your-dei-strategy-performative-or-sustainable/?sh=39db300c6aaa, viewed June 18, 2023.

3   https://www.documentcloud.org/documents/6936176-Autopsy-2020-3700-Floyd, viewed June 18, 2023.

4   Erin Donaghue, "Two Autopsies Both Find George Floyd Died by Homicide, But Differ on Some Key Details," CBS News, June 4, 2020, https://www.cbsnews.com/news/george-floyd-death-autopsies-homicide-axphyxiation-details/, viewed June 18, 2023.

5   Rahm Emanuel, "Let's Make Sure This Crisis Doesn't Go to Waste."

6   *New York Times*, "How George Floyd Died, and What Happened Next," July 29, 2022, https://www.nytimes.com/article/george-floyd.html, viewed June 14, 2023.

7   Christopher F. Rufo, "When 'Diversity Training' Is All About Feeding Racism," *New York Post*, July 10, 2020, https://manhattan.institute/article/when-diversity-training-is-all-about-feeding-racism, viewed June 6, 2023.

8   Rufo, "When 'Diversity Training' Is All About Feeding Racism."

9   Danielle Wiener-Bronner and Kristina Sgueglia, "Starbucks Says It Fired Her for an 'Absence of Leadership.' She Says It Was Because of Her Race. A Jury Returned a $25.6 Million Verdict in Her Favor," CNN, June 14, 2023, https://www.cnn.com/2023/06/14/business/starbucks-manager-racial-discrimination/index.html, viewed June 15, 2023.

10   Danielle Wiener-Bronner and Kristina Sgueglia, "Starbucks Says It Fired Her for an 'Absence of Leadership.' "

11   Heather Haddon, "Starbucks Closing Some Stores, Citing Safety Concerns in Certain Cafes," *Wall Street Journal*, July 12, 2022,

https://www.wsj.com/articles/starbucks-closing-some-stores-citing-safety-concerns-in-certain-cafes-11657588871, viewed June 15, 2023.

12   Sarah Rumpf-Whitten, "University of Minnesota Faces Backlash over Summer Research Program Restricted to Nonwhite Students," Fox News, May 21, 2023, https://www.foxnews.com/us/university-minnesota-faces-backlash-over-summer-research-pr

13   Rumpf-Whitten, "University of Minnesota Face Backlash over Summer Research Program Restricted to Nonwhite Students."

14   Dana Kennedy, "Inside the CEI System Pushing Brands to Endorse Celebs Like Dylan Mulvaney," *New York Post,* April 7, 2023, https://nypost.com/2023/04/07/inside-the-woke-scoring-system-guiding-american-companies/, viewed June 13, 2023.

15   Dana Kennedy, "Inside the CEI System Pushing Brands to Endorse Celebs Like Dylan Mulvaney."

16   Kennedy.

17   Kennedy.

18   Kennedy.

19   Cortney O'Brien, "Court Rules Against Employee Fired for Refusing to Attend LGBTQ Training Session," Fox News, March 15, 2023, https://www.foxnews.com/media/court-rules-against-employee-fired-refusing-attend-lgbtq-training-session, viewed June 16, 2023.

20   Charlotte Allen, "The DEI Invasion: Ideological Creep in Law and Medicine," *Epoch Times,* May 24, 2023, https://www.theepochtimes.com/the-dei-invasion-ideological-creep-in-law-and-medicine_5284040.html, viewed June 17, 2023.

21   Charlotte Allen, "The DEI Invasion: Ideological Creep in Law and Medicine."

22   Nadine El-Bawab and Melissa Repko, "One Year After George Floyd's Death: 6 Reflections on Corporate America's Progress," CNBC, May 26, 2021, https://www.cnbc.com/2021/05/26/one-year-after-george-floyds-death-6-reflections-on-corporate-americas-progress.html, viewed June 18, 2023.

Chapter 5

1   James A. Lindsay, "The Marxist Roots of DEI Workshop: Session 2—Diversity," New Discourses video presentation, April 4, 2023, https://newdiscourses.com/2023/04/marxist-roots-of-dei-workshop-all-sessions/, viewed June 23, 2023.

2   Jathon Sapsford, "Republican Attorneys General Warn Top U.S. Businesses

over 'Discrimination,'" *Wall Street Journal*, July 14, 2023, https://www.wsj.com/articles/republican-attorneys-general-warn-top-u-s-businesses-over-discrimination-1eb78d29, viewed July 14, 2023.

3   Darlene McCormick Sanchez, "UT Austin Spends over $13 million on Diversity, Equity, and Inclusion Salaries: Documents," *Epoch Times*, May 20, 2023, https://www.theepochtimes.com/ut-austin-spends-over-13-million-on-diversity-equity-and-inclusion-salaries-documents_5280452.html, viewed Jun 20, 2023.

4   Darlene McCormick Sanchez, "UT Austin Spends over $13 million on Diversity, Equity, and Inclusion Salaries: Documents."

5   McCormick Sanchez.

6   Sherry Sylvester, "Texas War to End DEI is Just Beginning," Cannononlline.com, July 5, 2023, https://thecannononline.com/texas-war-to-end-dei-is-just-beginning/, viewed July 17, 2023.

7   Olivia Land, "Former Penn State Professor Zack DePiero Claims College Said English Language Is 'Racist,'" *New York Post*, June 26, 2023, www.msn.com/en-us/news/us/former-penn-state-professor-zack-depiero-claims-college-said-english-language-is-racist/ar-AA1d7yRn, viewed July 2, 2023.

8   Land, "Former Penn State Professor Zack DePiero Claims College Said English Language Is 'Racist.'"

9   https://www.linkedin.com/showcase/hr-dive-human-resources-and-workforce-management-news/, viewed June 26, 2023.

10   Laura Kalser, "Some DEI Policies Send the Wrong Message, Survey Warns," *HR Dive*, November 16, 2022, https://www.hrdive.com/news/dei-policies-reverse-discrimination/636561/, viewed June 27, 2023.

11   Jonathan Turley, "Chicago-Area Teacher Sues After Being Fired for Criticism of Protests After George Floyd Murder," jonathanturley.org, July 26, 2021, https://jonathanturley.org/2021/07/26/chicago-area-teacher/Chicago-Area Teacher Sues After Being Fired For Criticism Of Protests After George Floyd Murder, viewed July 12, 2023.

12   Kenneth R. Timmerman, *Shakedown: Exposing the Real Jesse Jackson* (Washington, DC: Regnery, 2012).

13   Turley, "Chicago-Area Teacher Sues After Being Fired for Criticism of Protests After George Floyd Murder."

14   Timmerman, *Shakedown: Exposing the Real Jesse Jackson*.

15   Zachary Faria, "The NFL Meets with Race-Baiter Al Sharpton to Discuss Racial Quotas," *Washington Examiner*, February 9, 2022, https://www.washingtonexaminer.com/opinion/the-nfl-meets-with-race-

baiter-al-sharpton-to-discuss-racial-quotas, viewed July 12, 2023.

16   Khorri Atkinson, "Corporate Diversity Pledges Fizzle Amid Layoffs, GOP Backlash," news.bloomberglaw.com, March 9, 2023, https://news.bloomberglaw.com/daily-labor-report/corporate-diversity-pledges-fizzle-amid-layoffs-gop-backlash, viewed June 27, 2023.

17   Kelsey Minor, "Three Years After George Floyd's Murder: Where Is DEI Now, and What Have Companies Learned?" *Senior Executive*, February 10, 2023, https://seniorexecutive.com/three-years-after-george-floyds-murder-where-is-dei-now-and-what-have-companies-learned/#:~:text=The%20result%20of%20the%20company's,includes%20equity%20pay%20and%20promotions, viewed June 27, 2023.

18   Jonathan Turley, " 'What's More Tragic Is Capitalism': BLM Faces Bankruptcy as Founder Cullors Is Cut by Warner Bros.," jonathanturley.org, May 28, 2023, https://jonathanturley.org/2023/05/28/the-stuff-that-dreams-are-made-of-blm-faces-bankruptcy-as-founder-cullors-is-cut-by-warner-bros/, viewed June 7, 2023.

19   Morrison Foerster Law Firm, "Are Workplace Diversity Programs in Jeopardy if the Supreme Court Ends Affirmative Action in College Admissions?" March 29, 2023, https://www.mofo.com/resources/insights/230329-are-workplace-diversity-programs-in-jeopardy, viewed May 24, 2023.

20   Erika Johnson, "Top 4 Reasons Diversity and Inclusion Programs Fail," *Forbes*, March 29, 2021, https://www.forbes.com/sites/forbeseq/2021/03/29/top-4-reasons-diversity-and-inclusion-programs-fail/, viewed July 1, 2023.

21   Frank Dobbin and Alexandra Kalev, "Spotlight on Building a Diverse Organization: Why Diversity Programs Fail," *Harvard Business Review*, July-August 2016, https://hbr.org/2016/07/why-diversity-programs-fail, viewed June 15, 2023.

22   Dobbin and Kalev, "Spotlight on Building a Diverse Organization: Why Diversity Programs Fail."

Chapter 6

1   U.S. Supreme Court Chief Justice John Roberts, Majority Opinion, *Students for Fair Admissions v. President and Fellows of Harvard College*, https://supreme.justia.com/cases/federal/us/600/20-1199/#tab-opinion-4758916, viewed July 10, 2023.

2   U.S. Supreme Court Justice Clarence Thomas, Concurring Opinion, *Students for Fair Admissions v. President and Fellows of Harvard College*. https://supreme.justia.com/cases/federal/us/600/20-1199/, viewed July 10, 2023.

3   Deborah White, "Barack Obama's Inspiring 2004 Democratic Convention Speech," thoughtco.com, October 16, 2017, www.thoughtco.com/obama-speech-2004-democratic-convention-3325333, viewed July 4, 2023.

4   Carol M. Swain, "Is America Ready for a Black President? America is Ready, But It Won't Be A Veteran of the Civil Rights Movement," *Ebony* 62, no. 3 (January 2007) p. 141, as quoted in Carol M. Swain, "Racial Politics, President Obama and Me," Ch. 7, *Be the People: A Call to Reclaim America's Faith and Promise* (Nashville, Thomas Nelson Press, 2011), p. 191.

5   Te-Ping Chen and Ray A. Smith, "No One Is Happy about Diversity Efforts at Work," *Wall Street Journal*, July 3, 2023, https://www.wsj.com/articles/diversity-workplace-affirmative-action-dei-3646683b, viewed July 9, 2023.

6   Chen and Smith, "No One Is Happy about Diversity Efforts at Work," *Wall Street Journal*, July 3, 2023.

7   Stephen R. Covey, *The Seven Habits of Highly Effective People: Restoring the Character Ethic* (New York, Simon and Schuster, 1989).

8   Peter Lencioni, *The Five Dysfunctions of a Team* (London: Jossey-Bass, 2002).

9   Carol M. Swain, *The New White Nationalism in America: Its Challenge to Integration* (New York: Cambridge University Press, 2002).

10   Richard Sander and Stuart Taylor Jr., *Mismatch: How Affirmative Action Hurts Students It's Intended to Help, and Why Universities Won't Admit It* (New York: Basic Books, 2012).

11   Amazon book summary, *Mismatch: How Affirmative Action Hurts Students It's Intended to Help, and Why Universities Won't Admit It*, by Richard Sander and Stuart Taylor Jr., https://www.amazon.com/Mismatch-Affirmative-Students-%C2%92s-Universities/dp/0465029965/ref=sr_1_11?crid=3N3B4WC82DYM2&keywords=richard+sanders&qid=1689092071&s=books&sprefix=richard+sanders%2Cstripbooks%2C192&sr=1-11, viewed July 11, 2023.

12   WorldBlu, business management company, https://www.worldblu.com, viewed July 25, 2023.

13   Mike Hardwick, Churchill Mortgage Corporation, interview with Carol Swain, October 26, 2022.

14   "A Plan To Make 'Diversity, Equity, And Inclusion' Die," *The Federalist*, October 28, 2022, https://unitytrainingsolutions.com/a-plan-to-make-diversity-equity-and-inclusion-die/, viewed July 10, 2023.

APPENDIX A

Students for Fair Admissions, Inc. v. President and Fellows of Harvard College, 600 U.S. ___ (2023)

I. Majority Opinion

NOTICE: This opinion is subject to formal revision before publication in the United States Reports. Readers are requested to notify the Reporter of Decisions, Supreme Court of the United States, Washington, D. C. 20543, pio@supremecourt.gov, of any typographical or other formal errors.

SUPREME COURT OF THE UNITED STATES

Nos. 20–1199 and 21–707

STUDENTS FOR FAIR ADMISSIONS, INC., PETITIONER
20–1199v.
PRESIDENT AND FELLOWS OF HARVARD COLLEGE
on writ of certiorari to the united states court of appeals for the first circuit
STUDENTS FOR FAIR ADMISSIONS, INC., PETITIONER
21–707v.
UNIVERSITY OF NORTH CAROLINA, et al.
on writ of certiorari before judgment to the united states court of appeals for the fourth circuit
[June 29, 2023]
Chief Justice Roberts delivered the opinion of the Court.
In these cases we consider whether the admissions systems used by Harvard College and the University of North Carolina, two of the oldest institutions of higher learning in the United States, are lawful under the Equal Protection Clause of the Fourteenth Amendment.

I

A

Founded in 1636, Harvard College has one of the most selective application processes in the country. Over 60,000 people applied to the school last year; fewer than 2,000 were admitted. Gaining admission to

Harvard is thus no easy feat. It can depend on having excellent grades, glowing recommendation letters, or overcoming significant adversity. See 980 F.3d 157, 166–169 (CA1 2020). It can also depend on your race.

The admissions process at Harvard works as follows. Every application is initially screened by a "first reader," who assigns scores in six categories: academic, extracurricular, athletic, school support, personal, and overall. Ibid. A rating of "1" is the best; a rating of "6" the worst. Ibid. In the academic category, for example, a "1" signifies "near-perfect standardized test scores and grades"; in the extracurricular category, it indicates "truly unusual achievement"; and in the personal category, it denotes "outstanding" attributes like maturity, integrity, leadership, kindness, and courage. Id., at 167–168. A score of "1" on the overall rating—a composite of the five other ratings—"signifies an exceptional candidate with >90% chance of admission." Id., at 169 (internal quotation marks omitted). In assigning the overall rating, the first readers "can and do take an applicant's race into account." Ibid.

Once the first read process is complete, Harvard convenes admissions subcommittees. Ibid. Each subcommittee meets for three to five days and evaluates all applicants from a particular geographic area. Ibid. The subcommittees are responsible for making recommendations to the full admissions committee. Id., at 169–170. The subcommittees can and do take an applicant's race into account when making their recommendations. Id., at 170.

The next step of the Harvard process is the full committee meeting. The committee has 40 members, and its discussion centers around the applicants who have been recommended by the regional subcommittees. Ibid. At the beginning of the meeting, the committee discusses the relative breakdown of applicants by race. The "goal," according to Harvard's director of admissions, "is to make sure that [Harvard does] not hav[e] a dramatic drop-off" in minority admissions from the prior class. 2 App. in No. 20–1199, pp. 744, 747–748. Each applicant considered by the full committee is discussed one by one, and every member of the committee must vote on admission. 980 F. 3d, at 170. Only when an applicant secures a majority of the full committee's votes is he or she tentatively accepted for admission. Ibid. At the end of the full committee meeting, the racial composition of the pool of tentatively admitted students is disclosed to the committee. Ibid.; 2 App. in No. 20–1199, at 861.

The final stage of Harvard's process is called the "lop," during which the list of tentatively admitted students is winnowed further to arrive at the final class. Any applicants that Harvard considers cutting at this stage are placed on a "lop list," which contains only four pieces of information: legacy status, recruited athlete status, financial aid eligibility, and race. 980 F. 3d, at 170. The full committee decides as a group which students to lop.

397 F. Supp. 3d 126, 144 (Mass. 2019). In doing so, the committee can and does take race into account. Ibid. Once the lop process is complete, Harvard's admitted class is set. Ibid. In the Harvard admissions process, "race is a determinative tip for" a significant percentage "of all admitted African American and Hispanic applicants." Id., at 178.

B

Founded shortly after the Constitution was ratified, the University of North Carolina (UNC) prides itself on being the "nation's first public university." 567 F. Supp. 3d 580, 588 (MDNC 2021). Like Harvard, UNC's "admissions process is highly selective": In a typical year, the school "receives approximately 43,500 applications for its freshman class of 4,200." Id., at 595.

Every application the University receives is initially reviewed by one of approximately 40 admissions office readers, each of whom reviews roughly five applications per hour. Id., at 596, 598. Readers are required to consider "[r]ace and ethnicity . . . as one factor" in their review. Id., at 597 (internal quotation marks omitted). Other factors include academic performance and rigor, standardized testing results, extracurricular involvement, essay quality, personal factors, and student background. Id., at 600. Readers are responsible for providing numerical ratings for the academic, extracurricular, personal, and essay categories. Ibid. During the years at issue in this litigation, underrepresented minority students were "more likely to score [highly] on their personal ratings than their white and Asian American peers," but were more likely to be "rated lower by UNC readers on their academic program, academic performance, . . . extracurricular activities," and essays. Id., at 616–617.

After assessing an applicant's materials along these lines, the reader "formulates an opinion about whether the student should be offered admission" and then "writes a comment defending his or her recommended decision." Id., at 598 (internal quotation marks omitted). In making that decision, readers may offer students a "plus" based on their race, which "may be significant in an individual case." Id., at 601 (internal quotation marks omitted). The admissions decisions made by the first readers are, in most cases, "provisionally final." Students for Fair Admissions, Inc. v. University of N. C. at Chapel Hill, No. 1:14–cv–954 (MDNC, Nov. 9, 2020), ECF Doc. 225, p. 7, ¶52.

Following the first read process, "applications then go to a process called 'school group review' . . . where a committee composed of experienced staff members reviews every [initial] decision." 567 F. Supp. 3d, at 599. The review committee receives a report on each student which contains, among other things, their "class rank, GPA, and test scores; the ratings assigned to them by their initial readers; and their status as residents, legacies, or special recruits." Ibid. (footnote omitted). The review committee either approves or rejects each admission recommendation made by the first reader, after which the admissions decisions are finalized. Ibid. In making those decisions, the review committee may also consider the applicant's race. Id., at 607; 2 App. in No. 21–707, p. 407.[1]

C

Petitioner, Students for Fair Admissions (SFFA), is a nonprofit organization founded in 2014 whose purpose is "to defend human and civil rights secured by law, including the right of individuals to equal protection under the law." 980 F. 3d, at 164 (internal quotation marks omitted). In November 2014, SFFA filed separate lawsuits against Harvard College and the University of North Carolina, arguing that their race-based admissions programs violated, respectively, Title VI of the Civil Rights Act of 1964, 78Stat. 252, 42 U. S. C. §2000d et seq., and the Equal Protection Clause of the Fourteenth Amendment.[2] See 397 F. Supp. 3d, at 131–132; 567 F. Supp. 3d, at 585–586. The District Courts in both cases held bench trials to evaluate SFFA's claims. See 980 F. 3d, at 179; 567 F. Supp. 3d, at 588. Trial in the Harvard case lasted 15 days and included testimony from 30 witnesses, after which the Court concluded that Harvard's admissions program comported with our precedents on the use of race in college admissions. See 397 F. Supp. 3d, at 132, 183. The First Circuit affirmed that determination. See 980 F. 3d, at 204. Similarly, in the UNC case, the District Court concluded after an eight-day trial that UNC's admissions program was permissible under the Equal Protection Clause. 567 F. Supp. 3d, at 588, 666.

We granted certiorari in the Harvard case and certiorari before judgment in the UNC case. 595 U. S. ___ (2022).

II

Before turning to the merits, we must assure ourselves of our jurisdiction. See Summers v. Earth Island Institute, 555 U.S. 488, 499 (2009). UNC argues that SFFA lacks standing to bring its claims because it is not a "genuine" membership organization. Brief for University Respondents in No. 21–707, pp. 23–26. Every court to have considered this argument has rejected it, and so do we. See Students for Fair Admissions, Inc. v. University of Tex. at Austin, 37 F. 4th 1078, 1084–1086, and n. 8 (CA5 2022) (collecting cases).

Article III of the Constitution limits "[t]he judicial power of the United States" to "cases" or "controversies," ensuring that federal courts act only "as a necessity in the determination of real, earnest and vital" disputes. Muskrat v. United States, 219 U.S. 346, 351, 359 (1911) (internal quotation marks omitted). "To state a case or controversy under Article III, a plaintiff must establish standing." Arizona Christian School Tuition Organization v. Winn, 563 U.S. 125, 133 (2011). That, in turn, requires a plaintiff to demonstrate that it has "(1) suffered an injury in fact, (2) that is fairly traceable to the challenged conduct of the defendant, and (3) that is likely to be redressed by a favorable judicial decision." Spokeo, Inc. v. Robins, 578 U.S. 330, 338 (2016).

In cases like these, where the plaintiff is an organization, the standing requirements of Article III can be satisfied in two ways. Either the organization can claim that it suffered an injury in its own right or, alternatively, it can assert "standing solely as the representative of its members." Warth v. Seldin, 422 U.S. 490, 511 (1975). The latter approach is known as representational or organizational standing. Ibid.; Summers, 555 U. S., at 497–498. To invoke it, an organization must demonstrate that "(a) its members would otherwise have standing to sue in their own right; (b) the interests it seeks to protect are germane to the organization's purpose; and (c) neither the claim asserted nor the relief requested requires the participation of individual members in the lawsuit." Hunt v. Washington State Apple Advertising Comm'n, 432 U.S. 333, 343 (1977).

Respondents do not contest that SFFA satisfies the three-part test for organizational standing articulated in Hunt, and like the courts below, we find no basis in the record to conclude otherwise. See 980 F. 3d, at 182–184; 397 F. Supp. 3d, at 183–184; No. 1:14-cv-954 (MDNC, Sept. 29, 2018), App. D to Pet. for Cert. in No. 21–707, pp. 237–245 (2018 DC Opinion). Respondents instead argue that SFFA was not a "genuine 'membership organization' " when it filed suit, and thus that it could not invoke the doctrine of organizational standing in the first place. Brief for University Respondents in No. 21–707, at 24. According to respondents, our decision in Hunt established that groups qualify as genuine membership organizations only if they are controlled and funded by their members. And because SFFA's members did neither at the time this litigation commenced, respondents' argument goes, SFFA could not represent its members for purposes of Article III standing. Brief for University Respondents in No. 21–707, at 24 (citing Hunt, 432 U. S., at 343).

Hunt involved the Washington State Apple Advertising Commission, a state agency whose purpose was to protect the local apple industry. The Commission brought suit challenging a North Carolina statute that imposed a labeling requirement on containers of apples sold in that State. The Commission argued that it had standing to challenge the requirement on behalf of Washington's apple industry. See id., at 336–341. We recognized, however, that as a state agency, "the Commission [wa]s not a traditional voluntary membership organization . . . , for it ha[d] no members at all." Id., at 342. As a result, we could not easily apply the three-part test for organizational standing, which asks whether an organization's members have standing. We nevertheless concluded that the Commission had standing because the apple growers and dealers it represented were effectively members of the Commission. Id., at 344. The growers and dealers "alone elect[ed] the members of the Commission," "alone . . . serve[d] on the Commission," and "alone finance[d] its activities"—they possessed, in other words, "all of the indicia of membership." Ibid. The Commission was therefore a genuine membership organization in substance, if not in form. And it was "clearly" entitled to rely on the doctrine of organizational standing under the three-part test recounted above. Id., at 343.

The indicia of membership analysis employed in Hunt has no applicability in these cases. Here, SFFA is indisputably a voluntary membership organization with identifiable members—it is not, as in Hunt, a state agency that concededly has no members. See 2018 DC Opinion 241–242. As the First Circuit in the Harvard litigation observed, at the time SFFA filed suit, it was "a validly incorporated 501(c)(3) nonprofit with forty-seven members who joined voluntarily to support its mission." 980 F. 3d, at 184. Meanwhile in the UNC litigation, SFFA represented four members in particular—high school graduates who were denied admission to UNC. See 2018 DC Opinion 234. Those members filed declarations with the District Court stating "that they have voluntarily joined SFFA; they support its mission; they receive updates about the status of the case from SFFA's President; and they have had the opportunity to have input and direction on SFFA's case." Id., at 234–235 (internal quotation marks omitted). Where, as here, an organization has identified members and represents them in good faith, our cases do not require further scrutiny into how the organization operates. Because SFFA complies with the standing requirements demanded of organizational plaintiffs in Hunt, its obligations under Article III are satisfied.

III

A

In the wake of the Civil War, Congress proposed and the States ratified the Fourteenth Amendment, providing that no State shall "deny to any person . . . the equal protection of the laws." Amdt. 14, §1. To its proponents, the Equal Protection Clause represented a "foundation[al] principle"—"the absolute equality of all citizens of the United States politically and civilly before their own laws." Cong. Globe, 39th Cong., 1st Sess., 431 (1866) (statement of Rep. Bingham) (Cong. Globe). The Constitution, they were determined, "should not permit any distinctions of law based on race or color," Supp. Brief for United States on Reargument in Brown v. Board of Education, O. T. 1953, No. 1 etc., p. 41 (detailing the history of the adoption of the Equal Protection Clause), because any "law which operates upon one man [should] operate equally upon all," Cong. Globe 2459 (statement of Rep. Stevens). As soon-to-be President James Garfield observed, the Fourteenth Amendment would hold "over every American citizen, without regard to color, the protecting shield of law." Id., at 2462. And in doing so, said Senator Jacob Howard of Michigan, the Amendment would give "to the humblest, the poorest, the most despised of the race the same rights and the same protection before the law as it gives to the most powerful, the most wealthy, or the most haughty." Id., at 2766. For "[w]ithout this principle of equal justice," Howard continued, "there is no republican government and none that is really worth maintaining." Ibid.

At first, this Court embraced the transcendent aims of the Equal Protection Clause. "What is this," we said of the Clause in 1880, "but declaring that the law in the States shall be the same for the black as for the white; that all persons, whether colored or white, shall stand equal before the laws of the States?" Strauder v. West Virginia, 100 U.S. 303, 307–309. "[T]he broad and benign provisions of the Fourteenth Amendment" apply "to all persons," we unanimously declared six years later; it is "hostility to . . . race and nationality" "which in the eye of the law is not justified." Yick Wo v. Hopkins, 118 U.S. 356, 368–369, 373–374 (1886); see also id., at 368 (applying the Clause to "aliens and subjects of the Emperor of China"); Truax v. Raich, 239 U.S. 33, 36 (1915) ("a native of Austria"); semble Strauder, 100 U. S., at 308–309 ("Celtic Irishmen") (dictum).

Despite our early recognition of the broad sweep of the Equal Protection Clause, this Court—alongside the country—quickly failed to live up to the Clause's core commitments. For almost a century after the Civil War, state-mandated segregation was in many parts of the Nation a regrettable norm. This Court played its own role in that ignoble history, allowing in Plessy v. Ferguson the separate but equal regime that would come to deface much of America. 163 U.S. 537 (1896). The aspirations of the framers of the Equal Protection Clause, "[v]irtually strangled in [their] infancy," would remain for too long only that—aspirations. J. Tussman & J. tenBroek, The Equal Protection of the Laws, 37 Cal. L. Rev. 341, 381 (1949).

After Plessy, "American courts . . . labored with the doctrine [of separate but equal] for over half a century." Brown v. Board of Education, 347 U.S. 483, 491 (1954). Some cases in this period attempted to curtail the perniciousness of the doctrine by emphasizing that it required States to provide black students educational opportunities equal to—even if formally separate from—those enjoyed by white students. See, e.g., Missouri ex rel. Gaines v. Canada, 305 U.S. 337, 349–350 (1938) ("The admissibility of laws separating the races in the enjoyment of privileges afforded by the State rests wholly upon the equality of the privileges which the laws give to the separated groups . . . ."). But the inherent folly of that approach—of trying to derive equality from inequality—soon became apparent. As the Court subsequently recognized, even racial distinctions that were argued to have no palpable effect worked to subordinate the afflicted students. See, e.g., McLaurin v. Oklahoma State Regents for Higher Ed., 339 U.S. 637, 640–642 (1950) ("It is said that the separations imposed by the State in this case are in form merely nominal. . . . But they signify that the State . . . sets [petitioner] apart from the other students."). By 1950, the inevitable truth of the Fourteenth Amendment had thus begun to reemerge: Separate cannot be equal.

The culmination of this approach came finally in Brown v. Board of Education. In that seminal decision, we overturned Plessy for good and set firmly on the path of invalidating all de jure racial discrimination by the States and Federal Government. 347 U. S., at 494–495. Brown concerned the permissibility of racial segregation in public schools. The school district maintained that such segregation was lawful because the schools provided to black students and white students were of roughly the same quality. But we held such segregation impermissible "even though the physical facilities and other 'tangible' factors may be equal." Id., at 493 (emphasis added). The mere act of separating "children . . . because of their race," we explained, itself "generate[d] a feeling of inferiority." Id., at 494.

The conclusion reached by the Brown Court was thus unmistakably clear: the right to a public education "must be made available to all on equal terms." Id., at 493. As the plaintiffs had argued, "no State has any authority under the equal-protection clause of the Fourteenth Amendment to use race as a factor in affording educational opportunities among its citizens." Tr. of Oral Arg. in Brown I, O. T. 1952, No. 8, p. 7 (Robert L. Carter, Dec. 9, 1952); see also Supp. Brief for Appellants on Reargument in Nos. 1, 2, and 4, and for Respondents in No. 10, in Brown v. Board of Education, O. T. 1953, p. 65 ("That the Constitution is color blind is our dedicated belief."); post, at 39, n. 7 (Thomas, J., concurring). The Court reiterated that rule just one year later, holding that "full compliance" with Brown required schools to admit students "on a racially nondiscriminatory basis." Brown v. Board of Education, 349 U.S. 294, 300–301 (1955). The time for making distinctions based on race had passed. Brown, the Court observed, "declar[ed] the fundamental principle that racial discrimination in public education is unconstitutional." Id., at 298.

So too in other areas of life. Immediately after Brown, we began routinely affirming lower court decisions that invalidated all manner of race-based state action. In Gayle v. Browder, for example, we summarily affirmed a decision invalidating state and local laws that required segregation in busing. 352 U.S. 903 (1956) (per curiam). As the lower court explained, "[t]he equal protection clause requires equality of treatment before the law for all persons without regard to race or color." Browder v. Gayle, 142 F. Supp. 707, 715 (MD Ala. 1956). And in Mayor and City Council of Baltimore v. Dawson, we summarily affirmed a decision striking down racial segregation at public beaches and bathhouses maintained by the State of Maryland and the city of Baltimore. 350 U.S. 877 (1955) (per curiam). "It is obvious that racial segregation in recreational activities can no longer be sustained," the lower court observed. Dawson v. Mayor and City Council of Baltimore, 220 F.2d 386, 387 (CA4 1955) (per curiam). "[T]he ideal of equality before the law which characterizes our institutions" demanded as much. Ibid.

In the decades that followed, this Court continued to vindicate the Constitution's pledge of racial equality. Laws dividing parks and golf courses; neighborhoods and businesses; buses and trains; schools and juries were undone, all by a transformative promise "stemming from our American ideal of fairness": " 'the Constitution . . . forbids . . . discrimination by the General Government, or by the States, against any citizen because of his race.' " Bolling v. Sharpe, 347 U.S. 497, 499 (1954) (quoting Gibson v. Mississippi, 162 U.S. 565, 591 (1896) (Harlan, J., for the Court)). As we recounted in striking down the State of Virginia's ban on interracial marriage 13 years after Brown, the Fourteenth Amendment "proscri[bes] . . . all invidious racial discriminations." Loving v. Virginia, 388 U.S. 1, 8 (1967). Our cases had thus "consistently denied the constitutionality of measures which restrict the rights of citizens on account of race." Id., at 11–12; see also Yick Wo, 118 U. S., at 373–375 (commercial property); Shelley v. Kraemer, 334 U.S. 1 (1948) (housing covenants); Hernandez v. Texas, 347 U.S. 475 (1954) (composition of juries); Dawson, 350 U. S., at 877 (beaches and bathhouses); Holmes v. Atlanta, 350 U.S. 879 (1955) (per curiam) (golf courses); Browder, 352 U. S., at 903 (busing); New Orleans City Park Improvement Assn. v. Detiege, 358 U.S. 54 (1958) (per curiam) (public parks); Bailey v. Patterson, 369 U.S. 31 (1962) (per curiam) (transportation facilities); Swann v. Charlotte-Mecklenburg Bd. of Ed., 402 U.S. 1 (1971) (education); Batson v. Kentucky, 476 U.S. 79 (1986) (peremptory jury strikes).

These decisions reflect the "core purpose" of the Equal Protection Clause: "do[ing] away with all governmentally imposed discrimination based on race." Palmore v. Sidoti, 466 U.S. 429, 432 (1984) (footnote omitted). We have recognized that repeatedly. "The clear and central purpose of the Fourteenth Amendment was to eliminate all official state sources of invidious racial discrimination in the States." Loving, 388 U. S., at 10; see also Washington v. Davis, 426 U.S. 229, 239 (1976) ("The central purpose of the Equal Protection Clause of the Fourteenth Amendment is the prevention of official conduct discriminating on the basis of race."); McLaughlin v. Florida, 379 U.S. 184, 192 (1964) ("[T]he historical fact [is] that the central purpose of the Fourteenth Amendment was to eliminate racial discrimination.").

Eliminating racial discrimination means eliminating all of it. And the Equal Protection Clause, we have accordingly held, applies "without regard to any differences of race, of color, or of nationality"—it is "universal in [its] application." Yick Wo, 118 U. S., at 369. For "[t]he guarantee of equal protection cannot mean one thing when applied to one individual and something else when applied to a person of another color." Regents of Univ. of Cal. v. Bakke, 438 U.S. 265, 289–290 (1978) (opinion of Powell, J.). "If both are not accorded the same protection, then it is not equal." Id., at 290.

Any exception to the Constitution's demand for equal protection must survive a daunting two-step examination known in our cases as "strict scrutiny." Adarand Constructors, Inc. v. Peña, 515 U.S. 200, 227 (1995). Under that standard we ask, first, whether the racial classification is used to "further compelling governmental interests." Grutter v. Bollinger, 539 U.S. 306, 326 (2003). Second, if so, we ask whether the government's use of race is "narrowly tailored"—meaning "necessary"—to achieve that interest. Fisher v. University of Tex. at Austin, 570 U.S. 297, 311–312 (2013) (Fisher I) (internal quotation marks omitted).

Outside the circumstances of these cases, our precedents have identified only two compelling interests that permit resort to race-based government action. One is remediating specific, identified instances of past discrimination that violated the Constitution or a statute. See, e.g., Parents Involved in Community Schools v. Seattle School Dist. No. 1, 551 U.S. 701, 720 (2007); Shaw v. Hunt, 517 U.S. 899, 909–910 (1996); post, at 19–20, 30–31 (opinion of Thomas, J.). The second is avoiding imminent and serious risks to human safety in prisons, such as a race riot. See Johnson v. California, 543 U.S. 499, 512–513 (2005).[3]

Our acceptance of race-based state action has been rare for a reason. "Distinctions between citizens solely because of their ancestry are by their very nature odious to a free people whose institutions are founded upon the doctrine of equality." Rice v. Cayetano, 528 U.S. 495, 517 (2000) (quoting Hirabayashi v. United States, 320 U.S. 81, 100 (1943)). That principle cannot be overridden except in the most extraordinary case.

B

These cases involve whether a university may make admissions decisions that turn on an applicant's race. Our Court first considered that issue in Regents of University of California v. Bakke, which involved a set-aside admissions program used by the University of California, Davis, medical school. 438 U. S., at 272–276. Each year, the school held 16 of its 100 seats open for members of certain minority groups, who were reviewed on a special admissions track separate from those in the main admissions pool. Id., at 272–275. The plaintiff, Allan Bakke, was denied admission two years in a row, despite the admission of minority applicants with lower grade point averages and MCAT scores. Id., at 276–277. Bakke subsequently sued the school, arguing that its set-aside program violated the Equal Protection Clause.

In a deeply splintered decision that produced six different opinions—none of which commanded a majority of the Court—we ultimately ruled in part in favor of the school and in part in favor of Bakke. Justice Powell announced the Court's judgment, and his opinion—though written for himself alone—would eventually come to "serv[e] as the touchstone for constitutional analysis of race-conscious admissions policies." Grutter, 539 U. S., at 323.

Justice Powell began by finding three of the school's four justifications for its policy not sufficiently compelling. The school's first justification of "reducing the historic deficit of traditionally disfavored minorities in medical schools," he wrote, was akin to "[p]referring members of any one group for no reason other than race or ethnic origin." Bakke, 438 U. S., at 306–307 (internal quotation marks omitted). Yet that was "discrimination for its own sake," which "the Constitution forbids." Id., at 307 (citing, inter alia, Loving, 388 U. S., at 11). Justice Powell next observed that the goal of "remedying . . . the effects of 'societal discrimination' " was also insufficient because it was "an amorphous concept of injury that may be ageless in its reach into the past." Bakke, 438 U. S., at 307. Finally, Justice Powell found there was "virtually no evidence in the record indicating that [the school's] special admissions program" would, as the school had argued, increase the number of doctors working in underserved areas. Id., at 310.

Justice Powell then turned to the school's last interest asserted to be compelling—obtaining the educational benefits that flow from a racially diverse student body. That interest, in his view, was "a constitutionally permissible goal for an institution of higher education." Id., at 311–312. And that was so, he opined, because a university was entitled as a matter of academic freedom "to make its own judgments as to . . . the selection of its student body." Id., at 312.

But a university's freedom was not unlimited. "Racial and ethnic distinctions of any sort are inherently suspect," Justice Powell explained, and antipathy toward them was deeply "rooted in our Nation's constitutional and demographic history." Id., at 291. A university could not employ a quota system, for example, reserving "a specified number of seats in each class for individuals from the preferred ethnic groups." Id., at 315. Nor could it impose a "multitrack program with a prescribed number of seats set aside for each identifiable category of applicants." Ibid. And neither still could it use race to foreclose an individual "from all consideration . . . simply because he was not the right color." Id., at 318.

The role of race had to be cabined. It could operate only as "a 'plus' in a particular applicant's file." Id., at 317. And even then, race was to be weighed in a manner "flexible enough to consider all pertinent elements of diversity in light of the particular qualifications of each applicant." Ibid. Justice Powell derived this approach from what he called the "illuminating example" of the admissions system then used by Harvard College. Id., at 316. Under that system, as described by Harvard in a brief it had filed with the Court, "the race of an applicant may tip the balance in his favor just as geographic origin or a life [experience] may tip the balance in other candidates' cases." Ibid. (internal quotation marks omitted). Harvard continued: "A farm boy from Idaho can bring something to Harvard College that a Bostonian cannot offer. Similarly, a black student can usually bring something that a white person cannot offer." Ibid. (internal quotation marks omitted). The result, Harvard proclaimed, was that "race has been"—and should be—"a factor in some admission decisions." Ibid. (internal quotation marks omitted).

No other Member of the Court joined Justice Powell's opinion. Four Justices instead would have held that the government may use race for the purpose of "remedying the effects of past societal discrimination." Id., at 362 (joint opinion of Brennan, White, Marshall, and Blackmun, JJ., concurring in judgment in part and dissenting in part). Four other Justices, meanwhile, would have struck down the Davis program as violative of Title VI. In their view, it "seem[ed] clear that the proponents of Title VI assumed that the Constitution itself required a colorblind standard on the part of government." Id., at 416 (Stevens, J., joined by Burger, C. J., and Stewart and Rehnquist, JJ., concurring in judgment in part and dissenting in part). The Davis program therefore flatly contravened a core "principle imbedded in the constitutional and moral understanding of the times": the prohibition against "racial discrimination." Id., at 418, n. 21 (internal quotation marks omitted).

C

In the years that followed our "fractured decision in Bakke," lower courts "struggled to discern whether Justice Powell's" opinion constituted "binding precedent." Grutter, 539 U. S., at 325. We accordingly took up the matter again in 2003, in the case Grutter v. Bollinger, which concerned the admissions system used by the University of Michigan law school. Id., at

311. There, in another sharply divided decision, the Court for the first time "endorse[d] Justice Powell's view that student body diversity is a compelling state interest that can justify the use of race in university admissions." Id., at 325.

The Court's analysis tracked Justice Powell's in many respects. As for compelling interest, the Court held that "[t]he Law School's educational judgment that such diversity is essential to its educational mission is one to which we defer." Id., at 328. In achieving that goal, however, the Court made clear—just as Justice Powell had—that the law school was limited in the means that it could pursue. The school could not "establish quotas for members of certain racial groups or put members of those groups on separate admissions tracks." Id., at 334. Neither could it "insulate applicants who belong to certain racial or ethnic groups from the competition for admission." Ibid. Nor still could it desire "some specified percentage of a particular group merely because of its race or ethnic origin." Id., at 329–330 (quoting Bakke, 438 U. S., at 307 (opinion of Powell, J.)).

These limits, Grutter explained, were intended to guard against two dangers that all race-based government action portends. The first is the risk that the use of race will devolve into "illegitimate . . . stereotyp[ing]." Richmond v. J. A. Croson Co., 488 U.S. 469, 493 (1989) (plurality opinion). Universities were thus not permitted to operate their admissions programs on the "belief that minority students always (or even consistently) express some characteristic minority viewpoint on any issue." Grutter, 539 U. S., at 333 (internal quotation marks omitted). The second risk is that race would be used not as a plus, but as a negative—to discriminate against those racial groups that were not the beneficiaries of the race-based preference. A university's use of race, accordingly, could not occur in a manner that "unduly harm[ed] nonminority applicants." Id., at 341.

But even with these constraints in place, Grutter expressed marked discomfort with the use of race in college admissions. The Court stressed the fundamental principle that "there are serious problems of justice connected with the idea of [racial] preference itself." Ibid. (quoting Bakke, 438 U. S., at 298 (opinion of Powell, J.)). It observed that all "racial classifications, however compelling their goals," were "dangerous." Grutter, 539 U. S., at 342. And it cautioned that all "race-based governmental action" should "remai[n] subject to continuing oversight to assure that it will work the least harm possible to other innocent persons competing for the benefit." Id., at 341 (internal quotation marks omitted).

To manage these concerns, Grutter imposed one final limit on race-based admissions programs. At some point, the Court held, they must end. Id., at 342. This requirement was critical, and Grutter emphasized it repeatedly. "[A]ll race-conscious admissions programs [must] have a termination point"; they "must have reasonable durational limits"; they "must be limited in time"; they must have "sunset provisions"; they "must have a logical end point"; their "deviation from the norm of equal treatment" must be "a temporary matter." Ibid. (internal quotation marks omitted). The importance of an end point was not just a matter of repetition. It was the reason the Court was willing to dispense temporarily with the Constitution's unambiguous guarantee of equal protection. The Court recognized as much: "[e]nshrining a permanent justification for racial preferences," the Court explained, "would offend this fundamental equal protection principle." Ibid.; see also id., at 342–343 (quoting N. Nathanson & C. Bartnik, The Constitutionality of Preferential Treatment for Minority Applicants to Professional Schools, 58 Chi. Bar Rec. 282, 293 (May–June 1977), for the proposition that "[i]t would be a sad day indeed, were America to become a quota-ridden society, with each identifiable minority assigned proportional representation in every desirable walk of life").

Grutter thus concluded with the following caution: "It has been 25 years since Justice Powell first approved the use of race to further an interest in student body diversity in the context of public higher education. . . . We expect that 25 years from now, the use of racial preferences will no longer be necessary to further the interest approved today." 539 U. S., at 343.

IV

Twenty years later, no end is in sight. "Harvard's view about when [race-based admissions will end] doesn't have a date on it." Tr. of Oral Arg. in No. 20–1199, p. 85; Brief for Respondent in No. 20–1199, p. 52. Neither does UNC's. 567 F. Supp. 3d, at 612. Yet both insist that the use of race in their admissions programs must continue.

But we have permitted race-based admissions only within the confines of narrow restrictions. University programs must comply with strict scrutiny, they may never use race as a stereotype or negative, and—at some point—they must end. Respondents' admissions systems—however well intentioned and implemented in good faith—fail each of these criteria. They must therefore be invalidated under the Equal Protection Clause of the Fourteenth Amendment.[4]

A

Because "[r]acial discrimination [is] invidious in all contexts," Edmonson v. Leesville Concrete Co., 500 U.S. 614, 619 (1991), we have required that universities operate their race-based admissions programs in a manner that is "sufficiently measurable to permit judicial [review]" under the rubric of strict scrutiny, Fisher v. University of Tex. at Austin, 579 U.S.

365, 381 (2016) (Fisher II). "Classifying and assigning" students based on their race "requires more than . . . an amorphous end to justify it." Parents Involved, 551 U. S., at 735.

Respondents have fallen short of satisfying that burden. First, the interests they view as compelling cannot be subjected to meaningful judicial review. Harvard identifies the following educational benefits that it is pursuing: (1) "training future leaders in the public and private sectors"; (2) preparing graduates to "adapt to an increasingly pluralistic society"; (3) "better educating its students through diversity"; and (4) "producing new knowledge stemming from diverse outlooks." 980 F. 3d, at 173–174. UNC points to similar benefits, namely, "(1) promoting the robust exchange of ideas; (2) broadening and refining understanding; (3) fostering innovation and problem-solving; (4) preparing engaged and productive citizens and leaders; [and] (5) enhancing appreciation, respect, and empathy, cross-racial understanding, and breaking down stereotypes." 567 F. Supp. 3d, at 656.

Although these are commendable goals, they are not sufficiently coherent for purposes of strict scrutiny. At the outset, it is unclear how courts are supposed to measure any of these goals. How is a court to know whether leaders have been adequately "train[ed]"; whether the exchange of ideas is "robust"; or whether "new knowledge" is being developed? Ibid.; 980 F. 3d, at 173–174. Even if these goals could somehow be measured, moreover, how is a court to know when they have been reached, and when the perilous remedy of racial preferences may cease? There is no particular point at which there exists sufficient "innovation and problem-solving," or students who are appropriately "engaged and productive." 567 F. Supp. 3d, at 656. Finally, the question in this context is not one of no diversity or of some: it is a question of degree. How many fewer leaders Harvard would create without racial preferences, or how much poorer the education at Harvard would be, are inquiries no court could resolve.

Comparing respondents' asserted goals to interests we have recognized as compelling further illustrates their elusive nature. In the context of racial violence in a prison, for example, courts can ask whether temporary racial segregation of inmates will prevent harm to those in the prison. See Johnson, 543 U. S., at 512–513. When it comes to workplace discrimination, courts can ask whether a race-based benefit makes members of the discriminated class "whole for [the] injuries [they] suffered." Franks v. Bowman Transp. Co., 424 U.S. 747, 763 (1976) (internal quotation marks omitted). And in school segregation cases, courts can determine whether any race-based remedial action produces a distribution of students "compar[able] to what it would have been in the absence of such constitutional violations." Dayton Bd. of Ed. v. Brinkman, 433 U.S. 406, 420 (1977).

Nothing like that is possible when it comes to evaluating the interests respondents assert here. Unlike discerning whether a prisoner will be injured or whether an employee should receive backpay, the question whether a particular mix of minority students produces "engaged and productive citizens," sufficiently "enhance[s] appreciation, respect, and empathy," or effectively "train[s] future leaders" is standardless. 567 F. Supp. 3d, at 656; 980 F. 3d, at 173–174. The interests that respondents seek, though plainly worthy, are inescapably imponderable.

Second, respondents' admissions programs fail to articulate a meaningful connection between the means they employ and the goals they pursue. To achieve the educational benefits of diversity, UNC works to avoid the underrepresentation of minority groups, 567 F. Supp. 3d, at 591–592, and n. 7, while Harvard likewise "guard[s] against inadvertent drop-offs in representation" of certain minority groups from year to year, Brief for Respondent in No. 20–1199, at 16. To accomplish both of those goals, in turn, the universities measure the racial composition of their classes using the following categories: (1) Asian; (2) Native Hawaiian or Pacific Islander; (3) Hispanic; (4) White; (5) African-American; and (6) Native American. See, e.g., 397 F. Supp. 3d, at 137, 178; 3 App. in No. 20–1199, at 1278, 1280–1283; 3 App. in No. 21–707, at 1234–1241. It is far from evident, though, how assigning students to these racial categories and making admissions decisions based on them furthers the educational benefits that the universities claim to pursue.

For starters, the categories are themselves imprecise in many ways. Some of them are plainly overbroad: by grouping together all Asian students, for instance, respondents are apparently uninterested in whether South Asian or East Asian students are adequately represented, so long as there is enough of one to compensate for a lack of the other. Meanwhile other racial categories, such as "Hispanic," are arbitrary or undefined. See, e.g., M. Lopez, J. Krogstad, & J. Passel, Pew Research Center, Who is Hispanic? (Sept. 15, 2022) (referencing the "long history of changing labels [and] shifting categories . . . reflect[ing] evolving cultural norms about what it means to be Hispanic or Latino in the U. S. today"). And still other categories are underinclusive. When asked at oral argument "how are applicants from Middle Eastern countries classified, [such as] Jordan, Iraq, Iran, [and] Egypt," UNC's counsel responded, "[I] do not know the answer to that question." Tr. of Oral Arg. in No. 21–707, p. 107; cf. post, at 6–7 (Gorsuch, J., concurring) (detailing the "incoherent" and "irrational stereotypes" that these racial categories further).

Indeed, the use of these opaque racial categories undermines, instead of promotes, respondents' goals. By focusing on underrepresentation, respondents would apparently prefer a class with 15% of students from Mexico over a class with 10% of students from several Latin American countries, simply because the former contains more Hispanic students than the latter. Yet "[i]t is hard to understand how a plan that could allow these results can be viewed as being concerned with achieving enrollment that is 'broadly diverse.' " Parents Involved, 551 U. S., at 724 (quoting Grutter, 539 U. S., at 329). And given the mismatch between the means respondents employ and the goals they seek, it is especially hard to understand how courts are supposed to scrutinize the admissions programs that respondents use.

The universities' main response to these criticisms is, essentially, "trust us." None of the questions recited above need answering, they say, because universities are "owed deference" when using race to benefit some applicants but not others. Brief for University Respondents in No. 21–707, at 39 (internal quotation marks omitted). It is true that our cases have recognized a "tradition of giving a degree of deference to a university's academic decisions." Grutter, 539 U. S., at 328. But we have been unmistakably clear that any deference must exist "within constitutionally prescribed limits," ibid., and that "deference does not imply abandonment or abdication of judicial review," Miller–El v. Cockrell, 537 U.S. 322, 340 (2003). Universities may define their missions as they see fit. The Constitution defines ours. Courts may not license separating students on the basis of race without an exceedingly persuasive justification that is measurable and concrete enough to permit judicial review. As this Court has repeatedly reaffirmed, "[r]acial classifications are simply too pernicious to permit any but the most exact connection between justification and classification." Gratz v. Bollinger, 539 U.S. 244, 270 (2003) (internal quotation marks omitted). The programs at issue here do not satisfy that standard.[5]

B

The race-based admissions systems that respondents employ also fail to comply with the twin commands of the Equal Protection Clause that race may never be used as a "negative" and that it may not operate as a stereotype.

First, our cases have stressed that an individual's race may never be used against him in the admissions process. Here, however, the First Circuit found that Harvard's consideration of race has led to an 11.1% decrease in the number of Asian-Americans admitted to Harvard. 980 F. 3d, at 170, n. 29. And the District Court observed that Harvard's "policy of considering applicants' race . . . overall results in fewer Asian American and white students being admitted." 397 F. Supp. 3d, at 178.

Respondents nonetheless contend that an individual's race is never a negative factor in their admissions programs, but that assertion cannot withstand scrutiny. Harvard, for example, draws an analogy between race and other factors it considers in admission. "[W]hile admissions officers may give a preference to applicants likely to excel in the Harvard-Radcliffe Orchestra," Harvard explains, "that does not mean it is a 'negative' not to excel at a musical instrument." Brief for Respondent in No. 20–1199, at 51. But on Harvard's logic, while it gives preferences to applicants with high grades and test scores, "that does not mean it is a 'negative' " to be a student with lower grades and lower test scores. Ibid. This understanding of the admissions process is hard to take seriously. College admissions are zero-sum. A benefit provided to some applicants but not to others necessarily advantages the former group at the expense of the latter.

Respondents also suggest that race is not a negative factor because it does not impact many admissions decisions. See id., at 49; Brief for University Respondents in No. 21–707, at 2. Yet, at the same time, respondents also maintain that the demographics of their admitted classes would meaningfully change if race-based admissions were abandoned. And they acknowledge that race is determinative for at least some—if not many—of the students they admit. See, e.g., Tr. of Oral Arg. in No. 20–1199, at 67; 567 F. Supp. 3d, at 633. How else but "negative" can race be described if, in its absence, members of some racial groups would be admitted in greater numbers than they otherwise would have been? The "[e]qual protection of the laws is not achieved through indiscriminate imposition of inequalities." Shelley, 334 U. S., at 22.[6]

Respondents' admissions programs are infirm for a second reason as well. We have long held that universities may not operate their admissions programs on the "belief that minority students always (or even consistently) express some characteristic minority viewpoint on any issue." Grutter, 539 U. S., at 333 (internal quotation marks omitted). That requirement is found throughout our Equal Protection Clause jurisprudence more generally. See, e.g., Schuette v. BAMN, 572 U.S. 291, 308 (2014) (plurality opinion) ("In cautioning against 'impermissible racial stereotypes,' this Court has rejected the assumption that 'members of the same racial group—regardless of their age, education, economic status, or the community in which they live—think alike . . . .' " (quoting Shaw v. Reno, 509 U.S. 630, 647 (1993))).

Yet by accepting race-based admissions programs in which some students may obtain preferences on the basis of race alone, respondents' programs tolerate the very thing that Grutter foreswore: stereotyping. The point of respondents' admissions programs is that there is an inherent benefit in race qua race—in race for race's sake. Respondents admit as much. Harvard's admissions process rests on the pernicious stereotype that "a black student can usually bring something that a white person cannot offer." Bakke, 438 U. S., at 316 (opinion of Powell, J.) (internal quotation marks omitted); see also Tr. of Oral Arg. in No. 20–1199, at 92. UNC is much the same. It argues that race in itself "says [something] about who you are." Tr. of Oral Arg. in No. 21–707, at 97; see also id., at 96 (analogizing being of a certain race to being from a rural area).

We have time and again forcefully rejected the notion that government actors may intentionally allocate preference to those "who may have little in common with one another but the color of their skin." Shaw, 509 U. S., at 647. The entire point of the Equal Protection Clause is that treating someone differently because of their skin color is not like treating them differently because they are from a city or from a suburb, or because they play the violin poorly or well.

"One of the principal reasons race is treated as a forbidden classification is that it demeans the dignity and worth of a person to be judged by ancestry instead of by his or her own merit and essential qualities." Rice, 528 U. S., at 517. But when a university admits students "on the basis of race, it engages in the offensive and demeaning assumption that [students] of a particular race, because of their race, think alike," Miller v. Johnson, 515 U.S. 900, 911–912 (1995) (internal quotation marks omitted)—at the very least alike in the sense of being different from nonminority students. In doing so, the university furthers "stereotypes that treat individuals as the product of their race, evaluating their thoughts and efforts—their very worth as citizens—according to a criterion barred to the Government by history and the Constitution." Id., at 912 (internal quotation marks omitted). Such stereotyping can only "cause[ ] continued hurt and injury," Edmonson, 500 U. S., at 631, contrary as it is to the "core purpose" of the Equal Protection Clause, Palmore, 466 U. S., at 432.

C

If all this were not enough, respondents' admissions programs also lack a "logical end point." Grutter, 539 U. S., at 342.

Respondents and the Government first suggest that respondents' race-based admissions programs will end when, in their absence, there is "meaningful representation and meaningful diversity" on college campuses. Tr. of Oral Arg. in No. 21–707, at 167. The metric of meaningful representation, respondents assert, does not involve any "strict numerical benchmark," id., at 86; or "precise number or percentage," id., at 167; or "specified percentage," Brief for Respondent in No. 20–1199, at 38 (internal quotation marks omitted). So what does it involve?

Numbers all the same. At Harvard, each full committee meeting begins with a discussion of "how the breakdown of the class compares to the prior year in terms of racial identities." 397 F. Supp. 3d, at 146. And "if at some point in the admissions process it appears that a group is notably underrepresented or has suffered a dramatic drop off relative to the prior year, the Admissions Committee may decide to give additional attention to applications from students within that group." Ibid.; see also id., at 147 (District Court finding that Harvard uses race to "trac[k] how each class is shaping up relative to previous years with an eye towards achieving a level of racial diversity"); 2 App. in No. 20–1199, at 821–822.

The results of the Harvard admissions process reflect this numerical commitment. For the admitted classes of 2009 to 2018, black students represented a tight band of 10.0%–11.7% of the admitted pool. The same theme held true for other minority groups:

Brief for Petitioner in No. 20–1199 etc., p. 23. Harvard's focus on numbers is obvious.[7]

UNC's admissions program operates similarly. The University frames the challenge it faces as "the admission and enrollment of underrepresented minorities," Brief for University Respondents in No. 21–707, at 7, a metric that turns solely on whether a group's "percentage enrollment within the undergraduate student body is lower than their percentage within the general population in North Carolina," 567 F. Supp. 3d, at 591, n. 7; see also Tr. of Oral Arg. in No. 21–707, at 79. The University "has not yet fully achieved its diversity-related educational goals," it explains, in part due to its failure to obtain closer to proportional representation. Brief for University Respondents in No. 21–707, at 7; see also 567 F. Supp. 3d, at 594.

The problem with these approaches is well established. "[O]utright racial balancing" is "patently unconstitutional." Fisher I, 570 U. S., at 311 (internal quotation marks omitted). That is so, we have repeatedly explained, because "[a]t the heart of the Constitution's guarantee of equal protection lies the simple command that the Government must treat citizens as individuals, not as simply components of a racial, religious, sexual or national class." Miller, 515 U. S., at 911 (internal quotation marks omitted). By promising to terminate their use of race only when some rough percentage of various racial groups is admitted, respondents turn that principle on its head. Their admissions programs "effectively assure[ ] that race will always be relevant . . . and that the ultimate goal of eliminating" race as a criterion "will never be achieved." Croson, 488 U. S., at 495 (internal quotation marks omitted).

Respondents' second proffered end point fares no better. Respondents assert that universities will no longer need to engage in race-based admissions when, in their absence, students nevertheless receive the educational benefits of diversity. But as we have already explained, it is not clear how a court is supposed to determine when stereotypes have broken down or "productive citizens and leaders" have been created. 567 F. Supp. 3d, at 656. Nor is there any way to know whether those goals would adequately be met in the absence of a race-based admissions program. As UNC itself acknowledges, these "qualitative standard[s]" are "difficult to measure."

Tr. of Oral Arg. in No. 21–707, at 78; but see Fisher II, 579 U. S., at 381 (requiring race-based admissions programs to operate in a manner that is "sufficiently measurable").

Third, respondents suggest that race-based preferences must be allowed to continue for at least five more years, based on the Court's statement in Grutter that it "expect[ed] that 25 years from now, the use of racial preferences will no longer be necessary." 539 U. S., at 343. The 25-year mark articulated in Grutter, however, reflected only that Court's view that race-based preferences would, by 2028, be unnecessary to ensure a requisite level of racial diversity on college campuses. Ibid. That expectation was oversold. Neither Harvard nor UNC believes that race-based admissions will in fact be unnecessary in five years, and both universities thus expect to continue using race as a criterion well beyond the time limit that Grutter suggested. See Tr. of Oral Arg. in No. 20–1199, at 84–85; Tr. of Oral Arg. in No. 21–707, at 85–86. Indeed, the high school applicants that Harvard and UNC will evaluate this fall using their race-based admissions systems are expected to graduate in 2028—25 years after Grutter was decided.

Finally, respondents argue that their programs need not have an end point at all because they frequently review them to determine whether they remain necessary. See Brief for Respondent in No. 20–1199, at 52; Brief for University Respondents in No. 21–707, at 58–59. Respondents point to language in Grutter that, they contend, permits "the durational requirement [to] be met" with "periodic reviews to determine whether racial preferences are still necessary to achieve student body diversity." 539 U. S., at 342. But Grutter never suggested that periodic review could make unconstitutional conduct constitutional. To the contrary, the Court made clear that race-based admissions programs eventually had to end—despite whatever periodic review universities conducted. Ibid.; see also supra, at 18.

Here, however, Harvard concedes that its race-based admissions program has no end point. Brief for Respondent in No. 20–1199, at 52 (Harvard "has not set a sunset date" for its program (internal quotation marks omitted)). And it acknowledges that the way it thinks about the use of race in its admissions process "is the same now as it was" nearly 50 years ago. Tr. of Oral Arg. in No. 20–1199, at 91. UNC's race-based admissions program is likewise not set to expire any time soon—nor, indeed, any time at all. The University admits that it "has not set forth a proposed time period in which it believes it can end all race-conscious admissions practices." 567 F. Supp. 3d, at 612. And UNC suggests that it might soon use race to a greater extent than it currently does. See Brief for University Respondents in No. 21–707, at 57. In short, there is no reason to believe that respondents will—even acting in good faith—comply with the Equal Protection Clause any time soon.

V

The dissenting opinions resist these conclusions. They would instead uphold respondents' admissions programs based on their view that the Fourteenth Amendment permits state actors to remedy the effects of societal discrimination through explicitly race-based measures. Although both opinions are thorough and thoughtful in many respects, this Court has long rejected their core thesis.

The dissents' interpretation of the Equal Protection Clause is not new. In Bakke, four Justices would have permitted race-based admissions programs to remedy the effects of societal discrimination. 438 U. S., at 362 (joint opinion of Brennan, White, Marshall, and Blackmun, JJ., concurring in judgment in part and dissenting in part). But that minority view was just that—a minority view. Justice Powell, who provided the fifth vote and controlling opinion in Bakke, firmly rejected the notion that societal discrimination constituted a compelling interest. Such an interest presents "an amorphous concept of injury that may be ageless in its reach into the past," he explained. Id., at 307. It cannot "justify a [racial] classification that imposes disadvantages upon persons . . . who bear no responsibility for whatever harm the beneficiaries of the [race-based] admissions program are thought to have suffered." Id., at 310.

The Court soon adopted Justice Powell's analysis as its own. In the years after Bakke, the Court repeatedly held that ameliorating societal discrimination does not constitute a compelling interest that justifies race-based state action. "[A]n effort to alleviate the effects of societal discrimination is not a compelling interest," we said plainly in Hunt, a 1996 case about the Voting Rights Act. 517 U. S., at 909–910. We reached the same conclusion in Croson, a case that concerned a preferential government contracting program. Permitting "past societal discrimination" to "serve as the basis for rigid racial preferences would be to open the door to competing claims for 'remedial relief' for every disadvantaged group." 488 U. S., at 505. Opening that door would shutter another—"[t]he dream of a Nation of equal citizens . . . would be lost," we observed, "in a mosaic of shifting preferences based on inherently unmeasurable claims of past wrongs." Id., at 505–506. "[S]uch a result would be contrary to both the letter and spirit of a constitutional provision whose central command is equality." Id., at 506.

The dissents here do not acknowledge any of this. They fail to cite Hunt. They fail to cite Croson. They fail to mention that the entirety of their analysis of the Equal Protection Clause—the statistics, the cases, the history—has been considered and rejected before. There is a reason the principal dissent must invoke Justice Marshall's partial dissent in Bakke nearly a dozen times while mentioning Justice Powell's controlling opinion barely once (Justice Jackson's opinion ignores Justice Powell altogether). For what one dissent denigrates as "rhetorical flourishes about colorblindness," post, at 14 (opinion of Sotomayor, J.), are in fact the proud pronouncements of cases like Loving and Yick Wo, like Shelley and Bolling—they are defining statements of law. We understand the dissents want that law to be different. They are entitled to that desire. But they surely cannot claim the mantle of stare decisis while pursuing it.[8]

The dissents are no more faithful to our precedent on race-based admissions. To hear the principal dissent tell it, Grutter blessed such programs indefinitely, until "racial inequality will end." Post, at 54 (opinion of Sotomayor, J.). But Grutter did no such thing. It emphasized—not once or twice, but at least six separate times—that race-based admissions programs "must have reasonable durational limits" and that their "deviation from the norm of equal treatment" must be "a temporary matter." 539 U. S., at 342. The Court also disclaimed "[e]nshrining a permanent justification for racial preferences." Ibid. Yet the justification for race-based admissions that the dissent latches on to is just that—unceasing.

The principal dissent's reliance on Fisher II is similarly mistaken. There, by a 4-to-3 vote, the Court upheld a "sui generis" race-based admissions program used by the University of Texas, 579 U. S., at 377, whose "goal" it was to enroll a "critical mass" of certain minority students, Fisher I, 570 U. S., at 297. But neither Harvard nor UNC claims to be using the critical mass concept—indeed, the universities admit they do not even know what it means. See 1 App. in No. 21–707, at 402 ("[N]o one has directed anybody to achieve a critical mass, and I'm not even sure we would know what it is." (testimony of UNC administrator)); 3 App. in No. 20–1199, at 1137–1138 (similar testimony from Harvard administrator).

Fisher II also recognized the "enduring challenge" that race-based admissions systems place on "the constitutional promise of equal treatment." 579 U. S., at 388. The Court thus reaffirmed the "continuing obligation" of universities "to satisfy the burden of strict scrutiny." Id., at 379. To drive the point home, Fisher II limited itself just as Grutter had—in duration. The Court stressed that its decision did "not necessarily mean the University may rely on the same policy" going forward. 579 U. S., at 388 (emphasis added); see also Fisher I, 570 U. S., at 313 (recognizing that "Grutter . . . approved the plan at issue upon concluding that it . . . was limited in time"). And the Court openly acknowledged that its decision offered limited "prospective guidance." Fisher II, 579 U. S., at 379.[9]

The principal dissent wrenches our case law from its context, going to lengths to ignore the parts of that law it does not like. The serious reservations that Bakke, Grutter, and Fisher had about racial preferences go unrecognized. The unambiguous requirements of the Equal Protection

Clause—"the most rigid," "searching" scrutiny it entails—go without note. Fisher I, 570 U. S., at 310. And the repeated demands that race-based admissions programs must end go overlooked—contorted, worse still, into a demand that such programs never stop.

Most troubling of all is what the dissent must make these omissions to defend: a judiciary that picks winners and losers based on the color of their skin. While the dissent would certainly not permit university programs that discriminated against black and Latino applicants, it is perfectly willing to let the programs here continue. In its view, this Court is supposed to tell state actors when they have picked the right races to benefit. Separate but equal is "inherently unequal," said Brown. 347 U. S., at 495 (emphasis added). It depends, says the dissent.

That is a remarkable view of the judicial role—remarkably wrong. Lost in the false pretense of judicial humility that the dissent espouses is a claim to power so radical, so destructive, that it required a Second Founding to undo. "Justice Harlan knew better," one of the dissents decrees. Post, at 5 (opinion of Jackson, J.). Indeed he did:

"[I]n view of the Constitution, in the eye of the law, there is in this country no superior, dominant, ruling class of citizens. There is no caste here. Our Constitution is color-blind, and neither knows nor tolerates classes among citizens." Plessy, 163 U. S., at 559 (Harlan, J., dissenting).

VI

For the reasons provided above, the Harvard and UNC admissions programs cannot be reconciled with the guarantees of the Equal Protection Clause. Both programs lack sufficiently focused and measurable objectives warranting the use of race, unavoidably employ race in a negative manner, involve racial stereotyping, and lack meaningful end points. We have never permitted admissions programs to work in that way, and we will not do so today.

At the same time, as all parties agree, nothing in this opinion should be construed as prohibiting universities from considering an applicant's discussion of how race affected his or her life, be it through discrimination, inspiration, or otherwise. See, e.g., 4 App. in No. 21–707, at 1725–1726, 1741; Tr. of Oral Arg. in No. 20–1199, at 10. But, despite the dissent's assertion to the contrary, universities may not simply establish through application essays or other means the regime we hold unlawful today. (A dissenting opinion is generally not the best source of legal advice on how to comply with the majority opinion.) "[W]hat cannot be done directly cannot be done indirectly. The Constitution deals with substance, not shadows," and the prohibition against racial discrimination is "levelled at the thing, not the name." Cummings v. Missouri, 4 Wall. 277, 325 (1867). A benefit to a student who overcame racial discrimination, for example, must be tied to that student's courage and determination. Or a benefit to a student whose heritage or culture motivated him or her to assume a leadership role or attain a particular goal must be tied to that student's unique ability to contribute to the university. In other words, the student must be treated based on his or her experiences as an individual—not on the basis of race.

Many universities have for too long done just the opposite. And in doing so, they have concluded, wrongly, that the touchstone of an individual's identity is not challenges bested, skills built, or lessons learned but the color of their skin. Our constitutional history does not tolerate that choice.

The judgments of the Court of Appeals for the First Circuit and of the District Court for the Middle District of North Carolina are reversed.

It is so ordered.

Justice Jackson took no part in the consideration or decision of the case in No. 20–1199.

II.

Concurrence (Thomas)

SUPREME COURT OF THE UNITED STATES

Nos. 20–1199 and 21–707

STUDENTS FOR FAIR ADMISSIONS, INC., PETITIONER
20–1199v.
PRESIDENT AND FELLOWS OF HARVARD COLLEGE
on writ of certiorari to the united states court of appeals for the first circuit
STUDENTS FOR FAIR ADMISSIONS, INC., PETITIONER
21–707v.
UNIVERSITY OF NORTH CAROLINA, et al.
on writ of certiorari before judgment to the united states court of appeals for the fourth circuit
[June 29, 2023]
Justice Thomas, concurring.
In the wake of the Civil War, the country focused its attention on restoring the Union and establishing the legal status of newly freed slaves. The Constitution was amended to abolish slavery and proclaim that all

persons born in the United States are citizens, entitled to the privileges or immunities of citizenship and the equal protection of the laws. Amdts. 13, 14. Because of that second founding, "[o]ur Constitution is color-blind, and neither knows nor tolerates classes among citizens." Plessy v. Ferguson, 163 U.S. 537, 559 (1896) (Harlan, J., dissenting).

This Court's commitment to that equality principle has ebbed and flowed over time. After forsaking the principle for decades, offering a judicial imprimatur to segregation and ushering in the Jim Crow era, the Court finally corrected course in Brown v. Board of Education, 347 U.S. 483 (1954), announcing that primary schools must either desegregate with all deliberate speed or else close their doors. See also Brown v. Board of Education, 349 U.S. 294 (1955) (Brown II). It then pulled back in Grutter v. Bollinger, 539 U.S. 306 (2003), permitting universities to discriminate based on race in their admissions process (though only temporarily) in order to achieve alleged "educational benefits of diversity." Id., at 319. Yet, the Constitution continues to embody a simple truth: Two discriminatory wrongs cannot make a right.

I wrote separately in Grutter, explaining that the use of race in higher education admissions decisions—regardless of whether intended to help or to hurt—violates the Fourteenth Amendment. Id., at 351 (opinion concurring in part and dissenting in part). In the decades since, I have repeatedly stated that Grutter was wrongly decided and should be overruled. Fisher v. University of Tex. at Austin, 570 U.S. 297, 315, 328 (2013) (concurring opinion) (Fisher I); Fisher v. University of Tex. at Austin, 579 U.S. 365, 389 (2016) (dissenting opinion). Today, and despite a lengthy interregnum, the Constitution prevails.

Because the Court today applies genuine strict scrutiny to the race-conscious admissions policies employed at Harvard and the University of North Carolina (UNC) and finds that they fail that searching review, I join the majority opinion in full. I write separately to offer an originalist defense of the colorblind Constitution; to explain further the flaws of the Court's Grutter jurisprudence; to clarify that all forms of discrimination based on race—including so-called affirmative action—are prohibited under the Constitution; and to emphasize the pernicious effects of all such discrimination.

I

In the 1860s, Congress proposed and the States ratified the Thirteenth and Fourteenth Amendments. And, with the authority conferred by these Amendments, Congress passed two landmark Civil Rights Acts. Throughout the debates on each of these measures, their proponents repeatedly affirmed their view of equal citizenship and the racial equality that flows from it. In fact, they held this principle so deeply that their crowning accomplishment—the Fourteenth Amendment—ensures racial equality with no textual reference to race whatsoever. The history of these measures' enactment renders their motivating principle as clear as their text: All citizens of the United States, regardless of skin color, are equal before the law.

I do not contend that all of the individuals who put forth and ratified the Fourteenth Amendment universally believed this to be true. Some Members of the proposing Congress, for example, opposed the Amendment. And, the historical record—particularly with respect to the debates on ratification in the States—is sparse. Nonetheless, substantial evidence suggests that the Fourteenth Amendment was passed to "establis[h] the broad constitutional principle of full and complete equality of all persons under the law," forbidding "all legal distinctions based on race or color." Supp. Brief for United States on Reargument in Brown v. Board of Education, O. T. 1953, No. 1 etc., p. 115 (U. S. Brown Reargument Brief).

This was Justice Harlan's view in his lone dissent in Plessy, where he observed that "[o]ur Constitution is color-blind." 163 U. S., at 559. It was the view of the Court in Brown, which rejected " 'any authority . . . to use race as a factor in affording educational opportunities.' " Parents Involved in Community Schools v. Seattle School Dist. No. 1, 551 U.S. 701, 747 (2007). And, it is the view adopted in the Court's opinion today, requiring "the absolute equality of all citizens" under the law. Ante, at 10 (internal quotation marks omitted).

A

In its 1864 election platform, the Republican Party pledged to amend the Constitution to accomplish the "utter and complete extirpation" of slavery from "the soil of the Republic." 2 A. Schlesinger, History of U. S. Political Parties 1860–1910, p. 1303 (1973). After their landslide victory, Republicans quickly moved to make good on that promise. Congress proposed what would become the Thirteenth Amendment to the States in January 1865, and it was ratified as part of the Constitution later that year. The new Amendment stated that "[n]either slavery nor involuntary servitude . . . shall exist" in the United States "except as a punishment for crime whereof the party shall have been duly convicted." §1. It thus not only prohibited States from themselves enslaving persons, but also obligated them to end enslavement by private individuals within their borders. Its Framers viewed the text broadly, arguing that it "allowed Congress to legislate not merely against slavery itself, but against all the badges and relics of a slave system." A. Amar, America's Constitution: A Biography 362 (2005) (internal quotation marks omitted). The Amendment also authorized "Congress

. . . to enforce" its terms "by appropriate legislation"—authority not granted in any prior Amendment. §2. Proponents believed this enforcement clause permitted legislative measures designed to accomplish the Amendment's broader goal of equality for the freedmen.

It quickly became clear, however, that further amendment would be necessary to safeguard that goal. Soon after the Thirteenth Amendment's adoption, the reconstructed Southern States began to enact "Black Codes," which circumscribed the newly won freedoms of blacks. The Black Code of Mississippi, for example, "imposed all sorts of disabilities" on blacks, "including limiting their freedom of movement and barring them from following certain occupations, owning firearms, serving on juries, testifying in cases involving whites, or voting." E. Foner, The Second Founding 48 (2019).

Congress responded with the landmark Civil Rights Act of 1866, 14Stat. 27, in an attempt to pre-empt the Black Codes. The 1866 Act promised such a sweeping form of equality that it would lead many to say that it exceeded the scope of Congress' authority under the Thirteenth Amendment. As enacted, it stated:

"Be it enacted by the Senate and House of Representatives of the United States of America in Congress assembled, That all persons born in the United States and not subject to any foreign power, excluding Indians not taxed, are hereby declared to be citizens of the United States; and such citizens, of every race and color, without regard to any previous condition of slavery or involuntary servitude, except as a punishment for crime whereof the party shall have been duly convicted, shall have the same right, in every State and Territory in the United States, to make and enforce contracts, to sue, be parties, and give evidence, to inherit, purchase, lease, sell, hold, and convey real and personal property, and to full and equal benefit of all laws and proceedings for the security of person and property, as is enjoyed by white citizens, and shall be subject to like punishment, pains, and penalties, and to none other, any law, statute, ordinance, regulation, or custom, to the contrary notwithstanding."

The text of the provision left no doubt as to its aim: All persons born in the United States were equal citizens entitled to the same rights and subject to the same penalties as white citizens in the categories enumerated. See M. McConnell, Originalism and the Desegregation Decisions, 81 Va. L. Rev. 947, 958 (1995) ("Note that the bill neither forbade racial discrimination generally nor did it guarantee particular rights to all persons. Rather, it required an equality in certain specific rights"). And, while the 1866 Act used the rights of "white citizens" as a benchmark, its rule was decidedly colorblind, safeguarding legal equality for all citizens "of every race and color" and providing the same rights to all.

The 1866 Act's evolution further highlights its rule of equality. To start, Dred Scott v. Sandford, 19 How. 393 (1857), had previously held that blacks "were not regarded as a portion of the people or citizens of the Government" and "had no rights which the white man was bound to respect." Id., at 407, 411. The Act, however, would effectively overrule Dred Scott and ensure the equality that had been promised to blacks. But the Act went further still. On January 29, 1866, Senator Lyman Trumbull, the bill's principal sponsor in the Senate, proposed text stating that "all persons of African descent born in the United States are hereby declared to be citizens." Cong. Globe, 39th Cong., 1st Sess., 474. The following day, Trumbull revised his proposal, removing the reference to "African descent" and declaring more broadly that "all persons born in the United States, and not subject to any foreign Power," are "citizens of the United States." Id., at 498.

"In the years before the Fourteenth Amendment's adoption, jurists and legislators often connected citizenship with equality," where "the absence or presence of one entailed the absence or presence of the other." United States v. Vaello Madero, 596 U. S. ___, ___ (2022) (Thomas, J., concurring) (slip op., at 6). The addition of a citizenship guarantee thus evidenced an intent to broaden the provision, extending beyond recently freed blacks and incorporating a more general view of equality for all Americans. Indeed, the drafters later included a specific carveout for "Indians not taxed," demonstrating the breadth of the bill's otherwise general citizenship language. 14Stat. 27.[1] As Trumbull explained, the provision created a bond between all Americans; "any statute which is not equal to all, and which deprives any citizen of civil rights which are secured to other citizens," was "an unjust encroachment upon his liberty" and a "badge of servitude" prohibited by the Constitution. Cong. Globe, 39th Cong., 1st Sess., at 474 (emphasis added).

Trumbull and most of the Act's other supporters identified the Thirteenth Amendment as a principal source of constitutional authority for the Act's nondiscrimination provisions. See, e.g., id., at 475 (statement of Sen. Trumbull); id., at 1152 (statement of Rep. Thayer); id., at 503–504 (statement of Sen. Howard). In particular, they explained that the Thirteenth Amendment allowed Congress not merely to legislate against slavery itself, but also to counter measures "which depriv[e] any citizen of civil rights which are secured to other citizens." Id., at 474.

But opponents argued that Congress' authority did not sweep so broadly. President Andrew Johnson, for example, contended that Congress lacked authority to pass the measure, seizing on the breadth of the citizenship text and emphasizing state authority over matters of state citizenship. See S. Doc. No. 31, 39th Cong., 1st Sess., 1, 6 (1866) (Johnson veto message). Consequently, "doubts about the constitutional authority conferred by that measure led supporters to supplement their Thirteenth Amendment arguments with other sources of constitutional authority."

R. Williams, Originalism and the Other Desegregation Decision, 99 Va. L. Rev. 493, 532–533 (2013) (describing appeals to the naturalization power and the inherent power to protect the rights of citizens). As debates continued, it became increasingly apparent that safeguarding the 1866 Act, including its promise of black citizenship and the equal rights that citizenship entailed, would require further submission to the people of the United States in the form of a proposed constitutional amendment. See, e.g., Cong. Globe, 39th Cong., 1st Sess., at 498 (statement of Sen. Van Winkle).

B

Critically, many of those who believed that Congress lacked the authority to enact the 1866 Act also supported the principle of racial equality. So, almost immediately following the ratification of the Thirteenth Amendment, several proposals for further amendments were submitted in Congress. One such proposal, approved by the Joint Committee on Reconstruction and then submitted to the House of Representatives on February 26, 1866, would have declared that "[t]he Congress shall have power to make all laws which shall be necessary and proper to secure to the citizens of each State all privileges and immunities of citizens in the several States, and to all persons in the several States equal protection in the rights of life, liberty, and property." Id., at 1033–1034. Representative John Bingham, its drafter, was among those who believed Congress lacked the power to enact the 1866 Act. See id., at 1291. Specifically, he believed the "very letter of the Constitution" already required equality, but the enforcement of that requirement "is of the reserved powers of the States." Cong. Globe, 39th Cong., 1st Sess., at 1034, 1291 (statement of Rep. Bingham). His proposed constitutional amendment accordingly would provide a clear constitutional basis for the 1866 Act and ensure that future Congresses would be unable to repeal it. See W. Nelson, The Fourteenth Amendment 48–49 (1988).

Discussion of Bingham's initial draft was later postponed in the House, but the Joint Committee on Reconstruction continued its work. See 2 K. Lash, The Reconstruction Amendments 8 (2021). In April, Representative Thaddeus Stevens proposed to the Joint Committee an amendment that began, "[n]o discrimination shall be made by any State nor by the United States as to the civil rights of persons because of race, color, or previous condition of servitude." S. Doc. No. 711, 63d Cong., 1st Sess., 31–32 (1915) (reprinting the Journal of the Joint Committee on Reconstruction for the Thirty-Ninth Congress). Stevens' proposal was later revised to read as follows: " 'No State shall make or enforce any law which shall abridge the privileges or immunities of citizens of the United States; nor shall any State deprive any person of life, liberty, or property without due process of law, nor deny to any person within its jurisdiction the equal protection of the laws.' " Id., at 39. This revised text was submitted to the full House on April 30, 1866. Cong. Globe, 39th Cong., 1st Sess., at 2286–2287. Like the eventual first section of the Fourteenth Amendment, this proposal embodied the familiar Privileges or Immunities, Due Process, and Equal Protection Clauses. And, importantly, it also featured an enforcement clause—with text borrowed from the Thirteenth Amendment—conferring upon Congress the power to enforce its provisions. Ibid.

Stevens explained that the draft was intended to "allo[w] Congress to correct the unjust legislation of the States, so far that the law which operates upon one man shall operate equally upon all." Id., at 2459. Moreover, Stevens' later statements indicate that he did not believe there was a difference "in substance between the new proposal and" earlier measures calling for impartial and equal treatment without regard to race. U. S. Brown Reargument Brief 44 (noting a distinction only with respect to a suffrage provision). And, Bingham argued that the need for the proposed text was "one of the lessons that have been taught . . . by the history of the past four years of terrific conflict" during the Civil War. Cong. Globe, 39th Cong., 1st Sess., at 2542. The proposal passed the House by a vote of 128 to 37. Id., at 2545.

Senator Jacob Howard introduced the proposed Amendment in the Senate, powerfully asking, "Ought not the time to be now passed when one measure of justice is to be meted out to a member of one caste while another and a different measure is meted out to the member of another caste, both castes being alike citizens of the United States, both bound to obey the same laws, to sustain the burdens of the same Government, and both equally responsible to justice and to God for the deeds done in the body?" Id., at 2766. In keeping with this view, he proposed an introductory sentence, declaring that " 'all persons born in the United States, and subject to the jurisdiction thereof, are citizens of the United States and of the States wherein they reside.' " Id., at 2869. This text, the Citizenship Clause, was the final missing element of what would ultimately become §1 of the Fourteenth Amendment. Howard's draft for the proposed citizenship text was modeled on the Civil Rights Act of 1866's text, and he suggested the alternative language to "remov[e] all doubt as to what persons are or are not citizens of the United States," a question which had "long been a great desideratum in the jurisprudence and legislation of this country." Id., at 2890. He further characterized the addition as "simply declaratory of what I regard as the law of the land already." Ibid.

The proposal was approved in the Senate by a vote of 33 to 11. Id., at 3042. The House then reconciled differences between the two measures, approving the Senate's changes by a vote of 120 to 32. See id., at 3149. And, in June 1866, the amendment was submitted to the States for their consideration and ratification. Two years later, it was ratified by the requisite number of States and became the Fourteenth Amendment to the United States Constitution. See 15Stat. 706–707; id., at 709–711. Its opening words instilled in our Nation's Constitution a new birth of freedom:

"All persons born or naturalized in the United States, and subject to the jurisdiction thereof, are citizens of the United States and of the State wherein they reside. No State shall make or enforce any law which shall abridge the privileges or immunities of citizens of the United States; nor shall any State deprive any person of life, liberty, or property, without due process of law; nor deny to any person within its jurisdiction the equal protection of the laws." §1.

As enacted, the text of the Fourteenth Amendment provides a firm statement of equality before the law. It begins by guaranteeing citizenship status, invoking the "longstanding political and legal tradition that closely associated the status of citizenship with the entitlement to legal equality." Vaello Madero, 596 U. S., at ___ (Thomas, J., concurring) (slip op., at 6) (internal quotation marks omitted). It then confirms that States may not "abridge the rights of national citizenship, including whatever civil equality is guaranteed to 'citizens' under the Citizenship Clause." Id., at ___, n. 3 (slip op., at 13, n. 3). Finally, it pledges that even noncitizens must be treated equally "as individuals, and not as members of racial, ethnic, or religious groups." Missouri v. Jenkins, 515 U.S. 70, 120–121 (1995) (Thomas, J., concurring).

The drafters and ratifiers of the Fourteenth Amendment focused on this broad equality idea, offering surprisingly little explanation of which term was intended to accomplish which part of the Amendment's overall goal. "The available materials . . . show," however, "that there were widespread expressions of a general understanding of the broad scope of the Amendment similar to that abundantly demonstrated in the Congressional debates, namely, that the first section of the Amendment would establish the full constitutional right of all persons to equality before the law and would prohibit legal distinctions based on race or color." U. S. Brown Reargument Brief 65 (citation omitted). For example, the Pennsylvania debate suggests that the Fourteenth Amendment was understood to make the law "what justice is represented to be, blind" to the "color of [one's] skin." App. to Pa. Leg. Record XLVIII (1867) (Rep. Mann).

The most commonly held view today—consistent with the rationale repeatedly invoked during the congressional debates, see, e.g., Cong. Globe, 39th Cong., 1st Sess., at 2458–2469—is that the Amendment was designed to remove any doubts regarding Congress' authority to enact the Civil Rights Act of 1866 and to establish a nondiscrimination rule that could not be repealed by future Congresses. See, e.g., J. Harrison, Reconstructing the Privileges or Immunities Clause, 101 Yale L. J. 1385, 1388

(1992) (noting that the "primary purpose" of the Fourteenth Amendment "was to mandate certain rules of racial equality, especially those contained in Section 1 of the Civil Rights Act of 1866").[2] The Amendment's phrasing supports this view, and there does not appear to have been any argument to the contrary predating Brown.

Consistent with the Civil Rights Act of 1866's aim, the Amendment definitively overruled Chief Justice Taney's opinion in Dred Scott that blacks "were not regarded as a portion of the people or citizens of the Government" and "had no rights which the white man was bound to respect." 19 How., at 407, 411. And, like the 1866 Act, the Amendment also clarified that American citizenship conferred rights not just against the Federal Government but also the government of the citizen's State of residence. Unlike the Civil Rights Act, however, the Amendment employed a wholly race-neutral text, extending privileges or immunities to all "citizens"— even if its practical effect was to provide all citizens with the same privileges then enjoyed by whites. That citizenship guarantee was often linked with the concept of equality. Vaello Madero, 596 U. S., at ___ (Thomas, J., concurring) (slip op., at 10). Combining the citizenship guarantee with the Privileges or Immunities Clause and the Equal Protection Clause, the Fourteenth Amendment ensures protection for all equal citizens of the Nation without regard to race. Put succinctly, "[o]ur Constitution is colorblind." Plessy, 163 U. S., at 559 (Harlan, J., dissenting).

C

In the period closely following the Fourteenth Amendment's ratification, Congress passed several statutes designed to enforce its terms, eliminating government-based Black Codes—systems of government-imposed segregation—and criminalizing racially motivated violence. The marquee legislation was the Civil Rights Act of 1875, ch. 114, 18Stat. 335–337, and the justifications offered by proponents of that measure are further evidence for the colorblind view of the Fourteenth Amendment.

The Civil Rights Act of 1875 sought to counteract the systems of racial segregation that had arisen in the wake of the Reconstruction era. Advocates of so-called separate-but-equal systems, which allowed segregated facilities for blacks and whites, had argued that laws permitting or requiring such segregation treated members of both races precisely alike: Blacks could not attend a white school, but symmetrically, whites could not attend a black school. See Plessy, 163 U. S., at 544 (arguing that, in light of the social circumstances at the time, racial segregation did not "necessarily imply the inferiority of either race to the other"). Congress was not persuaded. Supporters of the soon-to-be 1875 Act successfully countered that symmetrical restrictions did not constitute equality, and they did so on colorblind terms.

For example, they asserted that "free government demands the abolition of all distinctions founded on color and race." 2 Cong. Rec. 4083 (1874). And, they submitted that "[t]he time has come when all distinctions that grew out of slavery ought to disappear." Cong. Globe, 42d Cong., 2d Sess., 3193 (1872) ("[A]s long as you have distinctions and discriminations between white and black in the enjoyment of legal rights and privileges[,] you will have discontent and parties divided between black and white"). Leading Republican Senator Charles Sumner compellingly argued that "any rule excluding a man on account of his color is an indignity, an insult, and a wrong." Id., at 242; see also ibid. ("I insist that by the law of the land all persons without distinction of color shall be equal before the law"). Far from conceding that segregation would be perceived as inoffensive if race roles were reversed, he declared that "[t]his is plain oppression, which you . . . would feel keenly were it directed against you or your child." Id., at 384. He went on to paraphrase the English common-law rule to which he subscribed: "[The law] makes no discrimination on account of color." Id., at 385.

Others echoed this view. Representative John Lynch declared that "[t]he duty of the law-maker is to know no race, no color, no religion, no nationality, except to prevent distinctions on any of these grounds, so far as the law is concerned." 3 Cong. Rec. 945 (1875). Senator John Sherman believed that the route to peace was to "[w]ipe out all legal discriminations between white and black [and] make no distinction between black and white." Cong. Globe, 42d Cong., 2d Sess., at 3193. And, Senator Henry Wilson sought to "make illegal all distinctions on account of color" because "there should be no distinction recognized by the laws of the land." Id., at 819; see also 3 Cong. Rec., at 956 (statement of Rep. Cain) ("[M]en [are] formed of God equally . . . . The civil-rights bill simply declares this: that there shall be no discriminations between citizens of this land so far as the laws of the land are concerned"). The view of the Legislature was clear: The Constitution "neither knows nor tolerates classes among citizens." Plessy, 163 U. S., at 559 (Harlan, J., dissenting).

D

The earliest Supreme Court opinions to interpret the Fourteenth Amendment did so in colorblind terms. Their statements characterizing the Amendment evidence its commitment to equal rights for all citizens, regardless of the color of their skin. See ante, at 10–11.

In the Slaughter-House Cases, 16 Wall. 36 (1873), the Court identified the "pervading purpose" of the Reconstruction Amendments as "the freedom of the slave race, the security and firm establishment of that freedom, and the protection of the newly-made freeman and citizen from the oppressions of those who had formerly exercised unlimited dominion over him." Id., at 67–72. Yet, the Court quickly acknowledged that the language of the Amendments did not suggest "that no one else but the negro can share in this protection." Id., at 72. Rather, "[i]f Mexican peonage or the Chinese coolie labor system shall develop slavery of the Mexican or Chinese race within our territory, [the Thirteenth Amendment] may safely be trusted to make it void." Ibid. And, similarly, "if other rights are assailed by the States which properly and necessarily fall within the protection of these articles, that protection will apply, though the party interested may not be of African descent." Ibid.

The Court thus made clear that the Fourteenth Amendment's equality guarantee applied to members of all races, including Asian Americans, ensuring all citizens equal treatment under law.

Seven years later, the Court relied on the Slaughter-House view to conclude that "[t]he words of the [Fourteenth A]mendment . . . contain a necessary implication of a positive immunity, or right, most valuable to the colored race,—the right to exemption from unfriendly legislation against them distinctively as colored." Strauder v. West Virginia, 100 U.S. 303, 307–308 (1880). The Court thus found that the Fourteenth Amendment banned "expres[s]" racial classifications, no matter the race affected, because these classifications are "a stimulant to . . . race prejudice." Id., at 308. See also ante, at 10–11. Similar statements appeared in other cases decided around that time. See Virginia v. Rives, 100 U.S. 313, 318 (1880) ("The plain object of these statutes [enacted to enforce the Fourteenth Amendment], as of the Constitution which authorized them, was to place the colored race, in respect of civil rights, upon a level with whites. They made the rights and responsibilities, civil and criminal, of the two races exactly the same"); Ex parte Virginia, 100 U.S. 339, 344–345 (1880) ("One great purpose of [the Thirteenth and Fourteenth Amendments] was to raise the colored race from that condition of inferiority and servitude in which most of them had previously stood, into perfect equality of civil rights with all other persons within the jurisdiction of the States").

This Court's view of the Fourteenth Amendment reached its nadir in Plessy, infamously concluding that the Fourteenth Amendment "could not have been intended to abolish distinctions based upon color, or to enforce social, as distinguished from political equality, or a commingling of the two races upon terms unsatisfactory to either." 163 U. S., at 544. That holding stood in sharp contrast to the Court's earlier embrace of the Fourteenth Amendment's equality ideal, as Justice Harlan emphasized in dissent: The Reconstruction Amendments had aimed to remove "the race line from our systems of governments." Id., at 563. For Justice Harlan, the Constitution was colorblind and categorically rejected laws designed to protect "a dominant race—a superior class of citizens," while imposing a "badge of servitude" on others. Id., at 560–562.

History has vindicated Justice Harlan's view, and this Court recently acknowledged that Plessy should have been overruled immediately because it "betrayed our commitment to 'equality before the law.' " Dobbs v. Jackson Women's Health Organization, 597 U. S. ___, ___ (2022) (slip op., at 44). Nonetheless, and despite Justice Harlan's efforts, the era of state-sanctioned segregation persisted for more than a half century.

E

Despite the extensive evidence favoring the colorblind view, as detailed above, it appears increasingly in vogue to embrace an "antisubordination" view of the Fourteenth Amendment: that the Amendment forbids only laws that hurt, but not help, blacks. Such a theory lacks any basis in the original meaning of the Fourteenth Amendment. Respondents cite a smattering of federal and state statutes passed during the years surrounding the ratification of the Fourteenth Amendment. And, Justice Sotomayor's dissent argues that several of these statutes evidence the ratifiers' understanding that the Equal Protection Clause "permits consideration of race to achieve its goal." Post, at 6. Upon examination, however, it is clear that these statutes are fully consistent with the colorblind view.

Start with the 1865 Freedmen's Bureau Act. That Act established the Freedmen's Bureau to issue "provisions, clothing, and fuel . . . needful for the immediate and temporary shelter and supply of destitute and suffering refugees and freedmen and their wives and children" and the setting "apart, for the use of loyal refugees and freedmen," abandoned, confiscated, or purchased lands, and assigning "to every male citizen, whether refugee or freedman, . . . not more than forty acres of such land." Ch. 90, §§2, 4, 13Stat. 507. The 1866 Freedmen's Bureau Act then expanded upon the prior year's law, authorizing the Bureau to care for all loyal refugees and freedmen. Ch. 200, 14Stat. 173–174. Importantly, however, the Acts applied to freedmen (and refugees), a formally race-neutral category, not blacks writ large. And, because "not all blacks in the United States were former slaves," " 'freedman' " was a decidedly under-inclusive proxy for race. M. Rappaport, Originalism and the Colorblind Constitution, 89 Notre Dame L. Rev. 71, 98 (2013) (Rappaport). Moreover, the Freedmen's Bureau served newly freed slaves alongside white refugees. P. Moreno, Racial Classifications and Reconstruction Legislation, 61 J. So. Hist. 271, 276–277 (1995); R. Barnett & E. Bernick, The Original Meaning of the Fourteenth Amendment 119 (2021). And, advocates of the law explicitly disclaimed any view rooted in modern conceptions of antisubordination. To the contrary, they explicitly clarified that the equality sought by the law was not one in which all men shall be "six feet high"; rather, it strove to ensure that freedmen enjoy "equal rights before the law" such that "each man shall have the right to pursue in his own way life, liberty, and happiness." Cong. Globe, 39th Cong., 1st Sess., at 322, 342.

Several additional federal laws cited by respondents appear to classify based on race, rather than previous condition of servitude. For example, an 1866 law adopted special rules and procedures for the payment of "colored" servicemen in the Union Army to agents who helped them secure bounties, pensions, and other payments that they were due. 14Stat. 367–368. At the time, however, Congress believed that many "black servicemen were significantly overpaying for these agents' services in part because [the servicemen] did not understand how the payment system operated." Rappaport 110; see also S. Siegel, The Federal Government's Power To Enact Color-Conscious Laws: An Originalist Inquiry, 92 Nw. U. L. Rev. 477, 561 (1998). Thus, while this legislation appears to have provided a discrete race-based benefit, its aim—to prohibit race-based exploitation—may not have been possible at the time without using a racial screen. In other words, the statute's racial classifications may well have survived strict scrutiny. See Rappaport 111–112. Another law, passed in 1867, provided funds for "freedmen or destitute colored people" in the District of Columbia. Res. of Mar. 16, 1867, No. 4, 15Stat. 20. However, when a prior version of this law targeting only blacks was criticized for being racially discriminatory, "it was defended on the grounds that there were various places in the city where former slaves . . . lived in densely populated shantytowns." Rappaport 104–105 (citing Cong. Globe, 39th Cong., 1st Sess., at 1507). Congress thus may have enacted the measure not because of race, but rather to address a special problem in shantytowns in the District where blacks lived.

These laws—even if targeting race as such—likely were also constitutionally permissible examples of Government action "undo[ing] the effects of past discrimination in [a way] that do[es] not involve classification by race," even though they had "a racially disproportionate impact." Richmond v. J. A. Croson Co., 488 U.S. 469, 526 (1989) (Scalia, J., concurring in judgment) (internal quotation marks omitted). The government can plainly remedy a race-based injury that it has inflicted—though such remedies must be meant to further a colorblind government, not perpetuate racial consciousness. See id., at 505 (majority opinion). In that way, "[r]ace-based government measures during the 1860's and 1870's to remedy state-enforced slavery were . . . not inconsistent with the colorblind Constitution." Parents Involved, 551 U. S., at 772, n. 19 (Thomas, J., concurring). Moreover, the very same Congress passed both these laws and the unambiguously worded Civil Rights Act of 1866 that clearly prohibited discrimination on the basis of race.[3] And, as noted above, the proponents of these laws explicitly sought equal rights without regard to race while disavowing any antisubordination view.

Justice Sotomayor argues otherwise, pointing to "a number of race-conscious" federal laws passed around the time of the Fourteenth Amendment's enactment. Post, at 6 (dissenting opinion). She identifies the Freedmen's Bureau Act of 1865, already discussed above, as one such law, but she admits that the programs did not benefit blacks exclusively. She also does not dispute that legislation targeting the needs of newly freed blacks in 1865 could be understood as directly remedial. Even today, nothing prevents the States from according an admissions preference to identified victims of discrimination. See Croson, 488 U. S., at 526 (opinion of Scalia, J.) ("While most of the beneficiaries might be black, neither the beneficiaries nor those disadvantaged by the preference would be identified on the basis of their race" (emphasis in original)); see also ante, at 39.

Justice Sotomayor points also to the Civil Rights Act of 1866, which as discussed above, mandated that all citizens have the same rights as those "enjoyed by white citizens." 14Stat. 27. But these references to the station of white citizens do not refute the view that the Fourteenth Amendment is colorblind. Rather, they specify that, in meeting the Amendment's goal of equal citizenship, States must level up. The Act did not single out a group of citizens for special treatment—rather, all citizens were meant to be treated the same as those who, at the time, had the full rights of citizenship. Other provisions of the 1866 Act reinforce this view, providing for equality in civil rights. See Rappaport 97. Most notably, §14 stated that the basic civil rights of citizenship shall be secured "without respect to race or color." 14Stat. 176–177. And, §8 required that funds from land sales must be used to support schools "without distinction of color or race, . . . in the parishes of " the area where the land had been sold. Id., at 175.

In addition to these federal laws, Harvard also points to two state laws: a South Carolina statute that placed the burden of proof on the defendant when a "colored or black" plaintiff claimed a violation, 1870 S. C. Acts pp. 387–388, and Kentucky legislation that authorized a county superintendent to aid "negro paupers" in Mercer County, 1871 Ky. Acts pp. 273–274. Even if these statutes provided race-based benefits, they do not support respondents' and Justice Sotomayor's view that the Fourteenth Amendment was contemporaneously understood to permit differential treatment based on race, prohibiting only caste legislation while authorizing antisubordination measures. Cf., e.g., O. Fiss, Groups and the Equal Protection Clause, 5 Philos. & Pub. Aff. 107, 147 (1976) (articulating the antisubordination view); R. Siegel, Equality Talk: Antisubordination and Anticlassification Values in Constitutional Struggles Over Brown, 117 Harv. L. Rev. 1470, 1473, n. 8 (2004) (collecting scholarship). At most, these laws would support the kinds of discrete remedial measures that our precedents have permitted.

If services had been given only to white persons up to the Fourteenth Amendment's adoption, then providing those same services only to previously excluded black persons would work to equalize treatment against a concrete baseline of government-imposed inequality. It thus may have been the case that Kentucky's county-specific, race-based public aid law was necessary because that particular county was not providing certain services to local poor blacks. Similarly, South Carolina's burden-shifting framework (where the substantive rule being applied remained notably race neutral) may have been necessary to streamline litigation around the most commonly litigated type of case: a lawsuit seeking to remedy discrimination against a member of the large population of recently freed black Americans. See 1870 S. C. Acts, at 386 (documenting "persist[ent]" racial discrimination by state-licensed entities).

Most importantly, however, there was a wide range of federal and state statutes enacted at the time of the Fourteenth Amendment's adoption and during the period thereafter that explicitly sought to discriminate against blacks on the basis of race or a proxy for race. See Rappaport 113–115. These laws, hallmarks of the race-conscious Jim Crow era, are precisely the sort of enactments that the Framers of the Fourteenth Amendment sought to eradicate. Yet, proponents of an antisubordination view necessarily do not take those laws as evidence of the Fourteenth Amendment's true meaning. And rightly so. Neither those laws, nor a small number of laws that appear to target blacks for preferred treatment, displace the equality vision reflected in the history of the Fourteenth Amendment's enactment. This is particularly true in light of the clear equality requirements present in the Fourteenth Amendment's text. See New York State Rifle & Pistol Assn., Inc. v. Bruen, 597 U. S. ___, ___–___ (2022) (slip op., at 26–27) (noting that text controls over inconsistent post-ratification history).

II

Properly understood, our precedents have largely adhered to the Fourteenth Amendment's demand for colorblind laws.[4] That is why, for example, courts "must subject all racial classifications to the strictest of scrutiny." Jenkins, 515 U. S., at 121 (Thomas, J., concurring); see also ante, at 15, n. 4 (emphasizing the consequences of an insufficiently searching inquiry). And, in case after case, we have employed strict scrutiny vigorously to reject various forms of racial discrimination as unconstitutional. See Fisher I, 570 U. S., at 317–318 (Thomas, J., concurring). The Court today rightly upholds that tradition and acknowledges the consequences that have flowed from Grutter's contrary approach.

Three aspects of today's decision warrant comment: First, to satisfy strict scrutiny, universities must be able to establish an actual link between racial discrimination and educational benefits. Second, those engaged in racial discrimination do not deserve deference with respect to their reasons for discriminating. Third, attempts to remedy past governmental discrimination must be closely tailored to address that particular past governmental discrimination.

A

To satisfy strict scrutiny, universities must be able to establish a compelling reason to racially discriminate. Grutter recognized "only one" interest sufficiently compelling to justify race-conscious admissions programs: the "educational benefits of a diverse student body." 539 U. S., at 328, 333. Expanding on this theme, Harvard and UNC have offered a grab bag of interests to justify their programs, spanning from " 'training future leaders in the public and private sectors' " to " 'enhancing appreciation, respect, and empathy,' " with references to " 'better educating [their] students through diversity' " in between. Ante, at 22–23. The Court today finds that each of these interests are too vague and immeasurable to suffice, ibid., and I agree.

Even in Grutter, the Court failed to clearly define "the educational benefits of a diverse student body." 539 U. S., at 333. Thus, in the years since Grutter, I have sought to understand exactly how racial diversity yields educational benefits. With nearly 50 years to develop their arguments, neither Harvard nor UNC—two of the foremost research institutions in the world—nor any of their amici can explain that critical link.

Harvard, for example, offers a report finding that meaningful representation of racial minorities promotes several goals. Only one of those goals—"producing new knowledge stemming from diverse outlooks," 980 F.3d 157, 174 (CA1 2020)—bears any possible relationship to educational benefits. Yet, it too is extremely vague and offers no indication that, for example, student test scores increased as a result of Harvard's efforts toward racial diversity.

More fundamentally, it is not clear how racial diversity, as opposed to other forms of diversity, uniquely and independently advances Harvard's goal. This is particularly true because Harvard blinds itself to other forms of applicant diversity, such as religion. See 2 App. in No. 20–1199, pp. 734–743. It may be the case that exposure to different perspectives and thoughts can foster debate, sharpen young minds, and hone students' reasoning skills. But, it is not clear how diversity with respect to race, qua race, furthers this goal. Two white students, one from rural Appalachia and one from a wealthy San Francisco suburb, may well have more diverse outlooks on this metric than two students from Manhattan's Upper East Side attending its most elite schools, one of whom is white and other of whom is black. If Harvard cannot even explain the link between racial diversity and education, then surely its interest in racial diversity cannot be compelling enough to overcome the constitutional limits on race consciousness.

UNC fares no better. It asserts, for example, an interest in training students to "live together in a diverse society." Brief for University Respondents in No. 21–707, p. 39. This may well be important to a university experience, but it is a social goal, not an educational one. See Grutter, 539 U. S., at 347–348 (Scalia, J., concurring in part and dissenting in part) (criticizing similar rationales as divorced from educational goals). And, again, UNC offers no reason why seeking a diverse society would not be equally supported by admitting individuals with diverse perspectives and backgrounds, rather than varying skin pigmentation.

Nor have amici pointed to any concrete and quantifiable educational benefits of racial diversity. The United States focuses on alleged civic benefits, including "increasing tolerance and decreasing racial prejudice." Brief for United States as Amicus Curiae 21–22. Yet, when it comes to educational benefits, the Government offers only one study purportedly showing that "college diversity experiences are significantly and positively related to cognitive development" and that "interpersonal interactions with racial diversity are the most strongly related to cognitive development." N. Bowman, College Diversity Experiences and Cognitive Development: A Meta-Analysis, 80 Rev. Educ. Research 4, 20 (2010). Here again, the link is, at best, tenuous, unspecific, and stereotypical. Other amici assert that diversity (generally) fosters the even-more nebulous values of "creativity" and "innovation," particularly in graduates' future workplaces. See, e.g., Brief for Major American Business Enterprises as Amici Curiae 7–9; Brief for Massachusetts Institute of Technology et al. as Amici Curiae 16–17 (describing experience at IBM). Yet, none of those assertions deals exclusively with racial diversity—as opposed to cultural or ideological diversity. And, none of those amici demonstrate measurable or concrete benefits that have resulted from universities' race-conscious admissions programs.

Of course, even if these universities had shown that racial diversity yielded any concrete or measurable benefits, they would still face a very high bar to show that their interest is compelling. To survive strict scrutiny, any such benefits would have to outweigh the tremendous harm inflicted by sorting individuals on the basis of race. See Cooper v. Aaron, 358 U.S. 1, 16 (1958) (following Brown, "law and order are not here to be preserved by depriving the Negro children of their constitutional rights"). As the Court's opinions in these cases make clear, all racial stereotypes harm and demean individuals. That is why "only those measures the State must take to provide a bulwark against anarchy, or to prevent violence, will constitute a pressing public necessity" sufficient to satisfy strict scrutiny today. Grutter, 539 U. S., at 353 (opinion of Thomas, J.) (internal quotations marks omitted). Cf. Lee v. Washington, 390 U.S. 333, 334 (1968) (Black, J., concurring) (protecting prisoners from violence might justify narrowly tailored discrimination); Croson, 488 U. S., at 521 (opinion of Scalia, J.) ("At least where state or local action is at issue, only a social emergency rising to the level of imminent danger to life and limb . . . can justify [racial discrimination]"). For this reason, "just as the alleged educational benefits of segregation were insufficient to justify racial discrimination [in the 1950s], see Brown v. Board of Education, the alleged educational benefits of diversity cannot justify racial discrimination today." Fisher I, 570 U. S., at 320 (Thomas, J., concurring) (citation omitted).

B

The Court also correctly refuses to defer to the universities' own assessments that the alleged benefits of race- conscious admissions programs are compelling. It instead demands that the "interests [universities] view as compelling" must be capable of being "subjected to meaningful judicial review." Ante, at 22. In other words, a court must be able to measure the goals asserted and determine when they have been reached. Ante, at 22–24. The Court's opinion today further insists that universities must be able to "articulate a meaningful connection between the means they employ and the goals they pursue." Ante, at 24. Again, I agree. Universities' self-proclaimed righteousness does not afford them license to discriminate on the basis of race.

In fact, it is error for a court to defer to the views of an alleged discriminator while assessing claims of racial discrimination. See Grutter, 539 U. S., at 362–364 (opinion of Thomas, J.); see also Fisher I, 570 U. S., at 318–319 (Thomas, J., concurring); United States v. Virginia, 518 U.S. 515, 551, n. 19 (1996) (refusing to defer to the Virginia Military Institute's judgment that the changes necessary to accommodate the admission of women would be too great and characterizing the necessary changes as "manageable"). We would not offer such deference in any other context. In employment discrimination lawsuits under Title VII of the Civil Rights Act, for example, courts require only a minimal prima facie showing by a complainant before shifting the burden onto the shoulders of the alleged-discriminator employer. See McDonnell Douglas Corp. v. Green, 411 U.S. 792, 803–805 (1973). And, Congress has passed numerous laws—such as the Civil Rights Act of 1875—under its authority to enforce the Fourteenth Amendment, each designed to counter discrimination and each relying on courts to bring a skeptical eye to alleged discriminators.

This judicial skepticism is vital. History has repeatedly shown that purportedly benign discrimination may be pernicious, and discriminators may go to great lengths to hide and perpetuate their unlawful conduct. Take, for example, the university respondents here. Harvard's "holistic" admissions policy began in the 1920s when it was developed to exclude Jews. See M. Synnott, The Half-Opened Door: Discrimination and Admission at Harvard, Yale, and Princeton, 1900–1970, pp. 58–59, 61, 69, 73–74 (2010). Based on de facto quotas that Harvard quietly implemented, the proportion of Jews in Harvard's freshman class declined from 28% as late as 1925 to just 12% by 1933. J. Karabel, The Chosen: The Hidden History of Admission and Exclusion at Harvard, Yale, and Princeton 172 (2005). During this same period, Harvard played a prominent role in the eugenics movement. According to then-President Abbott Lawrence Lowell, excluding Jews from Harvard would help maintain admissions opportunities for Gentiles and perpetuate the purity of the Brahmin race—New England's white, Protestant upper crust. See D. Okrent, The Guarded Gate 309, and n. * (2019).

UNC also has a checkered history, dating back to its time as a segregated university. It admitted its first black undergraduate students in 1955—but only after being ordered to do so by a court, following a long legal battle in which UNC sought to keep its segregated status. Even then, UNC did not turn on a dime: The first three black students admitted as undergraduates enrolled at UNC but ultimately earned their bachelor's degrees elsewhere. See M. Beauregard, Column: The Desegregation of UNC, The Daily Tar Heel, Feb. 16, 2022. To the extent past is prologue, the university respondents' histories hardly recommend them as trustworthy arbiters of whether racial discrimination is necessary to achieve educational goals.

Of course, none of this should matter in any event; courts have an independent duty to interpret and uphold the Constitution that no university's claimed interest may override. See ante, at 26, n. 5. The Court today makes clear that, in the future, universities wishing to discriminate based on race in admissions must articulate and justify a compelling and measurable state interest based on concrete evidence. Given the strictures set out by the Court, I highly doubt any will be able to do so.

C

In an effort to salvage their patently unconstitutional programs, the universities and their amici pivot to argue that the Fourteenth Amendment permits the use of race to benefit only certain racial groups—rather than applicants writ large. Yet, this is just the latest disguise for discrimination. The sudden narrative shift is not surprising, as it has long been apparent that " 'diversity [was] merely the current rationale of convenience' " to support racially discriminatory admissions programs. Grutter, 539 U. S., at 393 (Kennedy, J., dissenting). Under our precedents, this new rationale is also lacking.

To start, the case for affirmative action has emphasized a number of rationales over the years, including: (1) restitution to compensate those who have been victimized by past discrimination, (2) fostering "diversity," (3) facilitating "integration" and the destruction of perceived racial castes, and (4) countering longstanding and diffuse racial prejudice. See R. Kennedy, For Discrimination: Race, Affirmative Action, and the Law 78 (2013); see also P. Schuck, Affirmative Action: Past, Present, and Future, 20 Yale L. & Pol'y Rev. 1, 22–46 (2002). Again, this Court has only recognized one interest as compelling: the educational benefits of diversity embraced in Grutter. Yet, as the universities define the "diversity" that they practice, it encompasses social and aesthetic goals far afield from the education-based interest discussed in Grutter. See supra, at 23. The dissents too attempt to stretch the diversity rationale, suggesting that it supports broad remedial interests. See, e.g., post, at 23, 43, 67 (opinion of Sotomayor, J.) (noting that UNC's black admissions percentages "do not reflect the diversity of the State"; equating the diversity interest under the Court's precedents with a goal of "integration in higher education" more broadly; and warning of "the dangerous consequences of an America where its leadership does not reflect the diversity of the People"); post, at 23 (opinion of Jackson, J.) (explaining that diversity programs close wealth gaps). But language—particularly the language of controlling opinions of this Court—is not so elastic. See J. Pieper, Abuse of Language—Abuse of Power 23 (L. Krauth transl. 1992) (explaining that propaganda, "in contradiction to the nature of language, intends not to communicate but to manipulate" and becomes an "[i]nstrument of power" (emphasis deleted)).

The Court refuses to engage in this lexicographic drift, seeing these arguments for what they are: a remedial rationale in disguise. See ante, at 34–35. As the Court points out, the interest for which respondents advocate has been presented to and rejected by this Court many times before. In Regents of University of California v. Bakke, 438 U.S. 265 (1978), the University of California made clear its rationale for the quota system it had established: It wished to "counteract effects of generations of pervasive discrimination" against certain minority groups. Brief for Petitioner, O. T. 1977, No. 76–811, p. 2. But, the Court rejected this distinctly remedial rationale, with Justice Powell adopting in its place the familiar "diversity" interest that appeared later in Grutter. See Bakke, 438 U. S., at 306 (plurality opinion). The Court similarly did not adopt the broad remedial rationale in Grutter; and it rejects it again today. Newly and often minted theories cannot be said to be commanded by our precedents.

Indeed, our precedents have repeatedly and soundly distinguished between programs designed to compensate victims of past governmental discrimination from so-called benign race-conscious measures, such as affirmative action. Croson, 488 U. S., at 504–505; Adarand Constructors, Inc. v. Peña, 515 U.S. 200, 226–227 (1995). To enforce that distinction, our precedents explicitly require that any attempt to compensate victims of past governmental discrimination must be concrete and traceable to the de jure segregated system, which must have some discrete and continuing discriminatory effect that warrants a present remedy. See United States v. Fordice, 505 U.S. 717, 731 (1992). Today's opinion for the Court reaffirms the need for such a close remedial fit, hewing to the same line we have consistently drawn. Ante, at 24–25.

Without such guardrails, the Fourteenth Amendment would become self-defeating, promising a Nation based on the equality ideal but yielding a quota- and caste-ridden society steeped in race-based discrimination. Even Grutter itself could not tolerate this outcome. It accordingly imposed a time limit for its race-based regime, observing that " 'a core purpose of the Fourteenth Amendment was to do away with all governmentally imposed discrimination based on race.' " 539 U. S., at 341–342 (quoting Palmore v. Sidoti, 466 U.S. 429, 432 (1984); alterations omitted).

The Court today enforces those limits. And rightly so. As noted above, both Harvard and UNC have a history of racial discrimination. But, neither have even attempted to explain how their current racially discriminatory programs are even remotely traceable to their past discriminatory conduct. Nor could they; the current race-conscious admissions programs take no account of ancestry and, at least for Harvard, likely have the effect of discriminating against some of the very same ethnic groups against which Harvard previously discriminated (i.e., Jews and those who are not part of the white elite). All the while, Harvard and UNC ask us to blind ourselves to the burdens imposed on the millions of innocent applicants denied admission because of their membership in a currently disfavored race.

The Constitution neither commands nor permits such a result. "Purchased at the price of immeasurable human suffering," the Fourteenth Amendment recognizes that classifications based on race lead to ruinous consequences for individuals and the Nation. Adarand Constructors, Inc., 515 U. S., at 240 (Thomas, J., concurring in part and concurring in judgment). Consequently, "all" racial classifications are "inherently suspect," id., at 223–224 (majority opinion) (emphasis added; internal quotation marks omitted), and must be subjected to the searching inquiry conducted by the Court, ante, at 21–34.

III

Both experience and logic have vindicated the Constitution's color-blind rule and confirmed that the universities' new narrative cannot stand. Despite the Court's hope in Grutter that universities would voluntarily end their race-conscious programs and further the goal of racial equality, the opposite appears increasingly true. Harvard and UNC now forthrightly state that they racially discriminate when it comes to admitting students, arguing that such discrimination is consistent with this Court's precedents. And they, along with today's dissenters, defend that discrimination as good. More broadly, it is becoming increasingly clear that discrimination on the basis of race—often packaged as "affirmative action" or "equity" programs—are based on the benighted notion "that it is possible to tell when discrimination helps, rather than hurts, racial minorities." Fisher I, 570 U. S., at 328 (Thomas, J., concurring).

We cannot be guided by those who would desire less in our Constitution, or by those who would desire more. "The Constitution abhors classifications based on race, not only because those classifications can harm favored races or are based on illegitimate motives, but also because every time the government places citizens on racial registers and makes race relevant to the provision of burdens or benefits, it demeans us all." Grutter, 539 U. S., at 353 (opinion of Thomas, J.).

A

The Constitution's colorblind rule reflects one of the core principles upon which our Nation was founded: that "all men are created equal." Those words featured prominently in our Declaration of Independence and were inspired by a rich tradition of political thinkers, from Locke to Montesquieu, who considered equality to be the foundation of a just government. See, e.g., J. Locke, Second Treatise of Civil Government 48 (J. Gough ed. 1948); T. Hobbes, Leviathan 98 (M. Oakeshott ed. 1962); 1 B. Montesquieu, The Spirit of Laws 121 (T. Nugent transl., J. Prichard ed. 1914). Several Constitutions enacted by the newly independent States at the founding reflected this principle. For example, the Virginia Bill of Rights of 1776 explicitly affirmed "[t]hat all men are by nature equally free and independent, and have certain inherent rights." Ch. 1, §1. The State Constitutions of Massachusetts, Pennsylvania, and New Hampshire adopted similar language. Pa. Const., Art. 1 (1776), in 2 Federal and State Constitutions 1541 (P. Poore ed. 1877); Mass. Const., Art. I (1780), in 1 id., at 957; N. H. Const., Art. I (1784), in 2 id., at 1280.[5] And, prominent Founders publicly mused about the need for equality as the foundation for government. E.g., 1 Cong. Register 430 (T. Lloyd ed. 1789) (Madison, J.); 1

Letters and Other Writings of James Madison 164 (J. Lippincott ed. 1867);
N. Webster, The Revolution in France, in 2 Political Sermons of the
Founding Era, 1730–1805, pp. 1236–1299 (1998). As Jefferson declared in
his first inaugural address, "the minority possess their equal rights, which
equal law must protect." First Inaugural Address (Mar. 4, 1801), in 8 The
Writings of Thomas Jefferson 4 (Washington ed. 1854).

Our Nation did not initially live up to the equality principle. The institution of slavery persisted for nearly a century, and the United States
Constitution itself included several provisions acknowledging the practice.
The period leading up to our second founding brought these flaws into
bold relief and encouraged the Nation to finally make good on the equality
promise. As Lincoln recognized, the promise of equality extended to all
people—including immigrants and blacks whose ancestors had taken no
part in the original founding. See Speech at Chicago, Ill. (July 10, 1858), in
2 The Collected Works of Abraham Lincoln 488–489, 499 (R. Basler ed.
1953). Thus, in Lincoln's view, " 'the natural rights enumerated in the Declaration of Independence' " extended to blacks as his " 'equal,' " and " 'the
equal of every living man.' " The Lincoln-Douglas Debates 285 (H. Holzer
ed. 1993).

As discussed above, the Fourteenth Amendment reflected that vision,
affirming that equality and racial discrimination cannot coexist. Under
that Amendment, the color of a person's skin is irrelevant to that individual's equal status as a citizen of this Nation. To treat him differently on the
basis of such a legally irrelevant trait is therefore a deviation from the
equality principle and a constitutional injury.

Of course, even the promise of the second founding took time to ma-
terialize. Seeking to perpetuate a segregationist system in the wake of the
Fourteenth Amendment's ratification, proponents urged a "separate but
equal" regime. They met with initial success, ossifying the segregationist
view for over a half century. As this Court said in Plessy:

"A statute which implies merely a legal distinction between the white
and colored races—a distinction which is founded in the color of the two
races, and which must always exist so long as white men are distinguished
from the other race by color—has no tendency to destroy the legal equality
of the two races, or reestablish a state of involuntary servitude." 163 U. S.,
at 543.

Such a statement, of course, is precisely antithetical to the notion that
all men, regardless of the color of their skin, are born equal and must be
treated equally under the law. Only one Member of the Court adhered to
the equality principle; Justice Harlan, standing alone in dissent, wrote:
"Our constitution is color-blind, and neither knows nor tolerates classes
among citizens. In respect of civil rights, all citizens are equal before the
law." Id., at 559. Though Justice Harlan rightly predicted that Plessy would,

"in time, prove to be quite as pernicious as the decision made . . . in the Dred Scott case," the Plessy rule persisted for over a half century. Ibid. While it remained in force, Jim Crow laws prohibiting blacks from entering or utilizing public facilities such as schools, libraries, restaurants, and theaters sprang up across the South.

This Court rightly reversed course in Brown v. Board of Education. The Brown appellants—those challenging segregated schools—embraced the equality principle, arguing that "[a] racial criterion is a constitutional irrelevance, and is not saved from condemnation even though dictated by a sincere desire to avoid the possibility of violence or race friction." Brief for Appellants in Brown v. Board of Education, O. T. 1952, No. 1, p. 7 (citation omitted).[6] Embracing that view, the Court held that "in the field of public education the doctrine of 'separate but equal' has no place" and "[s]eparate educational facilities are inherently unequal." Brown, 347 U. S., at 493, 495. Importantly, in reaching this conclusion, Brown did not rely on the particular qualities of the Kansas schools. The mere separation of students on the basis of race—the "segregation complained of," id., at 495 (emphasis added)—constituted a constitutional injury. See ante, at 12 ("Separate cannot be equal").

Just a few years later, the Court's application of Brown made explicit what was already forcefully implied: "[O]ur decisions have foreclosed any possible contention that . . . a statute or regulation" fostering segregation in public facilities "may stand consistently with the Fourteenth Amendment." Turner v. Memphis, 369 U.S. 350, 353 (1962) (per curiam); cf. A. Blaustein & C. Ferguson, Desegregation and the Law: The Meaning and Effect of the School Segregation Cases 145 (rev. 2d ed. 1962) (arguing that the Court in Brown had "adopt[ed] a constitutional standard" declaring "that all classification by race is unconstitutional per se").

Today, our precedents place this principle beyond question. In assessing racial segregation during a race- motivated prison riot, for example, this Court applied strict scrutiny without requiring an allegation of unequal treatment among the segregated facilities. Johnson v. California, 543 U.S. 499, 505–506 (2005). The Court today reaffirms the rule, stating that, following Brown, "[t]he time for making distinctions based on race had passed." Ante, at 13. "What was wrong" when the Court decided Brown "in 1954 cannot be right today." Parents Involved, 551 U. S., at 778 (Thomas, J., concurring). Rather, we must adhere to the promise of equality under the law declared by the Declaration of Independence and codified by the Fourteenth Amendment.

B

Respondents and the dissents argue that the universities' race-conscious admissions programs ought to be permitted because they accomplish positive social goals. I would have thought that history had by now taught a "greater humility" when attempting to "distinguish good from harmful uses of racial criteria." Id., at 742 (plurality opinion). From the Black Codes, to discriminatory and destructive social welfare programs, to discrimination by individual government actors, bigotry has reared its ugly head time and again. Anyone who today thinks that some form of racial discrimination will prove "helpful" should thus tread cautiously, lest racial discriminators succeed (as they once did) in using such language to disguise more invidious motives.

Arguments for the benefits of race-based solutions have proved pernicious in segregationist circles. Segregated universities once argued that race-based discrimination was needed "to preserve harmony and peace and at the same time furnish equal education to both groups." Brief for Respondents in Sweatt v. Painter, O. T. 1949, No. 44, p. 94; see also id., at 79 (" '[T]he mores of racial relationships are such as to rule out, for the present at least, any possibility of admitting white persons and Negroes to the same institutions' "). And, parties consistently attempted to convince the Court that the time was not right to disrupt segregationist systems. See Brief for Appellees in McLaurin v. Oklahoma State Regents for Higher Ed., O. T. 1949, No. 34, p. 12 (claiming that a holding rejecting separate but equal would "necessarily result . . . [i]n the abandoning of many of the state's existing educational establishments" and the "crowding of other such establishments"); Brief for State of Kansas on Reargument in Brown v. Board of Education, O. T. 1953, No. 1, p. 56 ("We grant that segregation may not be the ethical or political ideal. At the same time we recognize that practical considerations may prevent realization of the ideal"); Tr. of Oral Arg. in Davis v. School Bd. of Prince Edward Cty., O. T. 1954, No. 3, p. 208 ("We are up against the proposition: What does the Negro profit if he procures an immediate detailed decree from this Court now and then impairs or mars or destroys the public school system in Prince Edward County"). Litigants have even gone so far as to offer straight-faced arguments that segregation has practical benefits. Brief for Respondents in Sweatt v. Painter, at 77–78 (requesting deference to a state law, observing that " 'the necessity for such separation [of the races] still exists in the interest of public welfare, safety, harmony, health, and recreation . . .' " and remarking on the reasonableness of the position); Brief for Appellees in Davis v. County School Bd. of Prince Edward Cty., O. T. 1952, No. 3, p. 17 ("Virginia has established segregation in certain fields as a part of her public policy to prevent violence and reduce resentment. The result, in the view of an overwhelming Virginia majority, has been to improve the relationship between the different races"); id., at 25 ("If segregation be stricken down, the general welfare will be definitely harmed . . . there would be more friction developed" (internal quotation marks omitted)). In fact, slaveholders once "argued that slavery was a 'positive good' that civilized blacks and elevated them in every dimension of life," and "segregationists similarly asserted that segregation was not only benign, but good for black students." Fisher I, 570 U. S., at 328–329 (Thomas, J., concurring).

"Indeed, if our history has taught us anything, it has taught us to beware of elites bearing racial theories." Parents Involved, 551 U. S., at 780–781 (Thomas, J., concurring). We cannot now blink reality to pretend, as the dissents urge, that affirmative action should be legally permissible merely because the experts assure us that it is "good" for black students. Though I do not doubt the sincerity of my dissenting colleagues' beliefs, experts and elites have been wrong before—and they may prove to be wrong again. In part for this reason, the Fourteenth Amendment outlaws government-sanctioned racial discrimination of all types. The stakes are simply too high to gamble.[7] Then, as now, the views that motivated Dred Scott and Plessy have not been confined to the past, and we must remain ever vigilant against all forms of racial discrimination.

C

Even taking the desire to help on its face, what initially seems like aid may in reality be a burden, including for the very people it seeks to assist. Take, for example, the college admissions policies here. "Affirmative action" policies do nothing to increase the overall number of blacks and Hispanics able to access a college education. Rather, those racial policies simply redistribute individuals among institutions of higher learning, placing some into more competitive institutions than they otherwise would have attended. See T. Sowell, Affirmative Action Around the World 145–146 (2004). In doing so, those policies sort at least some blacks and Hispanics into environments where they are less likely to succeed academically relative to their peers. Ibid. The resulting mismatch places "many blacks and Hispanics who likely would have excelled at less elite schools . . . in a position where underperformance is all but inevitable because they are less academically prepared than the white and Asian students with whom they must compete." Fisher I, 570 U. S., at 332 (Thomas, J., concurring).

It is self-evident why that is so. As anyone who has labored over an algebra textbook has undoubtedly discovered, academic advancement results from hard work and practice, not mere declaration. Simply treating students as though their grades put them at the top of their high school classes does nothing to enhance the performance level of those students or otherwise prepare them for competitive college environments. In fact, studies suggest that large racial preferences for black and Hispanic applicants have led to a disproportionately large share of those students receiving mediocre or poor grades once they arrive in competitive collegiate environments. See, e.g., R. Sander, A Systemic Analysis of Affirmative Action in American Law Schools, 57 Stan. L. Rev. 367, 371–372 (2004); see also R. Sander & R. Steinbuch, Mismatch and Bar Passage: A School-Specific Analysis (Oct. 6, 2017), https://ssrn.com/ abstract=3054208. Take science, technology, engineering, and mathematics (STEM) fields, for example. Those students who receive a large admissions preference are more likely to drop out of STEM fields than similarly situated students who did not receive such a preference. F. Smith & J. McArdle, Ethnic and Gender Differences in Science Graduation at Selective Colleges With Implications for Admission Policy and College Choice, 45 Research in Higher Ed. 353 (2004). "Even if most minority students are able to meet the normal standards at the 'average' range of colleges and universities, the systematic mismatching of minority students begun at the top can mean that such students are generally overmatched throughout all levels of higher education." T. Sowell, Race and Culture 176–177 (1994).[8]

These policies may harm even those who succeed academically. I have long believed that large racial preferences in college admissions "stamp [blacks and Hispanics] with a badge of inferiority." Adarand, 515 U. S., at 241 (opinion of Thomas, J.). They thus "tain[t] the accomplishments of all those who are admitted as a result of racial discrimination" as well as "all those who are the same race as those admitted as a result of racial discrimination" because "no one can distinguish those students from the ones whose race played a role in their admission." Fisher I, 570 U. S., at 333 (opinion of Thomas, J.). Consequently, "[w]hen blacks" and, now, Hispanics "take positions in the highest places of government, industry, or academia, it is an open question . . . whether their skin color played a part in their advancement." Grutter, 539 U. S., at 373 (Thomas, J., concurring). "The question itself is the stigma—because either racial discrimination did play a role, in which case the person may be deemed 'otherwise unqualified,' or it did not, in which case asking the question itself unfairly marks those . . . who would succeed without discrimination." Ibid.

Yet, in the face of those problems, it seems increasingly clear that universities are focused on "aesthetic" solutions unlikely to help deserving members of minority groups. In fact, universities' affirmative action programs are a particularly poor use of such resources. To start, these programs are overinclusive, providing the same admissions bump to a wealthy black applicant given every advantage in life as to a black applicant from a poor family with seemingly insurmountable barriers to overcome. In doing so, the programs may wind up helping the most well-off members of minority races without meaningfully assisting those who struggle with real hardship. Simultaneously, the programs risk continuing to ignore the academic underperformance of "the purported 'beneficiaries'" of racial preferences and the racial stigma that those preferences generate. Grutter, 539 U. S., at 371 (opinion of Thomas, J.). Rather than performing their academic mission, universities thus may "see[k] only a facade—it is sufficient that the class looks right, even if it does not perform right." Id., at 372.

D

Finally, it is not even theoretically possible to "help" a certain racial group without causing harm to members of other racial groups. "It should be obvious that every racial classification helps, in a narrow sense, some races and hurts others." Adarand, 515 U. S., at 241, n. * (opinion of Thomas, J.). And, even purportedly benign race-based discrimination has secondary effects on members of other races. The antisubordination view thus has never guided the Court's analysis because "whether a law relying upon racial taxonomy is 'benign' or 'malign' either turns on 'whose ox is gored' or on distinctions found only in the eye of the beholder." Ibid. (citations and some internal quotation marks omitted). Courts are not suited to the impossible task of determining which racially discriminatory programs are helping which members of which races—and whether those benefits outweigh the burdens thrust onto other racial groups.

As the Court's opinion today explains, the zero-sum nature of college admissions—where students compete for a finite number of seats in each school's entering class—aptly demonstrates the point. Ante, at 27.[9] Petitioner here represents Asian Americans who allege that, at the margins, Asian applicants were denied admission because of their race. Yet, Asian Americans can hardly be described as the beneficiaries of historical racial advantages. To the contrary, our Nation's first immigration ban targeted the Chinese, in part, based on "worker resentment of the low wage rates accepted by Chinese workers." U. S. Commission on Civil Rights, Civil Rights Issues Facing Asian Americans in the 1990s, p. 3 (1992) (Civil Rights Issues); Act of May 6, 1882, ch. 126, 22Stat. 58–59.

In subsequent years, "strong anti-Asian sentiments in the Western States led to the adoption of many discriminatory laws at the State and local levels, similar to those aimed at blacks in the South," and "segregation in public facilities, including schools, was quite common until after the Second World War." Civil Rights Issues 7; see also S. Hinnershitz, A Different Shade of Justice: Asian American Civil Rights in the South 21 (2017) (explaining that while both Asians and blacks have at times fought "against similar forms of discrimination," "[t]he issues of citizenship and immigrant status often defined Asian American battles for civil rights and separated them from African American legal battles"). Indeed, this Court even sanctioned this segregation—in the context of schools, no less. In Gong Lum v. Rice, 275 U.S. 78, 81–82, 85–87 (1927), the Court held that a 9-year-old Chinese-American girl could be denied entry to a "white" school because she was "a member of the Mongolian or yellow race."

Also, following the Japanese attack on the U. S. Navy base at Pearl Harbor, Japanese Americans in the American West were evacuated and interned in relocation camps. See Exec. Order No. 9066, 3 CFR 1092 (1943). Over 120,000 were removed to camps beginning in 1942, and the last camp that held Japanese Americans did not close until 1948. National Park Service, Japanese American Life During Internment, www.nps.gov/articles/japanese-american-internment-archeology.htm. In the interim, this Court endorsed the practice. Korematsu v. United States, 323 U.S. 214 (1944).

Given the history of discrimination against Asian Americans, especially their history with segregated schools, it seems particularly incongruous to suggest that a past history of segregationist policies toward blacks should be remedied at the expense of Asian American college applicants.[10] But this problem is not limited to Asian Americans; more broadly, universities' discriminatory policies burden millions of applicants who are not responsible for the racial discrimination that sullied our Nation's past. That is why, "[i]n the absence of special circumstances, the remedy for de jure segregation ordinarily should not include educational programs for students who were not in school (or even alive) during the period of segregation." Jenkins, 515 U. S., at 137 (Thomas, J., concurring). Today's 17-year-olds, after all, did not live through the Jim Crow era, enact or enforce segregation laws, or take any action to oppress or enslave the victims of the past. Whatever their skin color, today's youth simply are not responsible for instituting the segregation of the 20th century, and they do not shoulder the moral debts of their ancestors. Our Nation should not punish today's youth for the sins of the past.

IV

Far from advancing the cause of improved race relations in our Nation, affirmative action highlights our racial differences with pernicious effect. In fact, recent history reveals a disturbing pattern: Affirmative action policies appear to have prolonged the asserted need for racial discrimination. Parties and amici in these cases report that, in the nearly 50 years since Bakke, 438 U.S. 265, racial progress on campuses adopting affirmative action admissions policies has stagnated, including making no meaningful progress toward a colorblind goal since Grutter. See ante, at 21–22. Rather, the legacy of Grutter appears to be ever increasing and strident demands for yet more racially oriented solutions.

A

It has become clear that sorting by race does not stop at the admissions office. In his Grutter opinion, Justice Scalia criticized universities for "talk[ing] of multiculturalism and racial diversity," but supporting "tribalism and racial segregation on their campuses," including through "minority only student organizations, separate minority housing opportunities, separate minority student centers, even separate minority-only graduation ceremonies." 539 U. S., at 349 (opinion concurring in part and dissenting in part). This trend has hardly abated with time, and today, such programs are commonplace. See Brief for Gail Heriot et al. as Amici Curiae 9. In fact, a recent study considering 173 schools found that 43% of colleges offered segregated housing to students of different races, 46% offered segregated orientation programs, and 72% sponsored segregated graduation ceremonies. D. Pierre & P. Wood, Neo-Segregation at Yale 16–17 (2019); see also D. Pierre, Demands for Segregated Housing at Williams College Are Not News, Nat. Rev., May 8, 2019. In addition to contradicting the universities' claims regarding the need for interracial interaction, see Brief for National Association of Scholars as Amicus Curiae 4–12, these trends increasingly encourage our Nation's youth to view racial differences as important and segregation as routine.

Meanwhile, these discriminatory policies risk creating new prejudices and allowing old ones to fester. I previously observed that "[t]here can be no doubt" that discriminatory affirmative action policies "injur[e] white and Asian applicants who are denied admission because of their race." Fisher I, 570 U. S., at 331 (concurring opinion). Petitioner here clearly demonstrates this fact. Moreover, "no social science has disproved the notion that this discrimination 'engenders attitudes of superiority or, alternatively, provokes resentment among those who believe that they have been wronged by the government's use of race.' " Grutter, 539 U. S., at 373 (opinion of Thomas, J.) (quoting Adarand, 515 U. S., at 241 (opinion of Thomas, J.) (alterations omitted)). Applicants denied admission to certain colleges may come to believe—accurately or not—that their race was responsible for their failure to attain a life-long dream. These individuals, and others who wished for their success, may resent members of what they perceive to be favored races, believing that the successes of those individuals are unearned.

What, then, would be the endpoint of these affirmative action policies? Not racial harmony, integration, or equality under the law. Rather, these policies appear to be leading to a world in which everyone is defined by their skin color, demanding ever-increasing entitlements and preferences on that basis. Not only is that exactly the kind of factionalism that the Constitution was meant to safeguard against, see The Federalist No. 10 (J. Madison), but it is a factionalism based on ever-shifting sands.

That is because race is a social construct; we may each identify as members of particular races for any number of reasons, having to do with our skin color, our heritage, or our cultural identity. And, over time, these ephemeral, socially constructed categories have often shifted. For example, whereas universities today would group all white applicants together, white elites previously sought to exclude Jews and other white immigrant groups from higher education. In fact, it is impossible to look at an individual and know definitively his or her race; some who would consider themselves black, for example, may be quite fair skinned. Yet, university admissions policies ask individuals to identify themselves as belonging to one of only a few reductionist racial groups. With boxes for only "black," "white," "Hispanic," "Asian," or the ambiguous "other," how is a Middle Eastern person to choose? Someone from the Philippines? See post, at 5–7 (Gorsuch, J., concurring). Whichever choice he makes (in the event he chooses to report a race at all), the form silos him into an artificial category. Worse, it sends a clear signal that the category matters.

But, under our Constitution, race is irrelevant, as the Court acknowledges. In fact, all racial categories are little more than stereotypes, suggesting that immutable characteristics somehow conclusively determine a person's ideology, beliefs, and abilities. Of course, that is false. See ante, at 28–30 (noting that the Court's Equal Protection Clause jurisprudence forbids such stereotyping). Members of the same race do not all share the exact same experiences and viewpoints; far from it. A black person from rural Alabama surely has different experiences than a black person from Manhattan or a black first-generation immigrant from Nigeria, in the same way that a white person from rural Vermont has a different perspective than a white person from Houston, Texas. Yet, universities' racial policies suggest that racial identity "alone constitutes the being of the race or the man." J. Barzun, Race: A Study in Modern Superstition 114 (1937). That is the same naked racism upon which segregation itself was built. Small wonder, then, that these policies are leading to increasing racial polarization and friction. This kind of reductionist logic leads directly to the "disregard for what does not jibe with preconceived theory," providing a "cloa[k] to conceal complexity, argumen[t] to the crown for praising or damning without the trouble of going into details"—such as details about an individual's ideas or unique background. Ibid. Rather than forming a more pluralistic society, these policies thus strip us of our individuality and undermine the very diversity of thought that universities purport to seek.

The solution to our Nation's racial problems thus cannot come from policies grounded in affirmative action or some other conception of equity. Racialism simply cannot be undone by different or more racialism. Instead, the solution announced in the second founding is incorporated in our Constitution: that we are all equal, and should be treated equally before the law without regard to our race. Only that promise can allow us to look past our differing skin colors and identities and see each other for what we truly are: individuals with unique thoughts, perspectives, and goals, but with equal dignity and equal rights under the law.

B

Justice Jackson has a different view. Rather than focusing on individuals as individuals, her dissent focuses on the historical subjugation of black Americans, invoking statistical racial gaps to argue in favor of defining and categorizing individuals by their race. As she sees things, we are all inexorably trapped in a fundamentally racist society, with the original sin of slavery and the historical subjugation of black Americans still determining our lives today. Post, at 1–26 (dissenting opinion). The panacea, she counsels, is to unquestioningly accede to the view of elite experts and reallocate society's riches by racial means as necessary to "level the playing field," all as judged by racial metrics. Post, at 26. I strongly disagree.

First, as stated above, any statistical gaps between the average wealth of black and white Americans is constitutionally irrelevant. I, of course, agree that our society is not, and has never been, colorblind. Post, at 2 (Jackson, J., dissenting); see also Plessy, 163 U. S., at 559 (Harlan, J., dissenting). People discriminate against one another for a whole host of reasons. But, under the Fourteenth Amendment, the law must disregard all racial distinctions:

"[I]n view of the constitution, in the eye of the law, there is in this country no superior, dominant, ruling class of citizens. There is no caste here. Our constitution is color-blind, and neither knows nor tolerates classes among citizens. In respect of civil rights, all citizens are equal before the law. The humblest is the peer of the most powerful. The law regards man as man, and takes no account of his surroundings or of his color when his civil rights as guaranteed by the supreme law of the land are involved." Ibid.

With the passage of the Fourteenth Amendment, the people of our Nation proclaimed that the law may not sort citizens based on race. It is this principle that the Framers of the Fourteenth Amendment adopted in the wake of the Civil War to fulfill the promise of equality under the law. And it is this principle that has guaranteed a Nation of equal citizens the privileges or immunities of citizenship and the equal protection of the laws. To now dismiss it as "two-dimensional flatness," post, at 25 (Jackson, J., dissenting), is to abdicate a sacred trust to ensure that our "honored dead . . . shall not have died in vain." A. Lincoln, Gettysburg Address (1863).

Yet, Justice Jackson would replace the second Founders' vision with an organizing principle based on race. In fact, on her view, almost all of life's outcomes may be unhesitatingly ascribed to race. Post, at 24–26. This is so, she writes, because of statistical disparities among different racial groups. See post, at 11–14. Even if some whites have a lower household net worth than some blacks, what matters to Justice Jackson is that the average white household has more wealth than the average black household. Post, at 11.

This lore is not and has never been true. Even in the segregated South where I grew up, individuals were not the sum of their skin color. Then as now, not all disparities are based on race; not all people are racist; and not all differences between individuals are ascribable to race. Put simply, "the fate of abstract categories of wealth statistics is not the same as the fate of a given set of flesh-and-blood human beings." T. Sowell, Wealth, Poverty and Politics 333 (2016). Worse still, Justice Jackson uses her broad observations about statistical relationships between race and select measures of health, wealth, and well-being to label all blacks as victims. Her desire to do so is unfathomable to me. I cannot deny the great accomplishments of black Americans, including those who succeeded despite long odds.

Nor do Justice Jackson's statistics regarding a correlation between levels of health, wealth, and well-being between selected racial groups prove anything. Of course, none of those statistics are capable of drawing a direct causal link between race—rather than socioeconomic status or any other factor—and individual outcomes. So Justice Jackson supplies the link herself: the legacy of slavery and the nature of inherited wealth. This, she claims, locks blacks into a seemingly perpetual inferior caste. Such a view is irrational; it is an insult to individual achievement and cancerous to young minds seeking to push through barriers, rather than consign themselves to permanent victimhood. If an applicant has less financial means (because of generational inheritance or otherwise), then surely a university may take that into account. If an applicant has medical struggles or a family member with medical concerns, a university may consider that too. What it cannot do is use the applicant's skin color as a heuristic, assuming that because the applicant checks the box for "black" he therefore conforms to the university's monolithic and reductionist view of an abstract, average black person.

Accordingly, Justice Jackson's race-infused world view falls flat at each step. Individuals are the sum of their unique experiences, challenges, and accomplishments. What matters is not the barriers they face, but how they choose to confront them. And their race is not to blame for everything—good or bad—that happens in their lives. A contrary, myopic world view based on individuals' skin color to the total exclusion of their personal choices is nothing short of racial determinism.

Justice Jackson then builds from her faulty premise to call for action, arguing that courts should defer to "experts" and allow institutions to discriminate on the basis of race. Make no mistake: Her dissent is not a vanguard of the innocent and helpless. It is instead a call to empower privileged elites, who will "tell us [what] is required to level the playing field" among castes and classifications that they alone can divine. Post, at 26; see also post, at 5–7 (Gorsuch, J., concurring) (explaining the arbitrariness of these classifications). Then, after siloing us all into racial castes and pitting those castes against each other, the dissent somehow believes that we will be able—at some undefined point—to "march forward together" into some utopian vision. Post, at 26 (opinion of Jackson, J.). Social movements that invoke these sorts of rallying cries, historically, have ended disastrously.

Unsurprisingly, this tried-and-failed system defies both law and reason. Start with the obvious: If social reorganization in the name of equality may be justified by the mere fact of statistical disparities among racial groups, then that reorganization must continue until these disparities are fully eliminated, regardless of the reasons for the disparities and the cost of their elimination. If blacks fail a test at higher rates than their white counterparts (regardless of whether the reason for the disparity has anything at all to do with race), the only solution will be race-focused measures. If those measures were to result in blacks failing at yet higher rates, the only solution would be to double down. In fact, there would seem to be no logical limit to what the government may do to level the racial playing field—outright wealth transfers, quota systems, and racial preferences would all seem permissible. In such a system, it would not matter how many innocents suffer race-based injuries; all that would matter is reaching the race-based goal.

Worse, the classifications that Justice Jackson draws are themselves race-based stereotypes. She focuses on two hypothetical applicants, John and James, competing for admission to UNC. John is a white, seventh-generation legacy at the school, while James is black and would be the first in his family to attend UNC. Post, at 3. Justice Jackson argues that race-conscious admission programs are necessary to adequately compare the two applicants. As an initial matter, it is not clear why James's race is the only factor that could encourage UNC to admit him; his status as a first-generation college applicant seems to contextualize his application. But, setting that aside, why is it that John should be judged based on the actions of his great-great-great-grandparents? And what would Justice Jackson say to John when deeming him not as worthy of admission:

Some statistically significant number of white people had advantages in college admissions seven generations ago, and you have inherited their incurable sin?

Nor should we accept that John or James represent all members of their respective races. All racial groups are heterogeneous, and blacks are no exception—encompassing northerners and southerners, rich and poor, and recent immigrants and descendants of slaves. See, e.g., T. Sowell, Ethnic America 220 (1981) (noting that the great success of West Indian immigrants to the United States—disproportionate among blacks more broadly—"seriously undermines the proposition that color is a fatal handicap in the American economy"). Eschewing the complexity that comes with individuality may make for an uncomplicated narrative, but lumping people together and judging them based on assumed inherited or ancestral traits is nothing but stereotyping.[11]

To further illustrate, let's expand the applicant pool beyond John and James. Consider Jack, a black applicant and the son of a multimillionaire industrialist. In a world of race-based preferences, James' seat could very well go to Jack rather than John—both are black, after all. And what about members of the numerous other racial and ethnic groups in our Nation? What about Anne, the child of Chinese immigrants? Jacob, the grandchild of Holocaust survivors who escaped to this Nation with nothing and faced discrimination upon arrival? Or Thomas, the great- grandchild of Irish immigrants escaping famine? While articulating her black and white world (literally), Justice Jackson ignores the experiences of other immigrant groups (like Asians, see supra, at 43–44) and white communities that have faced historic barriers.

Though Justice Jackson seems to think that her race-based theory can somehow benefit everyone, it is an immutable fact that "every time the government uses racial criteria to 'bring the races together,' someone gets excluded, and the person excluded suffers an injury solely because of his or her race." Parents Involved, 551 U. S., at 759 (Thomas, J., concurring) (citation omitted). Indeed, Justice Jackson seems to have no response—no explanation at all—for the people who will shoulder that burden. How, for example, would Justice Jackson explain the need for race-based preferences to the Chinese student who has worked hard his whole life, only to be denied college admission in part because of his skin color? If such a burden would seem difficult to impose on a bright-eyed young person, that's because it should be. History has taught us to abhor theories that call for elites to pick racial winners and losers in the name of sociological experimentation.

Nor is it clear what another few generations of race- conscious college admissions may be expected to accomplish. Even today, affirmative action programs that offer an admissions boost to black and Hispanic students discriminate against those who identify themselves as members of other races that do not receive such preferential treatment. Must others in the future make sacrifices to re-level the playing field for this new phase of racial subordination? And then, out of whose lives should the debt owed to those further victims be repaid? This vision of meeting social racism with government-imposed racism is thus self-defeating, resulting in a never-ending cycle of victimization. There is no reason to continue down that path. In the wake of the Civil War, the Framers of the Fourteenth Amendment charted a way out: a colorblind Constitution that requires the government to, at long last, put aside its citizens' skin color and focus on their individual achievements.

C

Universities' recent experiences confirm the efficacy of a colorblind rule. To start, universities prohibited from engaging in racial discrimination by state law continue to enroll racially diverse classes by race-neutral means. For example, the University of California purportedly recently admitted its "most diverse undergraduate class ever," despite California's ban on racial preferences. T. Watanabe, UC Admits Largest, Most Diverse Class Ever, But It Was Harder To Get Accepted, L. A. Times, July 20, 2021, p. A1. Similarly, the University of Michigan's 2021 incoming class was "among the university's most racially and ethnically diverse classes, with 37% of first-year students identifying as persons of color." S. Dodge, Largest Ever Student Body at University of Michigan This Fall, Officials Say, MLive.com (Oct. 22, 2021), https://www.mlive.com/news/ann-arbor/2021/10/largest-ever-student-body-at-university-of-michigan- this-fall-officials-say.html. In fact, at least one set of studies suggests that, "when we consider the higher education system as a whole, it is clear that the vast majority of schools would be as racially integrated, or more racially integrated, under a system of no preferences than under a system of large preferences." Brief for Richard Sander as Amicus Curiae 26. Race-neutral policies may thus achieve the same benefits of racial harmony and equality without any of the burdens and strife generated by affirmative action policies.

In fact, meritocratic systems have long refuted bigoted misperceptions of what black students can accomplish. I have always viewed "higher education's purpose as imparting knowledge and skills to students, rather than a communal, rubber-stamp, credentialing process." Grutter, 539 U. S., at 371–372 (opinion concurring in part and dissenting in part). And, I continue to strongly believe (and have never doubted) that "blacks can achieve in every avenue of American life without the meddling of university administrators." Id., at 350. Meritocratic systems, with objective grading scales, are critical to that belief. Such scales have always been a great equalizer—offering a metric for achievement that bigotry could not alter. Racial preferences take away this benefit, eliminating the very metric by which those who have the most to prove can clearly demonstrate their accomplishments—both to themselves and to others.

Schools' successes, like students' grades, also provide objective proof of ability. Historically Black Colleges and Universities (HBCUs) do not have a large amount of racial diversity, but they demonstrate a marked ability to improve the lives of their students. To this day, they have proved "to be extremely effective in educating Black students, particularly in STEM," where "HBCUs represent seven of the top eight institutions that graduate the highest number of Black undergraduate students who go on to earn [science and engineering] doctorates." W. Wondwossen, The Science Behind HBCU Success, Nat. Science Foundation (Sept. 24, 2020), https://beta.nsf.gov/science-matters/science-behind-hbcu-success. "HBCUs have produced 40% of all Black engineers." Presidential Proclamation No. 10451, 87 Fed. Reg. 57567 (2022). And, they "account for 80% of Black judges, 50% of Black doctors, and 50% of Black lawyers." M. Hammond, L. Owens, & B. Gulko, Social Mobility Outcomes for HBCU Alumni, United Negro College Fund 4 (2021) (Hammond), https://cdn.uncf.org/wp-content/uploads/ Social-Mobility-Report-FINAL.pdf; see also 87 Fed. Reg. 57567 (placing the percentage of black doctors even higher, at 70%). In fact, Xavier University, an HBCU with only a small percentage of white students, has had better success at helping its low-income students move into the middle class than Harvard has. See Hammond 14; see also Brief for Oklahoma et al. as Amici Curiae 18. And, each of the top 10 HBCUs have a success rate above the national average. Hammond 14.[12]

Why, then, would this Court need to allow other universities to racially discriminate? Not for the betterment of those black students, it would seem. The hard work of HBCUs and their students demonstrate that "black schools can function as the center and symbol of black communities, and provide examples of independent black leadership, success, and achievement." Jenkins, 515 U. S., at 122 (Thomas, J., concurring) (citing Fordice, 505 U. S., at 748 (Thomas, J., concurring)). And, because race-conscious college admissions are plainly not necessary to serve even the interests of blacks, there is no justification to compel such programs more broadly. See Parents Involved, 551 U. S., at 765 (Thomas, J., concurring).

* * *

The great failure of this country was slavery and its progeny. And, the tragic failure of this Court was its misinterpretation of the Reconstruction Amendments, as Justice Harlan predicted in Plessy. We should not repeat this mistake merely because we think, as our predecessors thought, that the present arrangements are superior to the Constitution.

The Court's opinion rightly makes clear that Grutter is, for all intents and purposes, overruled. And, it sees the universities' admissions policies for what they are: rudderless, race-based preferences designed to ensure a particular racial mix in their entering classes. Those policies fly in the face of our colorblind Constitution and our Nation's equality ideal. In short, they are plainly—and boldly—unconstitutional. See Brown II, 349 U. S., at 298 (noting that the Brown case one year earlier had "declare[d] the fundamental principle that racial discrimination in public education is unconstitutional").

While I am painfully aware of the social and economic ravages which have befallen my race and all who suffer discrimination, I hold out enduring hope that this country will live up to its principles so clearly enunciated in the Declaration of Independence and the Constitution of the United States: that all men are created equal, are equal citizens, and must be treated equally before the law.

APPENDIX B

Legislation Abolishing DEI Programs at Public Colleges and Universities

I. Text of Texas Law signed by Governor Greg Abbott ending DEI at public Colleges and Universities

AN ACT
relating to diversity, equity, and inclusion initiatives at public institutions of higher education.
BE IT ENACTED BY THE LEGISLATURE OF THE STATE OF TEXAS:
Section 1. Subchapter G, Chapter 51, Education Code, is amended by adding Section 51.3525 to read as follows:
Sec. 51.3525. RESPONSIBILITY OF GOVERNING BOARDS REGARDING DIVERSITY, EQUITY, AND INCLUSION INITIATIVES. (a) In this section, "diversity, equity, and inclusion office" means an office, division, or other unit of an institution of higher education established for the purpose of:
(1) influencing hiring or employment practices at the institution with respect to race, sex, color, or ethnicity, other than through the use of color-blind and sex-neutral hiring processes in accordance with any applicable state and federal antidiscrimination laws;
(2) promoting differential treatment of or providing special benefits to individuals on the basis of race, color, or ethnicity;
(3) promoting policies or procedures designed or implemented in reference to race, color, or ethnicity, other than policies or procedures approved in writing by the institution's general counsel and the Texas Higher Education Coordinating Board for the sole purpose of ensuring compliance with any applicable court order or state or federal law; or
(4) conducting trainings, programs, or activities designed or implemented in reference to race, color, ethnicity, gender identity, or sexual orientation, other than trainings, programs, or activities developed by an attorney and approved in writing by the institution's general counsel and the Texas Higher Education Coordinating Board for the sole purpose of ensuring compliance with any applicable court order or state or federal law.
(b) The governing board of an institution of higher education shall

ensure that each unit of the institution:

(1) does not, except as required by federal law:

(A) establish or maintain a diversity, equity, and inclusion office;

(B) hire or assign an employee of the institution or contract with a third party to perform the duties of a diversity, equity, and inclusion office;

(C) compel, require, induce, or solicit any person to provide a diversity, equity, and inclusion statement or give preferential consideration to any person based on the provision of a diversity, equity, and inclusion statement;

(D) give preference on the basis of race, sex, color, ethnicity, or national origin to an applicant for employment, an employee, or a participant in any function of the institution; or

(E) Require as a condition of enrolling at the institution or performing any institution function any person to participate in diversity, equity, and inclusion training, which:

(i) includes a training, program, or activity designed or implemented in reference to race, color, ethnicity, gender identity, or sexual orientation; and

(ii) does not include a training, program or activity developed by an attorney and approved in writing by the institution's general counsel and the Texas Higher Education Coordinating Board for the sole purpose of ensuring compliance with any applicable court order or state or federal law; and

(2) adopts policies and procedures for appropriately disciplining, including by termination, an employee or contractor of the institution who engages in conduct in violation of Subdivision (1).

(c) Nothing in this section may be construed to limit or prohibit an institution of higher education or any employee of an institution of higher education from, for purposes of applying for a grant or complying with the terms of accreditation by an accrediting agency, submitting to the grantor or accrediting agency a statement that:

(1) highlights the institution's work in supporting:

(A) first-generation college students

(B) low-income students; or

(C) underserved student populations; or

(2) Certifies compliance with state and federal antidiscrimination laws.

(d) Subsection (b)(1) may not be construed to apply to:

(1) academic course instruction;

(2) scholarly research or a creative work by an institution of higher education's students, faculty, or other research personnel or the dissemination of that research or work;

(3) an activity of a student organization registered with or

recognized by an institution of higher education;

(4) guest speakers or performers on short-term engagements;

(5) a policy, practice, procedure, program, or activity to enhance student academic achievement or postgraduate outcomes that is designed and implemented without regard to race, sex, color, or ethnicity;

(6) data collection; or

(7) student recruitment or admissions.

(e) An institution of higher education may not spend money appropriated to the institution for a state fiscal year until the governing board of the institution submits to the legislature and the Texas Higher Education Coordinating Board a report certifying the board's compliance with this section during the preceding state fiscal year.

(f) In the interim between each regular session of the legislature, the governing board of each institution of higher education, or the board's designee, shall testify before the standing legislative committees with primary jurisdiction over higher education at a public hearing of the committee regarding the board's compliance with this section.

(g) The state auditor shall periodically conduct a compliance audit of each institution of higher education to determine whether the institution has spent state money in violation of this section. The state auditor shall adopt a schedule by which the state auditor will conduct compliance audits under this subsection. The schedule must ensure that each institution of higher education is audited at least once every four years.

(h) If the state auditor determines pursuant to a compliance audit conducted under Subsection (g) that an institution of higher education has spent state money in violation of this section, the institution:

(1) must cure the violation not later than the 180th day after the date on which the determination is made; and

(2) if the institution fails to cure the violation during the period described by Subdivision (1), is ineligible to receive formula funding increases, institutional enhancements, or exceptional items during the state fiscal biennium immediately following the state fiscal biennium in which the determination is made.

(i) A student or employee of an institution of higher education who is required to participate in training in violation of Subsection (b)(1)(E) may bring an action against the institution for injunctive or declaratory relief.

(j) The Texas Higher Education Coordinating Board, in coordination with institutions of higher education, shall conduct a biennial study to identify the impact of the implementation of this section on the application rate, acceptance rate, matriculation rate, retention rate, grade point average, and graduation rate of students at institutions of higher education, disaggregated by race, sex, and ethnicity. Not later than December 1 of each even-numbered year, the coordinating board shall submit to the legislature a report on the results of the study and any recommendations for legislative or other action. This subsection expires September 1, 2029.

SECTION 2. A public institution of higher education may provide to each employee in good standing at the institution whose position is eliminated as a result of the implementation of Section 51.3525, Education Code, as added by this Act, a letter of recommendation for employment for a position at the institution or elsewhere.

SECTION 3. (a) Except as provided by Subsection (b) of this section, this Act applies beginning with the spring semester of the 2023-2024 academic year.

(b) Section 51.3525(e), Education Code, as added by this Act, applies beginning with money appropriated to a public institution of higher education for the state fiscal year beginning September 1, 2024.

SECTION 4. This Act takes effect immediately if it receives a vote of two-thirds of all the members elected to each house, as provided by Section 39, Article III, Texas Constitution. If this Act does not receive the vote necessary for immediate effect, this Act takes effect January 1, 2024.

II. Text of Florida Law signed by Ron DeSantis ending DEI in public College and Universities

An act relating to higher education; amending s. 1001.706, F.S.; revising the duties of the Board of Governors relating to the mission of each state university; revising requirements for the Board of Governors' strategic plan relating to the goals and the Board of Governors to annually require each state university to include certain information in its economic security report; requiring, rather than authorizing, a Board of Governors regulation to include a post-tenure review of state university faculty on a specified basis; amending s. 1001.7065, F.S.; requiring the Board of Governors Accountability Plan to annually report certain research expenditures of a specified amount; revising the number of standards an institution must meet to receive a specified designation; creating s. 1001.741, F.S.; providing that each state university president is responsible for hiring the provost, the deans, and full-time faculty; providing that the president has a duty to assess the performance of the provost and deans; authorizing the president to delegate hiring authority to specified individuals and entities; prohibiting a university from using specified methods in its admissions or personnel processes; providing that certain actions regarding personnel may not be appealed beyond the university president; requiring each state university board of trustees to have review procedures for the president's selection and reappointment of certain faculty; requiring each state university president to annually present specified performance evaluations and salaries to the board of trustees; amending s. 1004.06, F.S.; prohibiting specified educational institutions from expending funds for certain purposes; providing exceptions; requiring the State Board of Education and the Board of Governors to adopt rules and regulations, respectively; creating s. 1004.3841, F.S.; creating the Institute for Risk Management and Insurance Education within the College of Business at the University of Central Florida; requiring that the institute be located in a specified county; providing the purpose and goals of the institute; amending s. 1004.6496, F.S.; authorizing the Board of Trustees of the University of Florida to use charitable donations in addition to appropriated funds to fund the Hamilton Center for Classical and Civic Education; requiring the University of Florida to annually report to the Governor and Legislature on the transition of the center to a college; revising the goals of the center; requiring the University of Florida president to take specified actions; providing requirements for the use of appropriated funds; authorizing the university to provide additional funding to the center; amending s. 1004.6499, F.S.; renaming the Florida Institute of Politics at the Florida State University as the Florida Institute for Governance and Civics; providing the goals of the institute; amending s. 1004.64991, F.S.; authorizing the Adam Smith Center for the Study of Economic Freedom to perform certain tasks in order to carry out its established purpose; amending s. 1007.25, F.S.; revising how general education core courses are established; requiring the State Board of Education and the Board of Governors to consider approval of certain courses; requiring faculty committees to review and submit recommendations to the Articulation Coordinating Committee and the commissioner relating to certain courses by a specified date and periodically thereafter; prohibiting general education core courses from teaching certain topics or presenting information in specified ways; providing requirements for general education core courses; requiring specified educational institutions to offer certain courses; prohibiting public postsecondary educational institutions from requiring students to take certain additional general education core courses; creating s. 1007.55, F.S.; providing legislative findings; providing requirements for general education courses; requiring public postsecondary educational institution boards of trustees and presidents to annually review and approve general education requirements; requiring public postsecondary educational institutions to report certain courses to the department; requiring the Articulation Coordinating Committee to submit general education courses to the State Board of Education and the Board of Governors for action; providing a penalty for failing to meet such review and approval requirements; prohibiting public postsecondary educational institutions from requiring students to take certain additional general education courses; requiring the State Board of Education and the Board of Governors to adopt rules and regulations, respectively; amending s. 1008.47, F.S.; specifying a one-time limit on the requirement to change accrediting agencies; providing for expiration; prohibiting an accrediting entity from requiring a public postsecondary institution to violate state law; amending s. 1009.26, F.S.; requiring the Board of Governors to identify state-approved teacher preparation programs eligible for a tuition waiver; providing that certain postsecondary fee waivers continue until specified criteria are met; providing an effective date.

Be It Enacted by the Legislature of the State of Florida:

Section 1.   Paragraphs (a) through (d) of subsection (5) and paragraph (b) of subsection (6) of section 1001.706, Florida Statutes, are amended to read:

1001.706   Powers and duties of the Board of Governors.—

(5)   POWERS AND DUTIES RELATING TO ACCOUNTABILITY.—

(a)   The Legislature intends that the Board of Governors shall align the missions of each constituent university with the academic success of its students; the existing and emerging economic development needs of the state; the national reputation of its faculty and its academic and research programs; the quantity of externally generated research, patents, and licenses; and the strategic and accountability plans required in paragraphs (b) and (c). The Board of Governors shall periodically review the mission of each constituent university and make updates or revisions as needed. Upon completion of a review of the mission, the board shall review existing academic programs for alignment with the mission. The board shall include in its review a directive to each constituent university regarding its programs for any curriculum that violates s. 1000.05 or that is based on theories that systemic racism, sexism, oppression, and privilege are inherent in the institutions of the United States and were created to maintain social, political, and economic inequities. The mission alignment and strategic plan must consider peer institutions at the constituent universities. The mission alignment and strategic plan must acknowledge that universities that have a national and international impact have the greatest capacity to promote the state's economic development through: new discoveries, patents, licenses, and technologies that generate state businesses of global importance; research achievements through external grants and contracts that are comparable to nationally recognized and ranked universities; the creation of a resource rich academic environment that attracts high-technology business and venture capital to the state; and this generation's finest minds focusing on solving the state's economic, social, environmental, and legal problems in the areas of life sciences, water, sustainability, energy, and health care. A nationally recognized and ranked university that has a global perspective and impact must be afforded the opportunity to enable and protect the university's competitiveness on the global stage in fair competition with other institutions of other states in the highest Carnegie Classification.

(b)   The Board of Governors shall develop a strategic plan specifying goals and objectives for the State University System and each constituent university, including each university's contribution to overall system goals and objectives. The strategic plan must:

1.   Include performance metrics and standards common for all institutions and metrics and standards unique to institutions depending on institutional core missions, including, but not limited to, student admission requirements, retention, graduation, percentage of graduates who have attained employment, percentage of graduates enrolled in continued education, licensure passage, nondegree credential attainment, average wages of employed graduates, average cost per graduate, excess hours, student loan burden and default rates, faculty awards, total annual research expenditures, patents, licenses and royalties, intellectual property, startup companies, annual giving, endowments, and well-known, highly respected national rankings for institutional and program achievements.

2.   Consider reports and recommendations of the Florida Talent Development Council under s. 1004.015 and the Articulation Coordinating Committee under s. 1007.01.

3.   Include student enrollment and performance data delineated by method of instruction, including, but not limited to, traditional, online, and distance learning instruction.

4.   Include criteria for designating baccalaureate degree and master's degree programs at specified universities as high demand programs of emphasis. The programs of emphasis list adopted by the Board of Governors before July 1, 2021, shall be used for the 2021-2022 academic year. Beginning in the 2022-2023 academic year, the Board of Governors shall adopt the criteria to determine value for and prioritization of degree credentials and degree programs established by the Credentials Review Committee under s. 445.004 for designating high-demand programs of emphasis. The Board of Governors must review designated programs of emphasis, at a minimum, every 3 years to ensure alignment with the prioritization of degree credentials and degree programs identified by the Credentials Review Committee.

5.   Include criteria for nondegree credentials.

(c)   The Board of Governors shall develop an accountability plan for the State University System and each constituent university. The accountability plan must address institutional and system achievement of goals and objectives specified in the strategic plan adopted pursuant to paragraph (b) and must be submitted as part of its legislative budget request. Each university shall submit, as a component of the university's annual accountability plan:,

    1.   Information on the effectiveness of its plan for 199 improving 4-year graduation rates; and

    2.   The level of financial assistance provided to students pursuant to paragraph (h).

    (d) The Board of Governors shall annually require a state university prior to registration to provide each enrolled student electronic access to the economic security report of employment and earning outcomes prepared by the Department of Economic Opportunity pursuant to s. 445.07. In addition, the Board of Governors shall require a state university to provide each student electronic access to the following information each year prior to registration using the data described in s. 1008.39:

    1.   The top 25 percent of degrees reported by the university in terms of highest full-time job placement and highest average annualized earnings in the year after earning the degree.

    2.   The bottom 10 percent of degrees reported by the university in terms of lowest full-time job placement and lowest average annualized earnings in the year after earning the degree.

    (6)   POWERS AND DUTIES RELATING TO PERSONNEL.—

    (b)   The Board of Governors shall adopt a regulation requiring each tenured state university faculty member to undergo a comprehensive post-tenure review every 5 years. The board may include other considerations in the regulation, but the regulation must address:

    1.   Accomplishments and productivity;

    2.   Assigned duties in research, teaching, and service;

    3.   Performance metrics, evaluations, and ratings; and

    4.   Recognition and compensation considerations, as well as improvement plans and consequences for underperformance.

    Section 2.   Paragraph (m) is added to subsection (2) of section 1001.7065, Florida Statutes, and subsection (3) of that section is amended, to read:

    1001.7065   Preeminent state research universities program.—

    (2)   ACADEMIC AND RESEARCH EXCELLENCE STANDARDS.—The following academic and research excellence standards are established for the preeminent state research universities program and shall be reported annually in the Board of Governors Accountability Plan:

    (m)   Total annual STEM-related research expenditures, including federal research expenditures, of $50 million or more.

    (3)   PREEMINENT STATE RESEARCH UNIVERSITY DESIGNATION.—

(a)   The Board of Governors shall designate each state university that annually meets at least 12 of the 13 academic and research excellence standards identified in subsection (2) as a "preeminent state research university."

(b)   The Board of Governors shall designate each state university that annually meets at least 7 of the 13 academic and research excellence standards identified in subsection (2) as an "emerging preeminent state research university."

Section 3.   Section 1001.741, Florida Statutes, is created to read:

1001.741   State university personnel.—

(1)   Except as delegated pursuant to paragraph (a), each state university president has the final authority for hiring the provost, the deans, and all full-time faculty for the university, and has an ongoing duty to assess the performance, productivity, and employment practices of the university's provost and deans. The president of the university is encouraged to engage in faculty recruiting as appropriate, and shall provide a regular report and recommendations on employment practices to the board at least twice annually.

(a)   The president may delegate hiring authority to individuals on the university's executive management team within the president's office, to the provost, or to individual deans; however, the president or the person delegated such hiring authority is not bound by the recommendations or opinions of faculty or other individuals.

(b)   A state university may not require any statement, pledge, or oath other than to uphold general and federal law, the United States Constitution, and the State Constitution as a part of any admissions, hiring, employment, promotion, tenure, disciplinary, or evaluation process.

(2)   Notwithstanding s. 447.401 or any other law related to faculty grievance procedures, personnel actions or decisions regarding faculty, including in the areas of evaluations, promotions, tenure, discipline, or termination, may not be appealed beyond the level of a university president or designee. Such actions or decisions must have as their terminal step a final agency disposition, which must be issued in writing to the faculty member, and are not subject to arbitration. The filing of a grievance does not toll the action or decision of the university, including the termination of pay and benefits of a suspended or terminated faculty member.

(3)   Each state university board of trustees must have procedures for the review of the president's selection and reappointment of each member of the university's executive management team, and his or her respective contract and annual salary, before such contracts and salaries become effective, in accordance with the personnel program established by the Board of Governors.

(4)   Each state university president shall annually present to the state university board of trustees the results of performance evaluations and associated annual salaries for all evaluated academic and administrative personnel earning an annual salary of $200,000 or more, regardless of the funding source for such salaries. The results may be presented in a summary or written format.

Section 4.   Section 1004.06, Florida Statutes, is amended to read:

1004.06   Prohibited expenditures.—

(1)   A Florida College System institution, state university, Florida College System institution direct-support organization, or state university direct-support organization may not expend any funds, regardless of source, to purchase membership in, or goods and services from, any organization that discriminates on the basis of race, color,

308   national origin, sex, disability, or religion.

(2)   A Florida College System institution, state university, Florida College System institution direct-support organization, or state university direct-support organization may not expend any state or federal funds to promote, support, or maintain any programs or campus activities that:

(a)   Violate s. 1000.05; or

(b)   Advocate for diversity, equity, and inclusion, or promote or engage in political or social activism, as defined by rules of the State Board of Education and regulations of the Board of Governors.

Student fees to support student-led organizations are permitted notwithstanding any speech or expressive activity by such organizations which would otherwise violate this subsection, provided that the public funds must be allocated to student-led organizations pursuant to written policies or regulations of each Florida College System institution or state university, as applicable. Use of institution facilities by student-led organizations is permitted notwithstanding any speech or expressive activity by such organizations which would otherwise violate this subsection, provided that such use must be granted to student-led organizations pursuant to written policies or regulations of each Florida College System institution or state university, as applicable.

(3)   Subsection (2) does not prohibit programs, campus activities, or functions required for compliance with general or federal laws or regulations; for obtaining or retaining institutional or discipline-specific accreditation with the approval of either the State Board of Education or the Board of Governors; or for access programs for military veterans, Pell Grant recipients, first generation college students, nontraditional students, "2+2" transfer students from the Florida College System, students from low-income families, or students with unique abilities.

(4)   The State Board of Education and the Board of Governors

shall adopt rules and regulations, respectively, to implement this section.

Section 5.   Section 1004.3841, Florida Statutes, is created to read:

1004.3841   The Institute for Risk Management and Insurance Education.—The Institute for Risk Management and Insurance Education is established within the College of Business at the University of Central Florida. Since insurance and risk management is a major industry in this state, with a concentration of such industry in Volusia County, the institute must be located in Volusia County. Like many other industries in the state, the insurance and risk management industry is being revolutionized by, among other things, the integration of technology, predictive analytics, and data science, and is becoming more complex, given its exposure to transformative trends in the economy and environment. The purpose of the institute is to respond to the ever-evolving insurance and risk management industry and the present and emerging needs of this state and its residents. The goals of the institute are to:

(1)   Pursue technological innovations that advance risk valuation models and operational efficiencies in the insurance industry.

(2)   Drive the development of workforce competencies in data analytics, system-level thinking, technology integration, entrepreneurship, and actuarial science.

(3)   Leverage the University of Central Florida's world class assets in data science, artificial intelligence, computer science, engineering, finance, economics, and sales.

(4)   Take advantage of the University of Central Florida's robust portfolio of academic program offerings and draw on faculty and industry experts in diverse fields, including actuarial science, computer science, economics, engineering, environmental science, finance, forensics, law, management, marketing, and psychology.

(5)   Develop and offer risk management and insurance education, including education that recognizes risks in areas such as the environment, pandemic disease, and digital security.

(6)   Offer programs, workshops, case studies, and applied research studies that integrate technology and artificial intelligence with soft skills while preparing students and professionals for the technology-enabled insurance industry of the future.

Section 6.   Section 1004.6496, Florida Statutes, is amended to read:

1004.6496   Hamilton Center for Classical and Civic Education.—

(1)   The Board of Trustees of the University of Florida may use funds as provided in the General Appropriations Act and charitable donations to establish and fund the Hamilton Center for Classical and Civic Education as an academic unit within the University of Florida. The pur-

pose of the center is to support teaching and research concerning the ideas, traditions, and texts that form the foundations of Western and American civilization.

(2) Beginning January 1, 2025, and by each January 1 thereafter, the University of Florida must report to the Governor, the President of the Senate, and the Speaker of the House of Representatives on the progress toward establishing the center as a permanent college at the university. The report must include a timeline for establishing the college, enrollment and educational outcomes and future goals for enrollment and educational outcomes, current financial progress and future financial needs, and any recommendation for changes in general law.

(3) The goals of the center are to:

(a) Educate university students in core texts and great debates of Western civilization and the Great Books.

1. The center is responsible for developing curriculum and courses to satisfy the requirement for the competency in civil discourse.

2. Courses developed under this paragraph may be used to satisfy the requirements of s. 1007.25(5).

(b) Educate university students in the principles, ideals, and institutions of the American political order.

(c) Educate university students in the foundations of responsible leadership and informed citizenship.

(d) Provide programming and training related to civic education and the values of open inquiry and civil discourse to support the K-20 system.

(e) Coordinate with the Florida Institute for Governance and Civics created pursuant to s. 1004.6499 and the Adam Smith Center for the Study of Economic Freedom created pursuant to s. 1004.64991 and assist in the curation and implementation of Portraits in Patriotism created pursuant to s. 1003.44.

(f) Develop educational programming and a plan for the implementation of such programming to ensure that all university students demonstrate competency in civil discourse.

(4) In order to carry out the goals set forth in subsection (3), the president of the University of Florida must:

(a) Annually update the board of trustees on the center's progress toward developing educational programming to ensure that all students at the university demonstrate competency in civil discourse. The president's report must identify a timeline and support necessary for the university to achieve this goal.

(b) Guide the university's leadership and the center to ensure that the center is able to enroll students, hire faculty, ensure a pathway to tenure for faculty, develop curricula and courses, establish certificate and degree programs, establish major and minor programs, and fulfill other actions approved by the president of the university.

(5)   Funds appropriated specifically to the center may not be used for any other purpose; however, the university may provide additional funding as available to the center.

Section 7.   Section 1004.6499, Florida Statutes, is amended to read:

1004.6499   Florida Institute for Governance and Civics.—

(1)   The Florida Institute for Governance and Civics is established at the Florida State University.

(2)   The goals of the institute are to:

(a)   Provide students with access to an interdisciplinary hub that will develop academically rigorous scholarship and coursework on the origins of the American system of government, its foundational documents, its subsequent political traditions and evolutions, and its impact on comparative political systems.

(b)   Encourage civic literacy in this state through the development of educational tools and resources for K-12 and postsecondary students which foster an understanding of how individual rights, constitutionalism, separation of powers, and federalism function within the American system.

(c)   Model civic discourse that recognizes the importance of viewpoint diversity, intellectual rigor, and an evidence-based approach to history.

(d)   Plan and host forums to allow students and guests to hear from exceptional individuals who have excelled in a wide range of sectors of American life, to highlight the possibilities created by individual achievement and entrepreneurial vision.

(e)   Become a national and state resource on using polling instruments and other assessments to measure civic literacy and make recommendations for improving civic education.

(f)   Provide fellowships and internship opportunities to students in government.

(g)   Create through scholarship, original research, publications, symposia, testimonials, and other means a body of resources that can be accessed by students, scholars, and government officials to understand the innovations in public policy in this state over a rolling 30-year time period.

Section 8.   Subsection (3) is added to section 1004.64991, Florida Statutes, to read:

1004.64991   The Adam Smith Center for the Study of Economic Freedom.—

(3)   In order to carry out the purpose set forth in this section, the institute is authorized to:

(a)   Hire necessary faculty and staff pursuant to s. 1001.741;

(b)   Enroll students;

(c)   Develop curriculum and offer new courses, including honors courses, certificates, and major and minor programs;

(d)   Hold events, including fundraisers;

(e)   Fulfill other actions approved by the president of the university; and enrollment, in the same manner as any college within the institution.

Section 9.   Subsection (3) of section 1007.25, Florida Statutes, is amended to read:

1007.25   General education courses; common prerequisites; other degree requirements.—

(3)   The chair of the State Board of Education and the chair of the Board of Governors, or their designees, shall jointly appoint faculty committees to review and recommend to the Articulation Coordinating Committee for approval by the State Board of Education and the Board of Governors statewide general education core course options for inclusion in the statewide course numbering system established under s. 1007.24. Faculty committees shall, by July 1, 2024, and by July 1 every 4 years thereafter, review and submit recommendations to the Articulation Coordinating Committee and the commissioner for the removal, alignment, realignment, or addition of general education core courses that satisfy the requirements of this subsection.

(a)   General education core course options shall consist of a maximum of five courses within each of the subject areas of communication, mathematics, social sciences, humanities, and natural sciences. The core courses may be revised, or the five course maximum within each subject area may be exceeded, if approved by the State Board of Education and the Board of Governors, as recommended by the subject area faculty committee and approved by the Articulation Coordinating Committee as necessary for a subject area.

(b)   Each general education core course option must contain high-level academic and critical thinking skills and common competencies that students must demonstrate to successfully complete the course.

(c)   General education core courses may not distort significant historical events or include a curriculum that teaches identity politics, violates s. 1000.05, or is based on theories that systemic racism, sexism, oppression, and privilege are inherent in the institutions of the United States and were created to maintain social, political, and economic inequities.

(d)   General education core courses must meet the following standards:

1.   Communication courses must afford students the ability to communicate effectively, including the ability to write clearly and engage

in public speaking.

    2.   Humanities courses must afford students the ability to think critically through the mastering of subjects concerned with human culture, especially literature, history, art, music, and philosophy, and must include selections from the Western canon.

    3.   Social science courses must afford students an understanding of the basic social and behavioral science concepts and principles used in the analysis of behavior and past and present social, political, and economic issues.

    4.   Natural science courses must afford students the ability to critically examine and evaluate the principles of the scientific method, model construction, and use the scientific method to explain natural experiences and phenomena.

    5.   Mathematics courses must afford students a mastery of foundational mathematical and computation models and methods by applying such models and methods in problem solving.

    (e)   Beginning with students initially entering a Florida College System institution or state university in 2015-2016 and thereafter, each student must complete at least one identified core course in each subject area as part of the general education course requirements. Beginning in the 2022-2023 academic year and thereafter, students entering a technical degree education program as defined in s. 1004.02(13) must complete at least one identified core course in each subject area as part of the general education course requirements before a degree is awarded.

    (f)   All public postsecondary educational institutions shall offer at least one general education core course in each of the identified subject areas and accept courses as meeting general education core course requirements upon transfer, regardless of whether the receiving institution offers the identical general education core courses. The remaining general education course requirements shall be identified by each institution as approved in accordance with this section and listed in the statewide course numbering system.

    (g)   A public postsecondary educational institution may not require a student to complete an additional course to meet a subject area distribution requirement that was completed by the student with a course that has since been removed as a general education core course.

    (h)   The general education core course options shall be adopted in rule by the State Board of Education and in regulation by the Board of Governors.

    Section 10.   Section 1007.55, Florida Statutes, is created to read:

    1007.55   General education course principles, standards, and content.—

    (1)   The Legislature finds it necessary to ensure that every un-

dergraduate student of a Florida public postsecondary educational institution graduates as an informed citizen through participation in rigorous general education courses that promote and preserve the constitutional republic through traditional, historically accurate, and high-quality coursework. General education courses should provide broad foundational knowledge to help students develop intellectual skills and habits that enable them to become more effective and lifelong learners. Courses with a curriculum based on unproven, speculative, or exploratory content are best suited as elective or specific program prerequisite credit, not general education credit. General education courses must:

(a) Meet the course standards as provided in s. 1007.25; and

(b) Whenever applicable, provide instruction on the historical background and philosophical foundation of Western civilization and this nation's historical documents, such as the Declaration of Independence, the United States Constitution, the Bill of Rights and subsequent amendments, and the Federalist Papers.

(2) Public postsecondary educational institution boards of trustees and presidents are responsible for annually reviewing and approving, at a public meeting, general education course requirements, as authorized and approved in accordance with ss. 1007.24 and 1007.25 and this section, at their respective institutions. The following must be included for each listed general education course:

(a) The general education distribution area;

(b) The number of state universities that offer the course and the number of Florida College System institutions that offer the course; and

(c) The course level.

(3) Public postsecondary educational institutions must report courses meeting institutional general education subject requirements to the department by their statewide course number.

(4) In performing it duties under ss. 1007.24 and 1007.25, by December 1, 2024, and each December 1 thereafter, the Articulation Coordinating Committee shall submit to the State Board of Education and the Board of Governors courses that have been approved by public postsecondary educational institutions as meeting general education requirements. The listing of general education courses must include the information in paragraphs (2)(a), (b), and (c). The State Board of Education and the Board of Governors must approve or reject the list of general education courses for each Florida College System institution and state university, respectively.

(5) Public postsecondary educational institutions that fail to comply with the requirements of this section are not eligible to receive performance-based funding pursuant to s. 1001.66 or s. 1001.92.

(6) A public postsecondary educational institution may not

require a student to take an additional course to meet a subject area distribution requirement that was completed by the student with a course that has since been removed as a general education course.

(7)   The State Board of Education and the Board of Governors shall adopt rules and regulations, respectively, to implement this section.

Section 11.   Present subsections (3) and (4) of section 1008.47, Florida Statutes, are redesignated as subsections (4) and (5), respectively, a new subsection (3) is added to that section, and subsection (2) and present subsection (3) of that section are amended, to read:

1008.47   Postsecondary education institution accreditation.—

(2)   ACCREDITATION.—

(a)   By September 1, 2022, the Board of Governors or the State Board of Education, as applicable, shall identify and determine the accrediting agencies or associations best suited to serve as an accreditor for public postsecondary institutions. Such accrediting agencies or associations must be recognized by the database created and maintained by the United States Department of Education. In the year following reaffirmation or fifth-year review by its accrediting agencies or associations, each public postsecondary institution must seek and obtain accreditation from an accrediting agency or association identified by the Board of Governors or State Board of Education, respectively, before its next reaffirmation or fifth-year review date. The requirements in this section are limited to a one-time change in accreditation. The requirements of this subsection are not applicable to those professional, graduate, departmental, or certificate programs at public postsecondary institutions that have specific accreditation requirements or best practices, including, but not limited to, law, pharmacy, engineering, or other similarly situated educational programs.

(b)   Once a public postsecondary institution is required to seek and obtain accreditation from an agency or association identified pursuant to paragraph (a), the institution shall seek accreditation from a regional accrediting agency or association and provide quarterly reports of its progress to the Board of Governors or State Board of Education, as applicable. If each regional accreditation agency or association identified pursuant to paragraph (a) has refused to grant candidacy status to an institution, the institution must seek and obtain accreditation from any accrediting agency or association that is different from its current accrediting agency or association and is recognized by the database created and maintained by the United States Department of Education. If a public postsecondary institution is not granted candidacy status before its next reaffirmation or fifth-year review date, the institution may remain with its current accrediting agency or association.

(c)   This subsection expires December 31, 2032.

(3)   PROHIBITION.—An accrediting agency or association

may not compel any public postsecondary institution to violate state law, and any adverse action upon the institution based upon the institution's compliance with state law constitutes a violation of this section that may be enforced through subsection (4), except to the extent that state law is preempted by a federal law that recognizes the necessity of the accreditation standard or requirement.

  (4) CAUSE OF ACTION.—A postsecondary education institution negatively impacted by retaliatory or adverse action taken against the postsecondary education institution by an accrediting agency or association may bring an action against the accrediting agency or association in a court of competent jurisdiction and may obtain liquidated damages in the amount of federal financial aid received by the postsecondary education institution, court costs, and reasonable attorney fees.

  Section 12. Paragraphs (a), (b), and (c) of subsection (18) of section 1009.26, Florida Statutes, are amended to read:

  1009.26 Fee Waivers.—

  (18)(a) For every course in a Program of Strategic Emphasis, or in a state-approved teacher preparation program identified by the Board of Governors, as identified in subparagraph 3., in which a student is enrolled, a state university shall waive 100 percent of the tuition and fees for an equivalent course in such program for a student who:

  1. Is a resident for tuition purposes under s. 1009.21.

  2. Has earned at least 60 semester credit hours towards a baccalaureate degree within 2 academic years after initial enrollment at a Florida public postsecondary institution.

  3. Enrolls in one of 10 Programs of Strategic Emphasis as adopted by the Board of Governors or in one of two state approved teacher preparation programs identified by the Board of Governors. The Board of Governors shall adopt eight Programs of Strategic Emphasis in science, technology, engineering, or math; beginning with the 2022-2023 academic year, two Programs of Strategic Emphasis in the critical workforce gap analysis category; and beginning with the 2023-2024 academic year, two state-approved teacher preparation programs for which a student may be eligible to receive the tuition and fee waiver authorized by this subsection. The programs identified by the board must reflect the priorities of the state and be offered at a majority of state universities at the time the Board of Governors approves the list.

  (b) A waiver granted under this subsection is applicable only for upper-level courses and up to 110 percent of the number of required credit hours of the baccalaureate degree program for which the student is enrolled. A student granted a waiver under this subsection shall continue receiving the waiver until the student graduates, exceeds the number of allowable credit hours, or withdraws from an eligible program, regardless of whether the program is removed from the approved list of eligible programs subsequent to the student's enrollment.

(c)   Upon enrollment in a Program of Strategic Emphasis or in one of two teacher preparation programs identified by the Board of Governors, the tuition and fees waived under this subsection must be reported for state funding purposes under ss. 1009.534 and 1009.535 and must be disbursed to the student. The amount disbursed to the student must be equal to the award amount the student has received under s. 1009.534(2) or s. 1009.535(2).

Section 13.   This act shall take effect July 1, 2023.

APPENDIX C

14th Amendment to the U.S. Constitution

Section 1.

All persons born or naturalized in the United States, and subject to the jurisdiction thereof, are citizens of the United States and of the State wherein they reside. No State shall make or enforce any law which shall abridge the privileges or immunities of citizens of the United States; nor shall any State deprive any person of life, liberty, or property, without due process of law; nor deny to any person within its jurisdiction the equal protection of the laws.

Section 2.

Representatives shall be apportioned among the several States according to their respective numbers, counting the whole number of persons in each State, excluding Indians not taxed. But when the right to vote at any election for the choice of electors for President and Vice-President of the United States, Representatives in Congress, the Executive and Judicial officers of a State, or the members of the Legislature thereof, is denied to any of the male inhabitants of such State, being twenty-one years of age, and citizens of the United States, or in any way abridged, except for participation in rebellion, or other crime, the basis of representation therein shall be reduced in the proportion which the number of such male citizens shall bear to the whole number of male citizens twenty-one years of age in such State.

Section 3.

No person shall be a Senator or Representative in Congress, or elector of President and Vice-President, or hold any office, civil or military, under the United States, or under any State, who, having previously taken an oath, as a member of Congress, or as an officer of the United States, or as a member of any State legislature, or as an executive or judicial officer of any State, to support the Constitution of the United States, shall have engaged in insurrection or rebellion against the same, or given aid or comfort to the enemies thereof. But Congress may by a vote of two-thirds of each House, remove such disability.

Section 4.

The validity of the public debt of the United States, authorized by law, including debts incurred for payment of pensions and bounties for services in suppressing insurrection or rebellion, shall not be questioned. But neither the United States nor any State shall assume or pay any debt or obligation incurred in aid of insurrection or rebellion against the United States, or any claim for the loss or emancipation of any slave; but all such debts, obligations and claims shall be held illegal and void.

Section 5.

The Congress shall have the power to enforce, by appropriate legislation, the provisions of this article.

Author Bios

Born into abject poverty in rural southwest Virginia, **Dr. Carol Swain**, a high school dropout, went on to earn five degrees. Holding a Ph.D. from University of North Carolina at Chapel Hill and an M.S.L. from Yale, she also earned early tenure at Princeton and full professorship at Vanderbilt where she was professor of political science and a professor of law. Today she is a sought-after cable news contributor and guest expert, a best-selling author, and a prominent national speaker.

In addition to having three Presidential appointments, Carol is a former Distinguished Senior Fellow for Constitutional Studies with the Texas Public Policy Foundation who has also served on the Tennessee Advisory Committee to the U.S. Civil Rights Commission, the National Endowment for the Humanities, and the 1776 Commission.

An award-winning political scientist, cited three times by the U.S. Supreme Court, she has authored or edited 11 published books including the bestseller, *Black Eye for America: How Critical Race Theory is Burning Down the House* and the timely *Countercultural Living: What Jesus Has to Say About Life, Marriage, Race, Gender, and Materialism.*

Ms. Swain is an expert on critical race theory, American politics, and race relations with television appearances that include BBC Radio and TV, CSPAN, ABC's Headline News, CNN, Fox News, Newsmax and more.

In addition, she has published opinion pieces in the *New York Times*, the *Washington Post,* the *Wall Street Journal*, the *Epoch Times*, the *Financial Times*, and *USA Today.*

She is the founder and CEO of Carol Swain Enterprises, REAL Unity Training Solutions, Your Life Story for Descendants, and her non-profit, Be The People.

Carol is a mother, grandmother, and great-grandmother. She resides in Nashville, Tennessee.

Mike Towle is a former newspaper reporter, editor, and general manager who has worked for the *St. Albans (Vermont) Messenger*, the *Fort Worth Star-Telegram*, *The National Sports Daily*, and the *Nashville Tennessean*, for whom he won six statewide Tennessee Press Association awards for his newspaper column writing. His work has also been published in or on numerous other publications/websites ranging from the *San Jose Mercury-News* and the *Washington Times* to *The Sporting News, Golf World*, and yahoo.com.

A native of Vermont and a graduate of the University of Notre Dame, Mike served four years active duty in the Army and four more in the Army Reserves as a signal officer and later as a public affairs officer. During this time he won two Army-wide writing awards and was awarded the Army Commendation Award before leaving service as a captain. He has authored or collaborated on more than twenty books published by the likes of HarperCollins/Thomas Nelson, WND Books, Triumph Books, Rutledge Hill Press, TowleHouse Publishing, and Brown Books.

Mike lives in the Nashville, Tennessee, area. His son, Andrew, is an Eagle Scout and honors college graduate preparing for Christian ministry and evangelism.